Christian Apologetics and Philosophy

CHRISTIAN APOLOGETICS AND PHILOSOPHY

AN INTRODUCTION

PAUL HERRICK

University of Notre Dame Press
Notre Dame, Indiana

Copyright © 2024 by the University of Notre Dame
Notre Dame, Indiana 46556
undpress.nd.edu

All Rights Reserved

Published in the United States of America

Library of Congress Control Number: 2024941584

ISBN: 978-0-268-20892-9 (Hardback)
ISBN: 978-0-268-20893-6 (Paperback)
ISBN: 978-0-268-20894-3 (WebPDF)
ISBN: 978-0-268-20895-0 (Epub3)

To Lucca and Benjamin

CONTENTS

Acknowledgments ix

Introduction xi

ONE
What Is Apologetics? 1

Interlude One
The Socratic Method and the Christian Examination of Conscience 11

TWO
Does God Exist? Part 1 15

THREE
Does God Exist? Part 2 55

Interlude Two
Christianity's Contributions to World Culture 89

FOUR
Why Would God Permit Evil? 99

FIVE
Hasn't Science Proved That Life after Death Is Impossible? 117

SIX
Isn't It Illogical to Believe That a Miracle Occurred?   151

SEVEN
Is the New Testament Historically Reliable?   163

EIGHT
Did Jesus Christ Rise Miraculously from the Dead?   179

NINE
Reason to the Best Explanation   205

Notes   211

Index   235

ACKNOWLEDGMENTS

Many colleagues gave me valuable feedback as I wrote this book. Steven Duncan and Jim Slagle read an early draft and made helpful suggestions. Art DiQuattro and Andrew Jeffery read and criticized parts of various drafts. Conversations with them and with Tom Kerns, Mark Storey, Michael Matriotti, Andrew Tadie, Michael Adeney, Steve Layman, Robert Bolger, Evan Burkholder, Tom McAuliffe, my cousins Charles Herrick and John Herrick, Father Brad Hagelin, Jean and Ruth Blanchett, and Larry Stern improved the manuscript.

I thank Emily King, senior editor, University of Notre Dame Press, for her encouragement and support during two rounds of review. I also thank the four anonymous reviewers for the University of Notre Dame Press for their very constructive comments.

I thank the students who have taken my classes over the years. Every quarter I am impressed by their thoughtful responses to class readings. I have learned as much from them as (I hope) they have learned from me.

I thank Karen Olson and Sheila Berg for their excellent copyediting.

I thank my fellow members of Philosophers on Holiday. Our weekly meetings since 1981 have helped me sort out many of the issues that I cover in this book. The members of this informal discussion group, formed by graduate students in philosophy at the University of Washington, have collectively been the Socrates in my life: John Burke, Jeff Clausen, Todd Currier, Richard Curtis, Art DiQuattro, Steven Duncan, Mitch Erickson, George Goodall, Richard Kang, Bob Kirk, Richard Kopczynski, Terry Mazurak, Shawn Mintek, Brad Rind, Michael Schmitt, Liz Ungar, and Carol Weibel.

I have also learned much from the conferences of the Society of Christian Philosophers that I have attended over the years and from the feedback I received on several papers I read at those conferences.

Finally, I thank my wife, Joan, our daughter, Lauren, and her husband, Aaron, and our grandsons, Lucca and Benjamin, for their love and support during the time I spent writing this book.

INTRODUCTION

Many people today believe that science is our only path to truth. And science, they say, has proved that God does not exist, that life after death is impossible, and that it is irrational to even hope for a miracle. If they are right, then the Bible is not a credible source of truth and Christianity is an elaborate falsehood. Of those who hold these views, quite a few draw the pessimistic conclusion expressed vividly by the British philosopher Bertrand Russell (1872–1970) in his famous essay emphatically rejecting belief in God, "A Free Man's Worship."

> That man is the product of causes which had no prevision of the end they were achieving; that his origin, his growth, his hopes and fears, his loves and beliefs are but accidental collocations of atoms; that [nothing] can preserve an individual life beyond the grave. That all the labors of the ages, all the devotion, all the inspiration, all the noonday brightness of human genius, are destined to extinction in the vast death of the solar system, and that the whole temple of man's achievement must inevitably be buried beneath a universe in ruins . . . only within the scaffolding of these truths, only in the firm foundation of unyielding despair, can the soul's habitation henceforth safely be built.[1]

But what if it can be shown with plain logic that science is not our only path to truth? What if, contrary to current intellectual fashion, there are deep philosophical reasons to believe in God, in life after death, and in miracles? What if the same form of reasoning that underlies modern science actually points strongly to the historical reliability of the Bible and the miraculous Resurrection of Jesus Christ three days after his Crucifixion? What if the truth of the Christian message is the best overall explanation of everything? These are the great worldview issues that are addressed in this book.

ONE

What Is Apologetics?

We normally use the word *apologize* to express regret for something we have done. However, the word dates to the ancient Greeks and originally meant "to give a reasoned defense." In 399 BC, the Greek philosopher Socrates (470–399 BC) was put on trial by the city-state of Athens. The two charges against him (both carrying the death penalty) were corrupting the youth by causing them to ask too many questions and introducing new gods. Socrates's student Plato (427–347 BC) attended the trial and later wrote a philosophical dialogue detailing the carefully reasoned speech Socrates gave to the jury in his own defense, titled the *Apology*.

Socrates believed that we should follow trained and educated reason when we make choices in life and when we decide what to believe. Emotions and desires are part of who we are, but when left unchecked by sound reasoning, they can lead us astray. The speech he gave to the jury was a reasoned case for philosophy and for his life's mission: he urged people to look in the mirror every day and evaluate their assumptions and life values on the basis of reasonable criteria logically connected to reality. Today we call his method of thought "critical thinking."[1]

2 Christian Apologetics and Philosophy

The charges against Socrates were phony. As we will see in chapter 2, Socrates was actually a monotheist (from the Greek words *mono*, "one," and *Theos*, "God": a believer in one God or supreme being), and the questions he asked helped people improve their lives. Nevertheless, the jury sided with the prosecution and found Socrates guilty. The vote was 280 to 220 — proof that large groups of people can be swayed by unscrupulous demagogues (from the Greek *demos*, "people," and *agein*, "leader") appealing to prejudice, ignorance, and inflamed emotion rather than objective truth and calm reason. The *Apology* is still studied and discussed profitably by philosophers today, 2,400 years after it was written.

Today the word *apologist* reflects its Greek origin. An apologist is one who makes a reasoned case for their view. In the courtroom, the prosecution presents an apology when it argues that the defendant is guilty, and the defense presents an apology when it argues that the evidence is not sufficient to overcome reasonable doubt.

A *Christian apologist* is someone who offers a reasoned case for Christianity. Saint Peter endorsed apologetics when he said to the first Christians, "Always be prepared to give a defense to everyone who asks you the reason for the hope that is in you. But respond with gentleness and respect" (1 Peter 3:15, Majority Standard Bible). It is noteworthy that Peter urged Christians to reason for their faith "with gentleness and respect." Few people are moved by harsh or disrespectful talk. Peter was not the only apostle to endorse apologetics. Saint Paul reasoned with people on his missionary journeys.

Justin Martyr (ca. AD 100–ca. 165) is "generally regarded as the father of the Christian apologetical tradition."[2] Justin was a philosopher before he converted to Christianity, and he remained a philosopher after his conversion. Many people today are surprised by this fact. They ask, "How can anyone be a Christian and a philosopher at the same time?" The answer requires a brief look at philosophy and then at Justin's conversion to the Christian faith.

INTRODUCING PHILOSOPHY

In a nutshell, philosophy is the discipline that seeks carefully reasoned answers to the most fundamental questions of human existence. The following are among the most fundamental questions one can ask.

1. Why is the universe orderly or structured rather than totally random and unpredictable?
2. Why does something, rather than nothing at all, exist?
3. Does God or a supreme being exist?
4. Why does the world contain so much suffering?
5. Is there life after bodily death?
6. What is justice?
7. What is truth, and how do we find it?

A reasoned answer is one supported by an argument. In everyday life, we use the word *argument* in many ways, sometimes to refer to people yelling at each other. In philosophy, and in intellectual contexts generally, an argument is defined more strictly as one or more statements, called "premises," offered as reasons to believe that a further statement, called the "conclusion," is true. And by *true*, philosophers generally mean what we ordinarily mean by the word: a statement is true when it corresponds to the relevant facts.

In sum, philosophy is the search for reasoned answers to the most fundamental questions of all. Nothing in this description contradicts Christianity. Christians from the beginning have followed Peter's advice by giving "reasons for the hope within."

JUSTIN'S PHILOSOPHICAL CONVERSION

Justin Martyr's conversion to Christianity is a model of how Christian apologetics can work. The process has four parts:

1. Dissatisfaction with an existing philosophy of life
2. Rational challenge
3. Consideration of logical arguments
4. Following reason to where it points, aided perhaps by spiritual preparation, help from others, prayer, and God's grace.

Before he became a Christian, Justin spent years studying Greek philosophy. Initially, he concluded that Plato's philosophy comes closest to the truth. Plato and his teacher Socrates both stated deep philosophical arguments for the existence of God or a supreme being. Indeed, Socrates, Plato, and Plato's most famous student, Aristotle (384–322 BC), all argued that reason, when followed with an open mind and an open heart, points the soul toward a supreme deity who is the source of all things. Philosophy, as they taught the subject, is an ascent of the mind, heart, and soul toward God. Socrates, Plato, and Aristotle were monotheists.

Justin agreed with Plato's monotheism, but at some point in his life, he came to believe that Plato had left something out: the final stage, a personal and lived relationship with God. Consequently, he was still searching when he came across an old man near the seashore. The man was a Christian who challenged him to investigate the logical evidence for Christianity. Justin took up the challenge and with an open mind examined the apologetical arguments of the day—carefully, in the manner of a philosopher. After study accompanied by prayer, he became convinced that reason, when followed sincerely to its logical conclusion, points not just to God, but to God as revealed by Jesus Christ. Reason, in short, leads the inquiring mind toward the Christian faith. His conversion followed.

But after becoming a Christian, Justin did not give up philosophy. He moved to Rome, put on the purple robe of the philosopher, and opened a school of Christian philosophy. Here Justin and his students studied the works of Plato and the books of the New Testament, seeking to harmonize Plato's philosophy and the central tenets of the Christian faith, including the amazing claim that Jesus was the uniquely divine Son of God who entered into human history, died for our sake, and was miraculously raised from the dead. Justin was the first Christian Platonist (one who seeks to harmonize Christianity with central themes drawn from Plato's philosophy).

The list of Christian scholars influenced significantly by Plato's thought is long and includes most of the church fathers, many great philosophers such as Saint Augustine and Saint Bonaventure, and the most famous Christian apologist of the twentieth century, C. S. Lewis, who began his career at Oxford University teaching philosophical classics.[3] When Lewis began working on his doctorate at Oxford in 1924, the subject he chose was the philosophy of Plato as expressed in the work of the great Cambridge Plato scholar Henry More (1614–87). Plato was Lewis's favorite ancient philosopher.[4]

So there is no inherent conflict between philosophy and Christianity. Christian apologists from Justin Martyr in the first century to C. S. Lewis in the twentieth have employed the methodology found in philosophy to argue for their faith, namely, carefully reasoned arguments on fundamental matters, combined with the courage and spiritual strength to follow reason to where it points. Indeed, most of the historically significant philosophers in the Western tradition over the past two thousand years have been believing Christians. The Christian apologetical enterprise has been philosophical from the beginning.

Justin was probably well known in Rome: one of his books was addressed to Emperor Marcus Aurelius, himself a philosopher. When another emperor persecuted Christians, Justin wrote a letter arguing that this persecution was immoral and unjust. In 165, Justin was arrested, tried, and executed for refusing on principle to worship the Roman deities.

In this book, I reason for some of the central tenets of the Christian faith. I also use reason to answer strong objections to the arguments I present. None of the philosophical arguments I present and defend are novel or original to me. My aim is simply to introduce some of the fascinating arguments of the philosophical tradition that support the Christian faith and to answer some of the strongest objections, as clearly and systematically as I can. The rest of the journey is up to you, perhaps aided by God's calling and grace.

IS APOLOGETICS NEEDED?

Now more than ever, in my opinion. We live in an age in which large numbers of people have rejected the Christian worldview in favor of a purely secular and materialistic outlook on life. Some, because they no longer believe in God or in anything supernatural. Others, because they believe that science is the only source of real truth, and science, they suppose, can explain everything without reference to God or to anything supernatural. Belief in God, they claim, is as outmoded as the horse and buggy. Popular beliefs such as these are for many people intellectual roadblocks that prevent them from even considering the Christian message.

As I see it, a proper work of apologetics does not aim to prove with mathematical certainty that the Christian message is true. Rather, its first job

> ### Saint Paul the Apologist
>
> In the *Acts of the Apostles*, written by the author of the Gospel according to Luke, Saint Paul reasoned with people when he made his case.
>
>> Now when they had traveled through Amphipolis and Apollonia, they came to Thessalonica, where there was a synagogue of the Jews. And according to Paul's custom, he visited them, and for three Sabbaths reasoned with them from the Scriptures, explaining and giving evidence that the Christ had to suffer and rise from the dead, and *saying*, "This Jesus whom I am proclaiming to you is the Christ." And some of them were persuaded and joined Paul and Silas, along with a large number of the God-fearing Greeks and a significant number of the leading women. (Acts 17:1–4, New American Standard Bible)
>
> Saint Paul obviously saw no inherent conflict between reasoning and the Christian faith.

is to remove barriers to faith—cognitive blockages that prevent people from opening their minds to the Christian message. With intellectual roadblocks out of the way, the next step is to offer solid arguments for the Christian message and thoughtful replies to the most common objections. While not proofs in the strict mathematical sense, arguments like these can point the way.

The contemporary Christian philosopher William Lane Craig quotes J. Gresham Machen (1881–1937), a professor of the New Testament and theology at Princeton Seminary, on the value of apologetics:

> False ideas are the greatest obstacle to the reception of the Gospel. We may preach with all the fervor of a reformer and yet succeed only in winning a straggler here and there, if we permit the whole collective thought of the nation to be controlled by ideas which prevent Christianity from being regarded as anything more than a harmless delusion.[5]

Apologetics, Craig argues, creates an intellectual background that makes the Christian message a plausible option to be considered rather than an absurdity to be quickly rejected.

> ### On Fideism
>
> Some people of faith reject apologetics altogether. Faith and reason, they say, have nothing to do with each other. Their view is called "fideism" (from the Latin *fides*, "faith"). Arguments for and against God's existence, the historical reliability of the Bible, and so forth, seem pointless to them. But if you accept fideism, then in response to the question, "Why do you believe in God?," your answer must be, "No reason at all; I just do." And if you are a Christian fideist, then in response to the question, "Why are you a Christian rather than a Muslim, a Jew, a Hindu, or a Jain?," your response must be, "No reason at all."
>
> This intellectual attitude may suit some people, but there are problems. What happens when young Christians who have been taught that faith has nothing to do with reason enter college and encounter strong arguments against their beliefs? What happens when they are told that science has explained everything without any reference to God? Some of the arguments Christians encounter in college can sound pretty impressive—especially to someone whose faith lacks any reasoned basis or defense. Does a fideistic attitude render a student of faith defenseless in the face of the many arguments against faith that permeate our culture and academic institutions today? Does the lack of a reasoned defense make those arguments appear more impressive than they are? Is this why many Christians lose their faith during their college years?

THE PLAN OF THIS BOOK

Some apologetics books are very comprehensive. The second edition of Douglas Groothuis's masterpiece, *Christian Apologetics*, is 834 pages in length.[6] Most of the apologetics books in my library run to more than 400 pages. This book is much shorter. I have found that for many people today, as busy as they are, shorter is better. My aim is to introduce and defend just the basics, as clearly as I can, in the hope that this will satisfy some and lead others to investigate further.

Each chapter in this book employs a common form of reasoning that philosophers call "inference to the best explanation." Reduced to essentials, this kind of argument takes the following general form.

1. D is a collection of facts in need of explanation.
2. On the basis of common criteria, hypothesis H is the best explanation of the facts.
3. Therefore, H is the most reasonable conclusion to draw based on the facts.

Inference to the best explanation is the most common form of reasoning in everyday life. Mechanics employ it when they try to figure out why your car won't start. Doctors reason to the best explanation when they search for the cause of a patient's symptoms. Real estate agents think this way when they try to figure out why a house isn't selling. Most arguments in science, social science, and philosophy are also inferences to the best explanation. Almost everything we believe about the world is based on this kind of reasoning.

While each chapter in this book can be viewed as an inference to the best explanation, the chapters taken together form one overall inference to the best explanation, making the book as a whole what philosophers call a "cumulative case argument." We are all familiar with cumulative cases. Multiple lines of evidence are woven together, like the strands of a rope, to support one overall conclusion. A rope is stronger than any one of the strands of which it is made. Similarly, a cumulative case becomes stronger as each new piece of evidence is added. Scientists build cumulative cases in the laboratory. Attorneys build them in the courtroom. We all build cumulative cases in life as we figure things out over time. Each chapter in this book contributes its part to a cumulative argument for Christianity generally conceived.

At the end of each chapter, you will find references for further study. If this book is the beginning of a journey of faith for even one individual, it will have achieved its goal.

FOR FURTHER STUDY

Blomberg, Craig L. *Can We Still Believe the Bible? An Evangelical Engagement with Contemporary Questions*. Grand Rapids, MI: Brazos Press, 2014.

Craig, William Lane. *Reasonable Faith: Christian Truth and Apologetics*. 3rd ed. Wheaton, IL: Crossway Books, 2008.

——— (with Chad Meister). *God Is Great, God Is Good: Why Believing in God Is Reasonable and Responsible*. Downers Grove, IL: InterVarsity Press, 2009.

———. *On Guard: Defending Your Faith with Reason and Precision*. Colorado Springs, CO: David C. Cook, 2010.
Dulles, Avery Cardinal. *A History of Apologetics*. San Francisco: Ignatius Press, 1971; repr. Eugene, OR: Wipf and Stock, 1999.
Forrest, Benjamin, Joshua D. Chatraw, and Alister E. McGrath, eds. *The History of Apologetics: A Biographical and Methodological Introduction*. Grand Rapids, MI: Zondervan Academic, 2020.
Ganssle, Gregory. *A Reasonable God: Engaging the New Face of Atheism*. Waco, TX: Baylor University Press, 2009.
Geisler, Norman. *Christian Apologetics*. 2nd ed. Grand Rapids, MI: Baker Academic, 2013.
Geisler, Norman, and Patrick Zukeran. *The Apologetics of Jesus: A Caring Approach to Dealing with Doubters*. Grand Rapids, MI: Baker Books, 2009.
Groothuis, Douglas. *Christian Apologetics: A Comprehensive Case for Biblical Faith*. Westmont, IL: InterVarsity Press Academic, 2022.
Kreeft, Peter, and Ronald K. Tacelli. *Handbook of Christian Apologetics: Hundreds of Answers to Crucial Questions*. Westmont, IL: InterVarsity Press, 1994.
Lewis, C. S. *Mere Christianity*. New York: Macmillan, 1943.
McDowell, Josh, and Sean McDowell. *Evidence That Demands a Verdict: Life-Changing Truth for a Skeptical World*. Updated and exp. ed. Nashville, TN: Thomas Nelson, 2017.
Purtill, Richard L. *Reason to Believe*. Grand Rapids, MI: Eerdmans, 1974.
Rota, Michael. *Taking Pascal's Wager: Faith, Evidence, and the Abundant Life*. Downers Grove, IL: InterVarsity Press Academic, 2016.

interlude one

The Socratic Method and the Christian Examination of Conscience

I argued in chapter 1 that philosophy is compatible with Christianity. But is the practice of philosophy compatible with a Christian lifestyle? To reply to this concern, let's return to Socrates for a few moments. At some point around the middle of his life, he became convinced that many people *think* they know what they are talking about when they really do not. He came to believe that many people, including smug experts, famous figures, and powerful people, are in the grips of illusion. He also came to believe that many *believe* that they are doing the morally right thing when they are only fooling themselves — their actions cannot be rationally justified. As this realization sank in, Socrates found his life's purpose: he would help people discover their own ignorance as the first step to attaining more realistic beliefs and values and a better life. But how to proceed?

He asked people questions. Not just any questions, though. His questions were designed to cause people to examine their assumptions and actions on the basis of sound reasoning and realistic criteria. For example: Are my assumptions on this matter true? Are they based on good reasoning? Have I considered all the relevant evidence? Or am I mistaken? Are my actions those of a morally good person? Am I making the right choices in life? Or am I fooling myself? Am I only rationalizing bad behavior?

His unique style of back-and-forth conversation had such an impact on those he talked with and on all subsequent intellectual thought that it has been given its own name: the Socratic method.

I have known people who overcame self-destructive behaviors, addictions, and willful ignorance and changed their lives for the better through Socratic self-examination — helped along the way by true friends, good counselors, and in most cases (I believe) with God's grace. Groups such as Alcoholics Anonymous (AA) can also help. I note in passing that members of AA seeking to improve their lives are encouraged to call upon God or a higher power for help as they reflect on their lives.

Socratic therapy is hard work. It requires honesty and realism. It can be psychologically painful. Inner defense mechanisms and cognitive biases can block the way.[1] Outside help is almost always needed. There will be times of progress and times of retrogression. But Socrates believed that everyone has the power within themselves to overcome illusion and error and aim for truth, real goodness, and God. To be personal for a moment, when I look back on my life, I see many failures, wrong turns, and sins of commission and omission, each at a time when my choice would have been much better had I been practicing sincere Socratic self-examination. When we look back and say things like, "How could I have been so blind?" and "I was really deceiving myself," we are looking back in a Socratic way.[2]

AN OBJECTION AND A REPLY

Some people reject the Socratic method. "Why follow reason rather than emotion or desire?" they ask. "Reasoning can lead us astray and frequently does." This objection is based on a misunderstanding. While it is true that reasoning can sometimes be distorted by irrational influences and lead us to falsehood and moral error, a true Socratic thinker employs only trained and educated reasoning. Socrates was well aware that reasoning can lead us astray if it is not first trained, educated, and aimed at truth, that is, at correspondence with reality.

Sound reasoning, he argued, has a leading role to play in the well-balanced, integrated personality. Our souls have three parts: reason, emotion, and desire. To achieve a life of inner harmony and true integrity, sound reasoning must govern and control the emotions and desires. Life experience supports Socrates. It is common sense that when our raw or unexamined emotions overrule our best reasoning the result is often something we later realize was harmful. In such cases, we look back and wish we had followed the prompts of reason rather than unexamined emotion. Road rage, crime, and domestic violence are contemporary examples.

Similarly, when our unexamined bodily desires overcome our reason, the result is usually something that we later realize, again using our best reasoning, was unhealthy or morally wrong. In such cases, we look back and wish we had followed reason rather than uncontrolled bodily desire. Overeating and excessive drinking are examples.

Life problems usually become magnified when either the emotions or the bodily desires rule the soul unchecked by reason and regular self-examination. Our souls function the way they were meant by God to function when sound reasoning governs the emotions and desires so as to point our lives toward truth, God, and real goodness. So argued Socrates.

THE CHRISTIAN EXAMINATION OF CONSCIENCE

Parallels to the Socratic method can be found in most religions. In the Christian tradition, the "examination of conscience" occurs in a private moment when people of faith reflect critically on their life, past choices, and sins before seeking forgiveness and vowing to improve. Some Christians meditate on the parables of Jesus, for example, the story of the good Samaritan, when they examine their conscience. Others reflect on the Beatitudes, the Ten Commandments, favorite Bible verses, the lives of the saints, the corporal and spiritual works of mercy, or some other source of spiritual direction. In either case, Christians are urged to regularly evaluate their actions in the light of sound moral principles, biblical models, spiritual exemplars, and calm reason as they pray for forgiveness and promise to do better.[3] The Socratic method fits seamlessly within the Christian life.

TWO

Does God Exist?

Part 1

I was raised Roman Catholic. However, in my early twenties, I began doubting all my religious beliefs, including my belief in God. I shared my doubts with our parish priest, but I was not satisfied with the answers he gave me. The religious books he loaned me did not help. As my questions expanded, I began doubting the other beliefs framing my worldview.

When I look back, I see that my belief in God played a central role in my entire belief system, for my doubts about God's existence led to doubts about many other fundamental matters. For instance, if God doesn't exist and matter is all that exists, then there is no such thing as an immaterial soul and therefore likely no such thing as life after bodily death. In the final analysis, it seems to follow that each of us is nothing more than a collection of whirling atoms joined together by atomic bonds into a physical body destined to disintegrate after death. But atoms are not intrinsically valuable. What makes human persons beings of such great intrinsic moral worth if we are ultimately nothing but soulless collections of atoms? And what are universal human rights based on, if not the sacred and great intrinsic worth of each individual human being considered regardless of social status, income, nationality, religion, ethnicity, or color? And if life ends abruptly and forever at bodily death, then what is ultimately the point or meaning of it all?

I had studied some works of philosophy in high school but understood little of what I read. Now I was pointed back to the subject by reading, as part of my search for answers, *Mere Christianity* and *The Pilgrim's Regress* by C. S. Lewis. At the local public library, I found thick works of academic philosophy that hadn't been checked out in years. I was intrigued. I had dropped out of college several years before. At the time, I was driving a semi, hauling 40,000 pounds of frozen beef down the West Coast each week and 40,000 pounds of sausages back up. I began taking home an armload of philosophy textbooks every few weeks to read at truck stops along the way.

Initially, I thought philosophers were radicals who rejected all traditional beliefs while proposing the most unusual ideas imaginable. I soon discovered that I was mistaken. Philosophy is a discipline in which serious people seek answers to the most fundamental questions of life on the basis of careful reasoning and observation. I also found that philosophy is full of fascinating arguments about the very worldview questions that were troubling me, and many of these arguments consist of deep reasons to believe that God exists.[1]

Upon returning to college and studying the classic arguments for God's existence along with the objections to those arguments, I eventually concluded that nothing makes logical sense if there is no such being as God is said to be. Reason, I came to believe, when followed carefully, points the mind toward God as the source of all things, toward theism rather than atheism.

After studying the history of philosophy, I came to see that theism has actually been the mainstream in philosophy from the beginning. The first three philosophers in the historical record—Thales (ca. 624–546 BC), Anaximander (ca. 610–546 BC), and Anaximenes (ca. 586–526 BC)—argued for monotheism in one form or another. Nearly every historically significant, pathbreaking philosopher from the ancient period up to the twentieth century has presented arguments for God's existence. As I mentioned in chapter 1, Socrates, Plato, and Aristotle understood philosophy as a spiritual ascent of the mind, heart, and soul toward the source of all being, God. The Pythagoreans (fl. fifth century BC), the Stoics (fl. fourth century BC), Augustine (AD 354–430), Boethius (AD 477–524), Anselm (1033–1109), Aquinas (1224–74), John Duns Scotus (1265–1308), Descartes (1596–1650), Locke (1632–1704), Leibniz (1646–1716), and Kant (1724–1804)—all offered deep arguments for the existence of God.

It is true that two of the most famous philosophers of the nineteenth century were atheists, Karl Marx (1818–83) and Friedrich Nietzsche (1844–1900). But neither gave a single philosophical argument for his atheism, and neither rationally critiqued even one philosophical argument for God's existence. Their atheism was unsubstantiated.

It is also true that during the first half of the twentieth century, atheism was popular among many academic philosophers. But the pendulum has swung. Since the 1960s, many of the leading philosophers in such subfields as modal logic, metaphysics, epistemology, ethics, and philosophy of religion have been theists who offered and defended profound philosophical arguments for their belief in God.[2]

THE CHALLENGE OF SCIENTISM

Many college students today deny the existence of God. The argument I hear most often goes something like this: (1) science is our only way of knowing anything, our only path to truth; (2) science has explained everything down to just about the last details, without reference to God or to anything supernatural; (3) belief in God has thus become intellectually superfluous; (4) therefore, God does not exist. This popular line of reasoning requires a response before I present my first philosophical argument for God's existence.

The claim that science is our only way of knowing anything, our only path to truth, is called "scientism." When I survey students at the start of an academic quarter, I find that the majority initially believe that scientism is true. But is it true? As we proceed, keep in mind the distinction between science and scient*ism*. The two are not the same thing. "Science" refers to those subjects (physics, chemistry, biology, geology, etc.) that restrict themselves to research based on the scientific method of observation and hypothesis testing. The sciences have certainly enlarged our knowledge of the world. All philosophers today agree on this. The scientific method is surely *one* guide to truth. It doesn't follow, however, from the fact that science is one guide to truth that science is the *only* guide to truth. Scientism goes further and claims that science is our only guide to truth.

The problem with this position can be demonstrated quickly. Consider the following sentence, which I will name S.

> S: Science is our only path to truth; nothing is known unless it has been proved by science.

Now, exactly which scientific experiment or series of experiments has ever proved that S is true? Which verified scientific theory appearing in the standard textbooks validates S? No scientist has ever carried out an experiment or established a theory showing scientifically that S is true, which is why scientism is neither presented nor defended in any reputable physics, chemistry, or biology textbook.

The sentence S has not been proved by science because it is not a scientifically testable or confirmable thesis. But if scientism cannot be proved true using the only method it claims is valid—the scientific method—then why believe it? Indeed, considered critically, scientism is actually what philosophers call a "self-defeating" view because accepting it as true commits you to saying that you have no reason at all to think it is true.

I know of no scientists who explicitly endorse scientism. But I regularly see the view expressed in student papers. Certainly none of the seventeenth-century founders of modern science endorsed scientism; most gave philosophical arguments for God's existence. Some even included philosophical arguments for God's existence in their scientific treatises.[3] Numerous prominent scientists today have given philosophical arguments for the existence of God—indicating that they reject scientism. Francis Collins, for example, former director of the National Institutes of Health who served as the head of the Human Genome Project, wrote a book in which he argues philosophically for the existence of God based on the apparent design in the genetic code.[4] The mathematician and astrophysicist Georges Lemaître (1894–1966), a Catholic priest, founded big bang astrophysics, about which more in the next chapter.

Many beliefs about matters of fundamental importance are reasonable—and are supported by good reasoning—even though they have not been, and cannot be, proved within the natural sciences such as physics, biology, and chemistry. For instance, isn't it as certain as anything we know that love is an intrinsically good and beautiful thing? That each person, regardless of social status, nationality, ethnicity, income, or color, is a being of great intrinsic worth and deserving of equal concern and respect? That each human being possesses innate, universal rights? That Samuel Barber's *Adagio for Strings* is a beautiful composition? These statements are all true—and each can be supported by compelling reasoning—yet they cannot be proved by science. Beauty and intrinsic moral value are not properties listed in the standard handbooks of physics and chemistry. Scientific knowledge is thus a fraction of the sum total of all human knowledge and needs to be interpreted within that sum total.

To return to philosophy, since the 1960s, many of the cutting-edge and most respected philosophers, spanning every field of the discipline, have presented and defended thoughtful arguments for God's existence. Many of these arguments can be found in a recent volume edited by the philosophers Jerry Walls and Trent Dougherty, *Two Dozen (or so) Arguments for God: The Plantinga Project*.[5] Richard Swinburne, professor of philosophy (now emeritus) at Oxford University (b. 1934), examines and rigorously defends a number of the greatest theistic arguments in his seminal book, *The Existence of God*.[6]

Indeed, there are so many deep and thoughtful arguments for God's existence that only a sample can be presented in the space of this book. I'll introduce four, each a line of thought that has roots in ancient philosophy but that has been continuously updated and deepened with new observations. Two are versions of what philosophers call the "design argument," and two are versions of what philosophers call the "cosmological argument." None of these arguments is offered as a definitive "proof." Each is intended only as food for thought and as an invitation to further reflection—in an apologetical spirit of gentleness and respect.

THE ARGUMENT FROM DESIGN

One of the first philosophers to give this famous argument, if we go by the historical record, was Socrates, among the wisest of all philosophers, in my opinion. According to his student Xenophon's account, Socrates presented the argument from design in the form of an analogy or similarity drawn between the deep structure of the universe and the deep structure of intelligently designed things such as songs, buildings, cities, and works of art.[7] Here is my interpretation.

Think about nature's cycles: the seasons, the setting of the sun and the moon, the flow of rivers to the ocean. They appear woven together like the threads of a coat. The universe presents itself to us not as random chaos but as an orderly, interconnected system of many diverse things functioning together. We express our belief in the orderliness and consistency of nature every time we make a prediction, take a step, drink a glass of water, or wait for the sun to rise.

Now think about the products of intelligence: songs, buildings, city plans, works of poetry and art. Each also has many interlaced parts fitted together into a complex system that functions.

When we see a building under construction, the chief architect is the ultimate source of the building's design plan. When a song comes into existence, the composer is the source of the song's melody or structure. When we see a picture being painted, we see that the artist is the cause of the painting's order, and so forth. The root cause of the orders we observe in buildings, cities, songs, and works of art is in each case a mind, that is, an intelligent designer who imposed an observed order on underlying parts.

It is a sound principle of analogical reasoning that like effects probably have like causes. Therefore, since the order of nature is similar to the order we observe in intelligently designed things, the cause of nature's order is probably also an intelligent designer, albeit one great enough to have imposed an order on the universe as a whole. The order of the universe, in short, is the expression of a mind.

Note that the claim here is *not* that the premises prove the conclusion true with complete certainty. Rather, the claim is that the conclusion is the most reasonable conclusion to draw based on the premises.

Philosophers call this kind of argument "analogical" because it is rooted in an analogy or similarity drawn between two or more things. We reason by analogy all the time. Suppose that Lucca gets sick and has a specific set of symptoms. The next day his brother, Ben, gets sick and shows the same symptoms. On discovering the cause of Lucca's illness, the doctor naturally reasons by analogy that Ben's illness probably has the same cause. Why? Similar effects probably have similar causes. Or a teenager prepares to buy his first car. He doesn't have much money, but he wants it to be reliable. He reasons analogically: "Dad's car is a Chevrolet, and it's reliable. Mr. Cooper's car is a Chevrolet, and it's reliable. The car for sale down the street is also a Chevrolet, so it's probably also reliable."

Analogical reasoning is not only part of our shared common sense; it is also an integral part of science. Many of the great arguments of science are based on an analogy between two or more things. Here's an analogical argument from the health sciences. Human hearts and monkey hearts have many attributes in common. Drug X cures heart disease in monkeys. Like effects probably have like causes. Therefore, it is reasonable to believe that drug X will cure heart disease in humans.

Applied to the abstract, structured order of the universe, analogical reasoning points our minds toward the existence of an intelligent designer as the source of that order. So argued Socrates.

In one form or another, design arguments for God's existence can be found in the writings of most of the greatest philosophers and scientists in history. Versions of the argument also appear in the Jewish, Hindu, and Muslim philosophical traditions. In addition, the list of recent scholars, East and West, who have defended the argument is long and includes many of the most eminent philosophers and scientists of our time. The argument from design is not only historically significant and mainstream; it is also very contemporary.

Some may object at this point: Why just one designer? Why not many? After all, it takes many architects to design a skyscraper, and sometimes several artists jointly compose a song — Rodgers and Hammerstein, Lennon and McCartney, for instance.

This objection was actually made in ancient times. However, defenders of the design argument are not without a reply. They point to the highly integrated unity of the universe — the fact that the regularities of nature appear to be interlocking parts of a single highly interconnected system. This unity points our minds to one supreme or superintending designer rather than to many.

Let's consider this issue for a moment. Physicists have discovered that the behavior of matter and energy can be described using partial differential equations that fit together into one unified system of interrelated mathematical formulas. In *Dreams of a Final Theory*, the theoretical physicist and Nobel Prize winner Steven Weinberg, one of the greatest physicists of our time, comments:

Think of the space of scientific theories as being filled with arrows, pointing toward each principle and away from the others by which it is explained. These arrows of explanation have already revealed a remarkable pattern: They do not form separate disconnected clumps, representing independent sciences, and they do not wander aimlessly—rather they are all connected and if followed backward (to deeper levels) they all seem to flow from a common starting point.[8]

Weinberg's statement is worth pondering. All the evidence of astrophysics indicates that the universal order stems from a single cause, not from many. That fact alone argues against the suggestion of many designers. However, physicists—in their capacity as physicists—have never given a scientific explanation for why this unified order exists. Nor have they explained why the universe seems to be one great whole stemming from one cause.

The ancient Greeks saw the universe as a puzzle to be figured out, a phenomenon to be rationally explained, rather than just as something that is there. That attitude of mind led them to formulate their academic theories of philosophy, science, proof-based mathematics, history, ethics, democracy, scientific medicine, and versions of the design argument—in writing. Modern scientists look at the universe the same way, as a puzzle to be solved. The question Socrates asked is legitimate: Why is the universe orderly and predictable on a large scale rather than disorderly and totally random?

Inference to the Best Explanation

If you reject the conclusion of Socrates's design argument, then you face an extremely difficult task. How do *you* explain the fact that the material universe is orderly, unified, and predictable on a large scale rather than disorderly and unpredictable? More specifically, how do you explain the fact that the trillions and trillions of particles of matter and quanta of energy that compose our universe are not randomly and aimlessly flitting about with no predictable pattern but instead fit together into a unified order that can be described with mathematical equations that can be grasped by a rational mind?

Science does not answer the question. Look at a college physics textbook and you'll see hundreds of mathematical formulas describing the predictable behavior of matter and energy across every domain in the universe.

What you will *not* see is even an attempt at explaining—within physics—why matter obeys a system of universal laws.

The deep order of nature was known in ancient times. Thanks to the discoveries of the Greek mathematician and philosopher Pythagoras (570–495 BC), the ancient Greeks were aware that orderly mathematical substructures can be found at levels of reality too fundamental and abstract to observe, such as the mathematical order underlying the harmonic intervals of the musical scale.[9] They knew that nature is characterized by interlocking cycles and systems from the smallest to the largest scales. Since their time, scientists have found that the deeper they probe the material universe, the deeper the order becomes.

So how are we to explain the fact that the universe is orderly and predictable? The question suggests a different kind of design argument, one that takes the form of an inference to the best explanation. Again, the basic format goes about like this.

1. A collection of data (facts, observations) in need of explanation is presented.
2. On the basis of common criteria, it is argued that hypothesis H is the best overall explanation of the data.
3. Therefore, it is probable that H is true.
4. Therefore, H is the most reasonable conclusion to draw based on the data.

But how do we decide which of two competing explanations is best? We decide on the basis of rational and tested criteria, including the following:

1. A good explanation is consistent with already known facts.
2. A good explanation is internally consistent; that is, it is not self-contradictory.
3. One explanation is better than another if it explains a wider array of facts.
4. If the data is more expected on the basis of one proposed hypothesis than on the basis of another, then the first hypothesis is the likelier explanation.

5. If two explanations explain the very same set of facts, the simpler explanation—the one that makes fewer assumptions or posits fewer entities or both—is the more reasonable choice.

The fifth criterion requires some comment. Philosophers and scientists from earliest times have agreed that when two hypotheses equally explain the very same data, the simpler of the two is the more reasonable choice. Since the fourteenth century, this principle of explanation has been called Ockham's razor in honor of William of Ockham (1287–1347), a medieval logician and scientific pioneer who was the first to state it explicitly and defend it. Ockham's principle is now an integral part of scientific practice because scientists have discovered that (a) for every set of data, an infinite number of potential explanations are possible, each of increasing complexity, and (b) it is impossible to settle on one explanation without assuming Ockham's principle or one like it. We also employ this principle in everyday life.

Imagine this. Exactly 66 shoeprints are found at a crime scene. Investigators determine that all 66 are the same size, come from the same brand of shoe, and show identical patterns of wear. Hypothesis 1 is that all 66 were made by one person. Hypothesis 2 is that two people left the prints, each wearing identical shoes. Hypothesis 3 is that three individuals left the prints, and so forth. (It is even theoretically possible that 66 one-legged, hopping people each wearing identical (left or right) shoes with the same wear patterns and so forth left the prints. You can see where this is going. In the absence of contrary evidence, isn't the first hypothesis the most reasonable choice?[10]

Now here is Socrates's design argument reconfigured into an inference to the best explanation placed in textbook form with numbered steps.

An Inference to the Best Explanation Design Argument

1. Careful observation indicates that the material universe from the smallest to the largest scales is orderly, interlaced, and unified. (This is the data to be explained.)

2. Hypothesis 1 is that the universal order is the product of a superintending mind or intelligent designer.

3. Hypothesis 2 is that the universal order is the product of absolute, blind, unstructured, undirected random chance.

4. Hypothesis 3 is that nature simply *has* to be organized in just this specific form, just as 2 + 3 must be 5 or a whole has to be greater than its parts. In short, nature's order is due to necessity.

5. No one has suggested a plausible alternative to these three hypotheses.

6. The design hypothesis is the best available explanation of the data.

7. Therefore, the most reasonable conclusion to draw is that the order of the universe is the product of an intelligent designer.

Now for a subargument in defense of premise 6.

Argument for premise 6: Design is the best explanation. Here is a thought experiment to help you consider hypothesis 2, the suggestion that the order of the universe is the product of blind, unstructured chance. Imagine that you walk into class one day to find one hundred colorful leaves arranged on the floor in the form of this English sentence: "The professor is sick today; class is canceled." In addition, suppose that the professor is nowhere to be seen. Which hypothesis makes the best sense of the observed data?

A. The wind blew the leaves in from outside, and they happened to form the perfectly structured sentence by sheer, blind, random chance.

B. An intelligent being with a knowledge of the professor's illness arranged the leaves intentionally to convey a message.

How reasonable is hypothesis A? In everyday life, we never appeal to purely random chance when making sense of an order like this. And the reason we do not is that we know by experience that blind, unstructured chance alone never brings complex, improbable, and functional order into existence out of sheer disorder or chaos. A story is in order.

I once took my watch into a shop for repair. The watchmaker—a friend I had known in high school—opened my watch and dumped its many parts onto his workbench. (This was before the invention of digital watches.) I thought, "How is he ever going to put that thing back together?" When I returned a few weeks later, the watch was like brand-new. Now,

I would not have believed him if he had told me, "I put all the parts in a bag, shook it up, and when I dumped it all out, your watch was back together and working perfectly." In everyday life we never observe complex, functional order come into existence out of sheer unstructured randomness.

The "it's all due to pure chance" hypothesis goes back to ancient times. In the fifth century BC, the Greek philosopher Leucippus of Miletus founded the school of philosophy known as "atomism" based on the hypothesis that every observable object is composed of tiny, indivisible particles too small to be seen, which he named "atoms" (from the Greek word for "uncuttable"). Leucippus's atomic hypothesis anticipated modern physics by more than two thousand years.

Leucippus was aware that the universe is amazingly orderly, predictable, and highly integrated. However, he rejected intelligent design in favor of a pure chance hypothesis, which I paraphrase as follows:

> There is no intelligent designer. The most reasonable explanation of the unified order of nature is that it is all just one giant accident. Long ago, billions and billions of primeval atoms falling through the void (empty space) happened by sheer chance to swerve and fall into the predictable order we call nature—for no reason at all. Blind, random chance is the ultimate explanation of all things.[11]

Let's reflect on this proposal for a moment. Suppose that we are playing five-card stud poker and I am dealing. Imagine that I deal myself a royal flush ten times in a row and win every game. When you question my honesty, I reply, "It was just an amazing run of pure, dumb luck—one big chance accident after another." Would that be an intellectually satisfying explanation? Would that make the best sense of the highly improbable pattern of the hands I dealt? (The odds against drawing one royal flush in five-card stud once are 649,000 to 1.) Or would intelligent design—in this case the hypothesis that I cheated—make better sense of the data?

But if blind, random chance is not a good explanation for a small-scale order such as a winning streak in a crooked game of cards, why is it a reasonable explanation for the largest order of all, the universal pattern that has persisted for billions of years?

Turning to hypothesis 3, the possibility that necessity is the source of the universal order, contemporary physics reveals that there is nothing at all necessary about the way the world is structured. Later in this chapter, we will see that physicists have designed thousands of mathematical models, each expressing a different way a material universe could be structured. Each model contains different equations describing the different ways that laws of physics might structure a particular universe. Using computers to manage vast quantities of data, physicists have found that the laws of nature that govern our universe and give it its unified form could have been different in infinitely many alternative ways. So, there is nothing mathematically or physically necessary about the present form or order of the universe. Which raises the question: Why is it structured this way and not another?

Going Further

Consider the fourth common criterion we use when we judge competing explanations. If the data is more expected on the basis of one hypothesis (H1) than on another (H2), then H1 is the more likely explanation. For example, suppose that a jewelry store owner is shot during a robbery. Using video footage from the store's cameras, detectives focus on Sam Smith, a career criminal who lives nearby. The stolen jewels are found in Smith's possession immediately after the crime, and Smith's fingerprints are on the murder weapon that was left behind. This is the data in need of explanation.

Now consider two hypotheses:

H1: Smith robbed the store and shot the owner.

H2: Someone else robbed the store and shot the owner.

If we assume that H1 is true, the evidence is not surprising (Smith's fingerprints on the gun and the jewelry found in his possession shortly after the crime). For if Smith robbed the store, we would expect to find his fingerprints on the gun left behind, and we would not be surprised to learn that the jewels were found in his possession shortly after the crime.

However, if we suppose that H2 is true, the evidence is not expected. For if someone else committed the crime, it would be very surprising to find Smith's fingerprints on the murder weapon. It would also be surprising that the jewels would be found in Smith's possession shortly after the crime. The data is therefore more expected, more likely, on the basis of H1 than on H2. If so, that is a reason to suppose that H1 is the likelier explanation.

Now let H1 and H2 be defined as follows:

H1: The order of the universe is the product of an intelligent mind.

H2: The order of the universe is the product of blind, unstructured, purely random chance.

The data (the order of the cosmos) is expected on the basis of H1. Based on H2, the data is astonishingly surprising.

To test your educated intuition, suppose that one morning fifty white rocks are observed scattered randomly on the ground in front of Judy's house at 5133 Kensington Avenue. The next morning, they are observed in an arrangement that spells out in perfectly formed letters Judy's address, "5133." This is the data to be explained. Which of the following two hypotheses is more likely?

H1* During the night, the rocks were arranged by an intelligent agent on purpose (to display the correct address).

H2* During the night a blind, random gust of wind picked up the rocks, and then they accidentally dropped into the observed pattern—an arrangement that by blind chance just happened to give the correct address.

Isn't the fact in need of explanation—the orderly and correct arrangement of the rocks— expected on H1* and surprising on H2*?

Imagine standing there in the morning looking at the rocks spelling out the correct address. If you didn't know which hypothesis was true and were offered a chance to bet, would you bet your money on H2*? Or on H1*? What does this tell us regarding the choice between design and chance?

BACK TO THE QUESTION

Socrates would ask, If you do not believe that intelligent design is the best explanation, then how do you explain the fact that the universe is orderly and unified from the largest to the smallest scales? Why isn't it all just a completely random unpredictable chaos?

At the dawn of Western civilization, the Greek scholar Thales (ca. 625–ca. 545 BC), the first philosopher on record, asked a related question: What holds everything together? What is the One that makes this a *uni*verse rather than a chaotic, nonorderly *multi*verse? In philosophy, this pathbreaking question is known as "the problem of the One and the Many." The design argument, which Thales eventually reached, offers an answer to this, the first great philosophical question recorded in the Western tradition.

What are we to make of this inference to the best explanation version of Socrates's design argument? The first thing to keep in mind is that best explanation reasoning is common in everyday life. For example, Jan comes home hungry and finds that the leftover tomato soup is gone. She reasons, "My roommate Joe hates soup. My roommate Sue can't stand tomato soup. The cat would eat it, but he can't get into the refrigerator. However, my roommate Chris loves tomato soup, and he has done this before. The best explanation is that Chris ate the leftover soup. The most reasonable conclusion to draw is therefore that Chris is the culprit."

Best explanation arguments are also ubiquitous in civil and criminal courts of law. When a jury finds the defendant guilty, it is usually because the hypothesis—the defendant committed the offense—best explains the verified facts presented by the prosecution.

Inference to the best explanation reasoning is also routinely employed in the physical sciences, the social sciences, and the humanities. Einstein's arguments for his general and special theories of relativity, for example, are best explanation arguments. The case for every large-scale theory in science and in the social sciences ultimately boils down to the claim that the favored theory best explains the data at hand.

Indeed, best explanation reasoning is so common in life that if we were to reject it, we would have to give up most of what we believe about the world. Many philosophers maintain that the design argument is more compelling when stated as an inference to the best explanation rather than as an analogy. Compare the two versions of the argument and decide for yourself.

One thing is certain: the conclusion of the design argument contradicts nothing in physics or in any of the other branches of science. Indeed, the argument complements physics, and science in general, for it takes our explanation of the universe one level deeper.

HAS SCIENCE ALREADY EXPLAINED WHY THE UNIVERSE IS ORDERLY?

The answer is definitely no. The reason, in a nutshell, is that scientific accounts explain their target phenomena by reference to one or more interlaced laws of nature. However, no matter how broad thir scope, scientific explanations never explain why the laws of nature they cite exist in the first place.

This is why Michio Kaku, a famed physicist and public intellectual, writes in *The God Equation: The Quest for a Theory of Everything*, "Physics says nothing about where the laws of physics themselves come from. . . . The key feature of any [physical] theory of everything is likely to be its symmetry. But where does this symmetry come from? This symmetry would be a by-product of deep mathematical truths. But where does mathematics come from? On this question, [science] is again silent."[12]

In sum, every scientific explanation explains its data by reference to the laws of nature—universal regularities confirmed by observation. Left unanswered in each case is the question: Why do the laws of nature exist? Put another way: Why is nature governed by laws? Why is it not lawless? This, in brief, is why science will never, by itself, explain why the world is orderly rather than disorderly.

This is not to say that science is invalid or that science is all wrong. Science explains many things. Science has deepened our knowledge of the world. This is only to say that an overall explanation of the order of the universe is beyond its theoretical reach. The point is not new. More than two thousand years ago, the Greek philosophers Socrates, Plato, and Aristotle argued that the physical sciences alone cannot explain everything.

DAVID HUME'S CRITIQUE OF ALL DESIGN ARGUMENTS

By the middle of the eighteenth century, the argument from design was accepted by most working scientists, and nearly everyone agreed that belief in God was in harmony with modern experimental science. Many scientists even included a design argument in their scientific treatises. This con-

> **Why Things Don't Fall Down**
>
> In his wonderful book, *Structures: Or Why Things Don't Fall Down*, J. E. Gordon writes:
>
>> Everything is structure—from the body of an earthworm and the skeleton of a kangaroo to medieval English longbows, ancient Greek triremes, and Chinese junks. And everything we do has a structural impact, both physically—climb the tower of a cathedral and it becomes shorter by your weight—and aesthetically: a bridge might be strong and safe, but, if designed inelegantly, it will have a negative impact on the landscape.[13]
>
> We are surrounded by structures. The movement of every atom in the universe is governed by the mathematically structured laws of physics. Every chemical reaction is governed by the structured laws of chemistry. Structured laws of biology govern the complex metabolism inside each cell. Going deeper still, mathematics is all structure. Read any standard math textbook, and every equation is a structure, albeit an abstract or immaterial one. The universe is saturated with structure. The philosophical question is: Where does all this amazing structure come from? Science doesn't answer the question. The design argument offers an answer.

sensus was finally challenged in 1778, with the posthumous publication of *Dialogues concerning Natural Religion* by the Scottish philosopher David Hume (1711–76). In this book Hume presented the first major, systematic, philosophical criticism of the design argument in modern times. Many in the New Atheist movement today believe that Hume's objections demolished the design argument and showed that theism is irrational. When I was a young philosophy student, the consensus in the classes I took was that Hume's objections had made the design argument obsolete.

However, since Hume wrote his famous book, theistic philosophers have offered reasonable replies to each of the objections he raised. And when you see Hume's final conclusion on the matter, after we have examined his objections, you may well suspect that he too believed that there are reasonable replies to the objections he raised.

Objection 1: Instead of an Intelligent Designer, Why Not an Unintelligent Spider?

Hume wrote the *Dialogues* in the form of a fictional conversation between three characters debating the existence of God. Philo, the first character, has a skeptical attitude toward religion; Cleanthes argues that we have good reason to believe in God; Demea is religious, but he is a fideist: he believes reason has nothing to do with religious belief. He claims to believe "by faith alone." In their discussion, Hume puts an interesting objection to the design argument into the mouth of Philo. Here is my summary.

If we must posit a cosmic designer, why assume that the designer is intelligent and personal? Why suppose it is a divine being we should worship? Why not hypothesize an unintelligent source of order? Consider a spider web. Seen glistening in the morning light, it has a complex and beautiful geometrical order. Yet this complex order is produced by an unintelligent beast. Complex order, therefore, does not always come from intelligence. Thus, it is just as reasonable to conclude that the order of the universe was produced by a gigantic, unintelligent spider, or something similar.[14]

This is a clever objection. But is Hume's alternative hypothesis—that an unintelligent being such as a large spider created the universal order—a reasonable explanation for the fundamental order of the entire cosmos, including the mathematical equations discovered by modern physics and the formulas discovered in modern chemistry? A defender of Hume might reply, "Why not? Although an ordinary spider may not be aware of the fact, its web follows complicated principles of geometry."

In reply, theists have argued that although it is unintelligent, a spider possesses an enormously complicated and functional organizational structure. Even tiny spiders are composed of billions of parts arranged in a special, interlaced, functional way. Anything that complex and functional yet lacking intelligence, they argue, only makes sense when understood as the product of an intelligence beyond itself. Furthermore, it is astronomically improbable that an order as vast as that of this universe would burst forth and persist from a purely nonrational source.

On hearing this reply, many ask: But wouldn't God also be an enormously complex and structured being that stands in need of further explanation? I'll take up this question below.

Objection 2: Why Not Many Designers?

When scientists and philosophers of Hume's day presented the design argument, they typically argued that one supreme designer exists. Essentially, Philo replies, Why not postulate many designers instead of one? After all, a machine, a temple, or a complex mechanism is typically the product of a committee. "A great number of men join in building a house or a ship," says Hume, "why may not several deities combine in framing a world?"[15] This is polytheism, or belief in many gods.

I've already touched on the theistic reply. Ockham's razor points us to one designer rather than many. Contemporary astrophysics also supports the conclusion that there is one designer rather than many. Recall the words of Steven Weinberg. Scientific explanations "are all connected and if followed backward (to deeper levels) they all seem to flow from a common starting point."[16] And in *The Little Book of the Big Bang: A Cosmic Primer*, the astrophysicist Craig Hogan presents the now-standard model of the universe in the form of a single, unified chain of causes and effects that traces back through many cosmic epochs to a single source.[17] Although they could not have known it, Thales, Socrates, and the scientists who advocated the design argument during the eighteenth century were all in line with contemporary astrophysics when they argued for a single source of order—a One over the Many—to explain the overall structure of the cosmos.

Objection 3: The Argument from Lack of Order

Expressed as an inference to the best explanation, the design argument concludes that the order of nature is best explained as the product of a mind. But the universe also contains evidence of a lack of order. Think about hurricanes, earthquakes, and cancers. We can add to this the poor "design" of the human spine—so prone to malfunction and pain. We also know that the universe contains "chaotic" systems in which a small change in one region leads to a massive and seemingly disconnected change in a region far distant. For instance, a flea falls off a mouse in Pakistan, causing a tornado in Kansas.

Hume's objection from disorder is that if order is evidence of a designer, then disorder is evidence against the existence of a designer. The design argument, expressed as an inference to the best explanation, needs to weigh both the evidence of order and the evidence of disorder before concluding that an intelligent designer exists. Perhaps the disorder present in the world exceeds the order and shows that there is likely no intelligent designer.

Defenders of the design argument are not without a reply. First, any significant amount of order points to an ordering intelligence, for order is the characteristic product of mind. Therefore, "some things don't seem ordered" doesn't negate the claim that other things do. Next, hurricanes are studied in the field of meteorology. Earthquakes are studied in the field of seismology, a branch of geophysics. Cancer is studied by oncologists, and chaotic systems are examined in chaos theory, a branch of mathematics. Hurricanes, earthquakes, and so forth must therefore be orderly at some level if each can be studied scientifically. The word *chaos* seems to connote disorder, but chaos theorists have discovered that chaotic systems are governed by mathematical laws reflecting deep underlying regularities. Thus, rather than being examples of disorder, hurricanes, cancer, and such are interlaced parts of one overall system.

Objection 4: Why Not a Finite, Limited Deity?

Many arguments from design conclude with the existence of God defined as an infinitely perfect being who is omnipotent (infinitely powerful), omniscient (infinitely knowing), and omnibenevolent (infinitely good). In *An Enquiry concerning Human Understanding* (1751), Hume objected to this way of concluding the design argument. When we infer any particular cause from an effect, we must proportion the one to the other, he argued. We should never "ascribe to the cause any qualities, but what are exactly sufficient to produce the effect. . . . Allowing, therefore, the gods to be the authors of the existence or order of the universe; it follows, that they possess [only] that . . . degree of power, intelligence, and benevolence, which appears in their workmanship."[18] So just as we cannot infer an infinite cause from a finite effect or a perfect cause from an imperfect effect, we cannot infer that the cause of the world is either infinite or perfect, for the world appears to be finite and imperfect. If we must hypothesize an intelligent designer then, we should attribute to it only finite power, limited intelligence, and limited goodness.

Hume makes a strong point here. However, his point does not apply to all versions of the design argument or to all philosophical thought about God. By "infinitely powerful," some philosophers mean simply that God's power is not limited or bound by anything we know in this world. God, they argue, must be an unimaginably powerful being whose power extends beyond anything we can possibly define or limit in analytic detail.

Similarly for God's knowledge, goodness, and love. Each must be great beyond anything we can possibly imagine or define in detail in this world. This way of thinking about God, I believe, avoids Hume's objection entirely.

Philosophers in the field of philosophical theology think deeply about the nature of God. This is a field that offers any serious searcher practically a lifetime of study.[19]

Objection 5: Who Designed the Designer?

This is perhaps Hume's strongest objection. With this question he seems to have the theist in a logical bind. If the theist replies, "A designer of the designer," then the question arises again: "Who designed that one?" If the theist replies, "A designer of the designer of the designer," the question again recycles and we get nowhere. If the theist says, "It's designers all the way back to infinity," then the theist is positing what is called an "infinite explanatory regression" of designers. What is this? An infinite explanatory regression is an unending series in which one item is explained in terms of a prior item, which is explained in terms of a prior item, and so forth back and back forever, with no first item in the series and no first explanation.

So, who or what designed the designer? Philosophical theists have offered deep and very involved answers to Hume's question. Rather than add another chapter to this book, I'll offer a compressed reply. First of all, since ancient times, philosophers and logicians have agreed that an infinite explanatory regression offered as an explanation of some phenomenon p does not, and by its nature, cannot explain p, for any p you care to mention.

Here is an example. Imagine that I am holding a book in my hand, and you ask me, "Where did you buy it?" Suppose I reply, "I didn't buy it. I borrowed it from a friend." When you ask me where the friend bought the book, I reply that the friend borrowed it from someone who already owned it. When you ask where that person bought the book, I answer that he borrowed it from a previous owner. Now imagine that after the question has recycled a few more times. I reply, "No one first owned or bought the book. It's borrowers all the way back to infinity." That would be an infinite regression explanation. It is obvious that an infinite regression of book borrowers is not going to answer this further question: Why does the particular book exist?

Next, given that an infinite regression will never explain its target phenomenon—that which is in need of explanation—an infinite regression is never a satisfying explanation. It follows that an infinite regression of designers will not explain the world's order. The appendix at the end of this chapter provides a more detailed reason why no infinite regression for the existence of some phenomenon p will ever explain p.

Now the design argument gives us good reason to believe that the world owes its order to an intelligent designer. So, with an infinite regression of designers ruled out, we are left with one ultimate designer. But if there is one ultimate designer, then that being's order must be intrinsic—not derived from a previous designer.

Some will surely reply: Why not suppose the material universe's order is intrinsic and not due to an intelligent designer? My reply is that the answer to that question has been given. The answer is contained within the design argument itself.[20]

Hume's Surprising Conclusion

After the conversation between Philo, Cleanthes, and Demea ends, Hume editorializes and sides with the theist Cleanthes. The order we observe in nature, Hume states, is indeed good evidence that the universe was designed by a superintending mind of immense magnitude.

> Cleanthes and Philo did not pursue this conversation much further; and as nothing ever made greater impression on me than all the reasonings of that day, so I confess that on carefully looking over the whole conversation I cannot help thinking that Philo's principles are more probable than Demea's, but that those of Cleanthes approach still nearer to the truth.[21]

THE FINE-TUNING DESIGN ARGUMENT

Although the design argument for the existence of God goes back to ancient times, it has been updated and deepened by contemporary physicists and philosophers. The latest version takes matters down to the level of the fundamental particles and forces of nature studied in atomic physics. Some context, however, is required before I continue.

After Darwin proposed his theory of evolution by natural selection in 1859, many scientists rejected theism and claimed that an unguided, purely natural process of evolution operating on random mutations in living things can explain all the order that needs explaining, including the amazing complexity we see in living organisms. Belief in God or an intelligent designer, they claimed, is no longer needed to make sense of our world. Theism, they said, is intellectually obsolete now that we have Darwin's theory of evolution.

However, during the second half of the twentieth century, theoretical physicists studying subatomic particles and the universal physical laws that govern their behavior made a surprising discovery. They discovered a complex background system functioning deep within the universe at the subatomic level, somewhat the way the operating system of a computer functions quietly in the background when an application is run. Furthermore, they found that the evolutionary process of natural selection by random mutation depends crucially on the operation of this background system; natural selection would not have occurred if this background system had not been in place and operating correctly *beforehand*.

To their great surprise, they soon discovered that no conceivable process of evolution by natural selection can even get started unless this background program, or one very similar to it, is already in place and running properly. It followed that the newly found background order operating deep within nature cannot itself be the product of the evolutionary process discovered by Darwin.

Even more surprising was the stunning degree of organized complexity displayed by this universal background order: it looked every bit as designed as a working watch. One famous scientist claimed that it looked as designed as a Boeing jetliner.[22]

What is this newly discovered background order? Why does it look purposely designed? The details are contained in the latest design argument, one initially stated by astrophysicists during the second half of the twentieth century, known today as the "fine-tuning argument."

Atomic Details

Since the new design argument rests on recent discoveries in particle physics, further background is required.[23] Early in the twentieth century, physicists began uncovering the atomic details of the material universe. According to the current model, the universe contains four fundamental kinds of particles:

- protons and neutrons, which exist in the nucleus of the atom;
- electrons, which orbit the atomic nucleus;
- photons, which carry electromagnetic radiation; and
- quarks, which exist inside protons and neutrons.

In addition, the behavior of all particles of matter and energy across the universe obeys four fundamental laws of nature:

- The electromagnetic force holds the negatively charged electrons in their orbits around the positively charged atomic nucleus.
- The strong nuclear force holds protons and neutrons together within the atom's nucleus.
- The weak nuclear force governs radioactivity.
- The gravitational force operates between all particles of matter.

Thanks to powerful computers and advanced telescopes, astrophysicists discovered that no matter which region of the universe we study, the basic properties of the particles of matter and the fundamental forces of nature remain constant. These unchanging properties have been measured in physics labs and are represented in mathematical formulas today by constants—numbers inside equations that do not change. Since these constants determine the deep structure of the whole universe, they are called the "universal constants."[24] The astrophysicists John Gribbin and Martin Rees write, "Physicists have now reduced nature still further. They now believe that the basic structure of the entire physical world . . . is in principle determined by a few basic 'constants.' These are the masses of a few so-called elementary particles, and the strengths of the forces — electric, nuclear, and gravitational—that bind those particles together and govern their motions."[25]

Once physicists had precise values for several universal constants, they asked an intriguing question: What would the universe have been like if these constants had taken different values? For instance, what would the universe be like if the force of gravity had been 1 percent less or 1 percent more than it actually is? What would the universe be like if protons were 1 percent heavier? To their amazement, when they plugged alternative constants into their mathematical models of the universe, they discovered that if even *one* of the universal constants had taken a slightly different value, by an astonishingly small amount, the universe would have been so disorderly that no evolutionary process of any kind would have occurred, and life in any conceivable form would not have been possible.[26]

For example, writing in *Nature*, one of the most prestigious scientific journals in the world, the physicists Brandon Carr and Martin Rees offer this assessment.

> The basic features of galaxies, stars, planets, and the everyday world are essentially determined by a few microphysical constants. . . . [S]everal aspects of our Universe—some of which seem to be prerequisites for the evolution of any form of life—depend rather delicately on apparent "coincidences" among the physical constants.[27]

Many other respected physicists have commented on the surprising arrangement of the universal constants, including Paul Davies:

> If we could play God, and select values for [the fundamental constants] by twiddling a set of knobs, we would find that almost all knob settings would render the universe uninhabitable. Some knobs would have to be fine-tuned to enormous precision if life is to flourish in the universe.[28]

And John Barrow and Frank Tippler:

> If we were to imagine a whole collection of hypothetical "other universes" in which all the [constants] that define the structure of our universe take on all possible permutations of values, then we find that almost all of these other possible universes we have created on paper are stillborn, unable to give rise to that type of chemical complexity that we call "life." The more we examine the other types of universes[,] . . . the more special and unusual do the properties of the actual universe appear to be.[29]

And Heinz Pagels:

> The universe, it seems, has been finely tuned for our comfort; its properties appear to be precisely conducive to intelligent life. The force of gravity, for example, could hardly have been set at a more ideal level.[30]

And John Gribbin:

> Our form of life depends, in delicate and subtle ways, on several apparent "coincidences" in the fundamental laws of nature which make the universe tick. Without these coincidences, we would not be here to puzzle over the problem of their existence.
> If we modify the value of one of the fundamental constants, something invariably goes wrong, leading to a universe that is inhospitable to life. Whenever we adjust a second constant in an attempt to fix the problem the result is generally to create three new problems for every one we "solve." The conditions in our universe really do seem to be uniquely suitable for life.[31]
> The universe seems to have been set up in such a way that interesting things can happen in it. It is very easy to imagine other kinds of universes, which would have been stillborn because the laws of physics in them would not have allowed anything interesting to evolve.[32]

Barrow draws together many threads when he notes that the universe's "deep unalterable structure" forms a "cosmic environment" for evolution stretching farther and wider than Darwin ever imagined.

> Before biological complexity can begin to develop, there must exist atoms and molecules with properties that permit the development of complexity and self-replication; there must exist stable environments; and there must exist sites that are temperate enough for those structures to exist. All these things must persist for enormous periods of time. Deep within the inner spaces of matter, unseen and unnoticed, exist the features that enable these conditions to be met. . . . [Without these features] all structures complex enough to evolve spontaneously by natural selection would be impossible.[33]

By the 1980s, astrophysicists generally agreed that no evolutionary process *of any kind* would have occurred and that no life in any form would exist if just *one* of the fundamental constants had taken a slightly different value. As an analogy, some of the settings on an automobile engine are so crucial to its operation that if one setting is at a slightly different value, the engine won't function. To many of the physicists who studied the matter, the delicate arrangement of the universal constants did not look random at all; it looked purposeful.

Let's look at some of the surprising numerical relationships that many scientists and philosophers today call the "cosmic coincidences." After this we'll take up the question: Is the arrangement of the universal constants evidence that the universe was intelligently designed?

Cosmic Coincidence 1: Electron-Proton Charges in Precise Balance

The positively charged proton (normally found in the nucleus of the atom) differs in many ways from the negatively charged electron (normally found gyrating outside the nucleus). For instance, the proton is about 1,836 times heavier than the electron. About a million electrons would theoretically fit inside a proton. The two particles also have different magnetic properties, and the proton participates in processes involving the strong nuclear force while the electron does not.

Given their many differences, it is amazing that the negative charge on the electron precisely balances the positive charge on the proton. The two charges could theoretically have been unbalanced. How accurate is the balance? Accurate at least to *one part in 100 billion*, according to the astrophysicist George Greenstein.[34] If the charges were to differ by just one part in 100 billion, our bodies would explode like sticks of dynamite.[35] If the balance were to be off by just one part in a *billion billion*, objects like the earth and sun would explode.[36] It follows that if the universe is to have any structure at all, let alone an evolutionary one, the charges of electrons and protons must be finely tuned to a mind-boggling degree.

Cosmic Coincidence 2: The Balance between Electromagnetic and Gravitational Forces

The strengths of the electromagnetic and gravitational forces appear to be fine-tuned to each other to an accuracy of one part in 10^{40}. If these two forces had been out of balance by one part in a billion billion billion billion, the explosion mechanism inside large stars would not have functioned, supernova explosions would not have scattered complex elements into interstellar space, complex elements would not have been available for the evolution of life, and life in any form would not have been possible.[37] Davies writes:

> In one of the categories of stars, the "red" stars, the stars do not become supernovas and so do not scatter heavy elements into the interstellar medium. In another category of stars, the "blue" stars, the stars burn too fast for life to form. To prevent all stars from crowding into one or the other category, the relative strengths of the electromagnetic force and the gravitational force must be balanced to one part in 10^{40}.[38]

Cosmic Coincidence 3: The Initial Expansion Rate of the Universe

We now know that the material universe began a finite time ago in an explosive event astrophysicists call the "big bang." (We'll examine this event in the next chapter.) When astrophysicists calculated the initial expansion rate of the universe, they discovered that if that rate had been different by one part in a billion billion billion billion billion, evolution in any form would not have occurred, and life of any kind would not have been possible.[39]

Specifically, if the initial expansion value had been higher by just one part in a billion billion billion billion billion, the universe would have expanded too fast for stars to form, and the universe would be unfit for any kind of evolved life. But if the initial expansion value had been less by the same infinitesimal amount, the expanding universe would have collapsed before stars could form, also producing a lifeless universe. Gribbin and Rees write, "The implication is that the relevant number, the so-called 'density parameter,' was set, in the beginning, with an accuracy of one part in 10^{60}. Changing that parameter, either way, by a fraction given by a decimal point followed by 60 zeroes and a 1, would have made the universe unsuitable for life as we know it."[40] These two physicists add that the density parameter is "the most accurately determined number in all of physics, and suggests a fine-tuning of the universe, to set up conditions suitable for the emergence of stars, galaxies, and life, of exquisite precision."[41]

Astrophysicists have discovered dozens of other cosmic coincidences, each an example of fine-tuning at the atomic level. Freeman Dyson, one of the twentieth century's leading physicists, writes that the more he studies the universe and its amazing architecture, "the more evidence I find that the universe in some sense must have known that we were coming."[42] Dyson also speaks of the "peculiar harmony between the structure of the universe and the needs of life and intelligence."[43]

Stephen Hawking (1942–2018), perhaps the most famous physicist of our time, writes in *A Brief History of Time*, "The laws of science, as we know them at present, contain many fundamental numbers, like the size of the electric charge of the electron and the ratio of the masses of the proton and the electron. . . . The values of these numbers seem to have been very finely adjusted to make possible the development of life."[44]

Best Explanation?

Now for the philosophical question: What best explains the amazing arrangement of the universal constants? As we proceed, keep in mind that most arguments in science, in the courtroom, and in everyday life are inferences to the best explanation. If you dismiss inference to the best explanation reasoning, then you ought to give up most of what you believe about the world, for (again) most of what we believe about our world derives from this form of reasoning. Two thought experiments will now help us proceed.

Imagine that the pizza maker Vincenzo Ramaglia invents an automatic pizza machine. When dough, vegetables, seasonings, sauce, and other ingredients are fed into one end of the device, intricately formed pizzas come out the other end—but only if the machine's fifty dials are set properly. The machine is so sensitive that each of the fifty dials must be set within a tolerance of one-millionth of an inch, or the product that comes out will not be edible.

Now imagine walking into Vincenzo's shop and seeing his famous machine cranking out intricately formed pizzas. Which hypothesis would make the best overall sense of the observed data?

1. The fifty dials are loose and were set at their present values by the wind—a blind, unconscious process that has no goal.

2. The dials were set on purpose by an intelligent being who intended to make intricately formed pizzas.

The second thought experiment involves an imaginary computer game that allows you to design a possible universe on your laptop. After loading the program onto your computer, you design a model universe by typing in fifty mathematical equations, each containing a constant that must be entered to sixty decimal places. Together these constants determine the way your model universe will function. Once you have typed in your numbers, the background order is in place, and the program cranks out a simulation of the universe you designed.

The goal of the game is to design a functional world containing an evolutionary process, diverse life-forms, and interesting activity. However, such a universe will not result unless the constants are set within very, very narrow limits.

On the first day, you load the program onto your laptop and begin typing in all fifty mathematical equations with your choice of fundamental constants. You are operating blindly because you lost the instruction manual and therefore have no hints at all. After you give the command, your universe starts to operate. But after one hour, you're bored. It isn't doing anything. It is just a disorderly chaotic blur.

This is a letdown because at the software store, the demo showed stars forming, galaxies coalescing, supernovas spewing out complex elements into space, and weird life-forms developing on planets with stable environments. After several days of effort, you give up. This was smart, because out of millions of billions of trillions of possible combinations of values for the fundamental constants, a vanishingly small fraction produces an active universe containing evolved life-forms.

Now suppose that a friend comes over and asks to give the game a try. The friend sits down and begins typing constants into the equations. Soon a complex, stable, interesting universe is developing, complete with stars, galaxies, and an evolutionary process leading to complicated life-forms. Would you believe your friend if she told you that she hit the right numbers by blind luck? With no foresight? Or would you be strongly inclined to suppose that she chose those numbers on purpose—based on preexisting knowledge of what it takes to produce the background order needed for a life-sustaining universe?

In light of our thought experiments, which hypothesis makes the best overall sense of the fine-tuning of the universal constants: intelligent design, natural necessity, or blind chance? This gives us a best explanation version of the fine-tuning argument.

Summary of the Fine-Tuning Argument

1. The values of the universal constants of physics are fine-tuned to each other in such a way that if even one constant had been different by an astonishingly small amount, no evolutionary process of any kind would have occurred anywhere in the universe, and life in any form would not have been possible. (This is the data to be explained.)

2. The arrangement of the fundamental constants is astronomically unlikely to occur on a chance hypothesis.

3. The natural necessity hypothesis is contradicted by modern astrophysics, which indicates that there is nothing necessary about the specific structure of the universe, for the universe could have been structured in infinitely many alternative ways.

4. The arrangement of the fundamental constants is expected on an intelligent design hypothesis.

5. No one has suggested a plausible alternative to these three hypotheses.

6. The best explanation is therefore intelligent design.

7. Therefore, it is reasonable to believe that the order of the universe is the product of a divine mind existing above the space-time fray, in short, an intelligent designer.

An important corollary of this argument is sometimes overlooked. It follows with strict logic that Darwin's theory of evolution, as presented in standard biology texts today, does not at all prove that God does not exist.

THE BIGGEST OBJECTION: THE MULTIVERSE HYPOTHESIS

Most critics of the fine-tuning argument agree that the intricate and almost unimaginably improbable arrangement of the universal constants of physics set at values that make life possible certainly *looks* designed. They also agree that the fortunate (for us) arrangement of the fundamental

> **Michio Kaku writes in *The God Equation*:**
>
> The universe is a remarkably beautiful, ordered, and simple place. I find it utterly staggering that all the known laws of the physical universe can be summarized on a single sheet of paper. Contained on the paper is Einstein's theory of relativity. The Standard Model is more complicated, taking up most of the page with its zoo of subatomic particles. They can describe everything in the known universe, from deep inside the proton to the very boundary of the visible universe. Given the utter brevity of this sheet of paper, it is hard to avoid the conclusion that this was all planned in advance, that its elegant design shows the hand of a cosmic designer. To me, this is the strongest argument for the existence of God.[45]

constants requires a rational explanation. However, the best explanation, they argue, is not God or an intelligent designer; rather, it is the multiverse hypothesis, also called the "many worlds hypothesis" and the "many universes hypothesis."

Their proposal has three parts. First, let's suppose that there is no intelligent designer, no creator, no god, and nothing supernatural in any sense. Second, let's suppose that the material universe we inhabit is just one universe embedded in a hyperspace containing an infinite number of other universes, each spatially and temporally discontinuous from the others.[46] Third, let's suppose that the fundamental constants of physics vary randomly from one universe within the hyperspace to the next, for no reason at all, without any intelligent designer responsible for the variations. The differences between universes result from nothing but blind, unstructured chance.[47]

However, they argue, *if* our universe is just one universe within a multiverse containing an infinite number of other universes and if the fundamental constants vary randomly from one universe to the next, then there are bound to be a few universes like ours just by chance alone. We just happen by chance to exist in one of the few universes accidentally fit for life.

If we adopt this hypothesis, they suggest, then we can explain the fine-tuning coincidences without reference to a higher intelligence, by arguing like this:

1. Suppose that there is no intelligent designer, no god; nothing supernatural exists.

2. Suppose our universe is just one universe within a multiverse containing an infinite number of universes each spatially and temporally discontinuous from the rest, with the fundamental constants varying randomly from one universe to the next. Nothing assigns values to the constants within a universe—they just pop into existence in each universe by pure random chance.
Comment. These premises constitute the multiverse hypothesis.

3. Out of an infinity of different universes, there is almost certain to be one or two like ours simply by blind chance alone.

4. We just happen by chance to live in one of the few universes suited for life.

5. This explains the fortuitous (for us) arrangement of the constants without reference to intelligent design.

6. This proposal is preferable because it avoids intelligent design.

7. The multiverse hypothesis is therefore the best explanation of the fine-tuning data.

If the multiverse hypothesis is true, then all order is indeed ultimately due to pure, random chance. But is the multiverse hypothesis the best explanation of the facts?

Problems with the Multiverse Hypothesis

The multiverse hypothesis may sound plausible at first, but there are deep problems. First, according to the hypothesis, the infinitely many universes are spatially and temporally discontinuous, which means that no signals or information can pass from one universe to the next. Thus, the other universes cannot be observed or detected in any way from within our universe. It follows that no strictly *scientific* evidence could ever prove the multiverse hypothesis true. Therefore, the multiverse hypothesis is not a scientific hypothesis. Of course, it does not follow from this that the theory is false. However, the multiverse theory will not be acceptable to those who seek a purely scientific explanation of the fine-tuning data.

Second, theism explains the arrangement of the fundamental constants in terms of one single underlying cause: God or an intelligent designer existing beyond space or time. In contrast, the multiverse hypothesis posits (for the most basic level of explanation) an *infinity* of empirically undetectable mini-universes existing beyond space and time. Both hypotheses offer explanations of the same data—the cosmic coincidences—but theism is theoretically simpler, for it posits one entity at the most fundamental level, while the multiverse theory posits an infinity. In this case, Ockham's razor, which as we have seen is absolutely essential to science and

---

Multiverse Mechanisms?

Some advocates of the multiverse avoid the question of what caused the whole ensemble to exist. Ask them what caused it all and they'll shrug their shoulders and say, "It's just there." Others hypothesize a mechanism that generates the multiverse. However, the multiverse-generating mechanisms commonly proposed all require significant fine-tuning. Fr. Robert Spitzer, a Catholic priest of the Jesuit order who has a background in physics, notes:

> All known multiverse theories have significant fine-tuning requirements. Linde's Chaotic Inflationary Multiverse cannot randomly cough out bubble universes because they would collide and make the bubble universes inhospitable to life; the bubble universes must be spaced out in a slow roll which requires considerable fine-tuning in the multiverse's initial parameters. Similarly, Susskind's String Theory Landscape requires considerable meta-level fine-tuning to explain its [ability to produce and support intelligent life].[48]

In short, a multiverse theory does not eliminate cosmic fine tuning; rather, it entails fine-tuning to an astonishing degree. Of course, we can also ask: Who or what caused the multiverse to exist in the first place? Father Spitzer presents further scientific and mathematical problems for the many worlds hypothesis in *New Proofs for the Existence of God: Contributions of Contemporary Physics and Philosophy*.[49] These are among the reasons a multiverse theory does not at all block the inference to God's existence.

indeed to every academic subject, points us toward theism. This observation led Davies to comment, "To explain the [fine-tuning] coincidences by invoking an infinity of useless universes seems like carrying excess [explanatory] baggage to the extreme."[50]

CONCLUDING REFLECTION

Where does this leave us? No one within the scientific community has ever given a scientific explanation of the fundamental fact that the universe on the largest scale is orderly rather than not. No one within the boundaries of science has ever explained the finely tuned background order needed if the universe is to have any evolutionary process—and any life—at all. And no one in science ever will, for every scientific explanation presupposes rather than explains the existence of the laws of nature—laws that give our universe its particular structure. It follows that science by itself cannot explain why the universe is orderly rather than not orderly in the large scale; that question is too fundamental for science. It also follows that science alone will never explain why the fundamental constants are improbably arranged so as to produce an orderly universe containing intelligent life.

However, the question is not too fundamental for philosophy. Philosophers from ancient times have asked: What is the source of the universal order? What is the One over the Many? And no philosophical hypothesis that does not involve mind as the ultimate source of order has ever succeeded in making deep sense of the fact that the universe is orderly from the largest scale to the most fundamental level. If the universe is the product of a supreme mind, that makes sense of the data. What is the best explanation? You decide, hopefully on the basis of critical thinking and on the best reasons of your heart, soul, and mind.

One final thought. Perhaps the design argument alone doesn't take us all the way to God as God is conceived within Christianity or within any one religion or faith community. Perhaps all the argument does is this. As we work through the steps, reason elevates our minds above matter, space, energy, and time and then gestures silently toward a majestic supernatural agency behind it all. Perhaps reason stops there and leaves the next step to each of us, as if to say, "This is as far as I can take you, but the journey is not finished. The next step must be your own." Perhaps the next step begins with faith.

APPENDIX: THE PROBLEM WITH INFINITE EXPLANATORY REGRESSIONS

The question of infinite regression is one of the most important in all of philosophy. Imagine a long line of boxcars rolling along railroad tracks up a hill. Why are the cars moving rather than standing still? The question arises because a boxcar, lacking a motor or any other internal source of motion, doesn't move itself. Suppose that someone offers the following explanation: "The boxcar in front—boxcar 1—is moving because it is being pushed by the boxcar behind it—boxcar 2." This explains why boxcar 1 is moving, but it doesn't explain why boxcar 2 is moving. It also doesn't explain why the series as a whole is moving (rather than standing still).

Now suppose that someone says, "Boxcar 2 is moving because it is being pushed by the car behind it, boxcar 3." This explains why boxcar 2 is moving, but it doesn't explain the motion of boxcar 3. It also doesn't explain why the series as a whole is in motion. Now imagine that the series of boxcars stretches as far as the eye can see. We stand before the tracks with the question still unanswered: Why are they all moving rather than standing still?

Someone steps forward and offers the following explanation: The series is infinite. Each boxcar is moved by the one behind it, which is moved by the one before it, without end. There is no first boxcar. This person is trying to explain the motion of the cars in terms of an infinite explanatory regression.

But does an infinite regression of boxcars explain what it is supposed to explain? Does it answer the question at issue? The question was: Why are the boxcars moving? The consensus in philosophy is that it does not answer the question. An infinite regression of boxcars leaves unanswered the following clearly meaningful contrastive question: Why are the (infinitely many) boxcars moving rather than standing still? Put another way: Why is the series in motion rather than idle? Infinite regression doesn't touch that question. (Think carefully about this before moving on.)

It follows that there is a fact that the infinite regression hypothesis doesn't explain: the motion of the series as a whole. Surprisingly, although the motion of each car in the series has an explanation (by reference to the car before it), the motion of the series as a whole remains unexplained. But all attempts to explain by infinite regression are like this: each link in the series has an explanation while the series as a whole remains unexplained. Infinite regressions never deliver the goods. They don't explain what they are supposed to explain.

Going deeper. Why does an infinite regression fail to explain what it is supposed to explain? Philosophers and mathematicians have thought a great deal about this question and about the nature of infinity. In a nutshell, the mainstream view is that an infinite regression fails to explain what it aims to explain because each of the linked explanations within its infinite series is only a hypothetical (if, then) explanation. Not a single one is categorical, or complete in itself. But only a categorical explanation can complete an explanatory series.

Consider the boxcars again. The motion of boxcar 1 is explained only if the motion of boxcar 2, which is pushing it, has already been explained. But the motion of boxcar 2 is explained only if the motion of boxcar 3 has been explained, and so on. Each explanation, being hypothetical, passes the explanatory bill to the previous explanation, like one broke concertgoer after another in an infinite line of concertgoers outside a venue telling the ticket taker that the person behind him will pay. No one explanation in an infinite series is categorical, or fully explanatory in its own right (no concertgoer ever hands over the money). Thus, the question that generated the regress is never answered (the venue never receives any cash).

Since the question of infinite regression is so crucial, yet so often misunderstood, here is one more analogy for you to ponder, this one adapted from an idea suggested by the philosopher Robert Martin. A group of extremely shy people have all been invited to the same party. Suppose that A will go if B will go but not otherwise. Suppose that B will go if C will go but not otherwise. Suppose that C will go only if D will go, and so forth. Each will hypothetically go; that is, each will go if someone else goes. Now if no one in the series categorically will go, that is, if no one will simply go with or without the others going, then no one goes—no matter how many shy people are added to the series.[51]

FOR FURTHER STUDY

Craig, William Lane, and Chad Meister, eds. *God Is Good, God Is Great: Why Believing in God Is Reasonable and Responsible.* Downers Grove, IL: InterVarsity Press, 2009.

Layman, C. Stephen. *God: Eight Enduring Questions.* Notre Dame, IN: University of Notre Dame Press, 2022.

———. *Letters to a Doubting Thomas: A Case for the Existence of God.* New York: Oxford University Press, 2007.

Plantinga, Alvin. *Where the Conflict Really Lies: Science, Religion, and Naturalism.* New York: Oxford University Press, 2011.

Rasmussen, Joshua. *How Reason Can Lead to God: A Philosopher's Bridge to Faith.* Downers Grove, IL: InterVarsity Press Academic, 2019.

Reppert, Victor. *C. S. Lewis's Dangerous Idea: In Defense of the Argument from Reason.* Downers Grove, IL: InterVarsity Press, 2003.

Slagle, Jim. *The Evolutionary Argument against Naturalism: Context, Exposition, and Repercussions.* New York: Bloomsbury Academic, 2021.

Spitzer, Robert. *New Proofs for the Existence of God: Contributions of Contemporary Physics and Philosophy.* Grand Rapids, MI: Eerdmans, 2010.

Swinburne, Richard. *The Existence of God.* 2nd ed. New York: Oxford University Press, 2004.

Walls, Jerry, and Trent Dougherty, eds. *Two Dozen (or so) Arguments for God: The Plantinga Project.* New York: Oxford University Press, 2018.

On the modern design argument

Collins, Robin. "The Argument from Physical Constants." In *Two Dozen (or so) Arguments for God: The Plantinga Project,* ed. Jerry Walls and Trent Dougherty, 89–107. New York: Oxford University Press, 2018.

Craig, William Lane, and J. P. Moreland, eds. *The Blackwell Companion to Natural Theology.* Hoboken, NJ: Wiley-Blackwell, 2012.

Layman, C. Stephen. *God: Eight Enduring Questions.* Notre Dame, IN: University of Notre Dame Press, 2022, chap. 2.

Walls, Jerry, and Trent Dougherty, eds. *Two Dozen (or so) Arguments for God: The Plantinga Project.* New York: Oxford University Press, 2018.

For those interested in biology

Behe, Michael. *Darwin's Black Box.* 2nd ed. New York: Free Press, 2001.

———. *A Mousetrap for Darwin: Michael J. Behe Answers His Critics.* Seattle: Discovery Institute, 2020.

Collins, Francis S. *The Language of God: A Scientist Presents Evidence for Belief.* New York: Free Press, 2007.

Meyer, Stephen C. *Darwin's Doubt: The Explosive Origin of Animal Life and the Case for Intelligent Design.* New York: HarperOne, 2013.

———. *Return of the God Hypothesis: Three Scientific Discoveries That Reveal the Mind behind the Universe.* New York: HarperOne, 2021.

———. *Signature in the Cell: DNA and the Evidence for Intelligent Design.* New York: HarperOne, 2010.

General works introducing arguments for God's existence

Craig, William Lane, and Michael Murray, eds. *Philosophy of Religion: A Reader and Guide*. New Brunswick, NJ: Rutgers University Press, 2002.
Evans, C. Stephen, and R. Zachary Manis. *Philosophy of Religion: Thinking about Faith*. 2nd ed. Downers Grove, IL: InterVarsity Press Academic, 2009.
Herrick, Paul. *Philosophy, Reasoned Belief, and Faith: An Introduction*. Notre Dame, IN: University of Notre Dame Press, 2022.
Swinburne, Richard. *The Existence of God*. 2nd. ed. New York: Oxford University Press, 2004.

For contemporary criticisms of the design argument

Mackie, J. L. *The Miracle of Theism: Arguments for and against the Existence of God*. New York: Oxford University Press, 1983.
Martin, Michael. *Atheism: A Philosophical Justification*. Philadelphia: Temple University Press, 1992.

On some of the deep philosophical issues that arise when we consider arguments for God

Layman, C. Stephen. *God: Eight Enduring Questions*. Notre Dame, IN: University of Notre Dame Press, 2022.
O'Conner, Timothy. *Theism and Ultimate Explanation: The Necessary Shape of Contingency*. Oxford: Wiley-Blackwell, 2012.
Pruss, Alexander. *The Principle of Sufficient Reason: A Reassessment*. Cambridge: Cambridge University Press, 2006.

For those willing to delve into philosophical theology — the study of the nature of God

Craig, William Lane, and Michael Murray, eds. *Philosophy of Religion: A Reader and Guide*. New Brunswick, NJ: Rutgers University Press, 2002.
Flint, Thomas P., and Michael C. Rea, eds. *The Oxford Handbook of Philosophical Theology*. New York: Oxford University Press, 2011.
Layman, C. Stephen. *God: Eight Enduring Questions*. Notre Dame, IN: University of Notre Dame Press, 2022, esp. chaps. 4–9.
Morris, Thomas V. *Our Idea of God: An Introduction to Philosophical Theology*. Notre Dame, IN: University of Notre Dame Press, 1991.
Swinburne, Richard, *The Coherence of Theism*. Oxford: Oxford University Press, 1977.

THREE

Does God Exist?

Part 2

PERHAPS THE BIGGEST QUESTION OF ALL

Aristotle stated that philosophy begins in wonder. The next argument for God's existence that I present and defend in this chapter is rooted in the wonder we feel when we contemplate the fact that the universe exists. Have you ever looked up at the night sky and wondered, "Where does it all come from?" and "Why is there a universe rather than just nothing at all?" In his autobiography, *A Life in Two Centuries*, the noted historian Bertram Wolfe (1896–1977) expressed the question this way:

> There was one large problem that I tackled that I could not solve at 11 or 12 or 13, and have not solved yet, nor do I expect to: Why does the universe exist at all, and why is there life on the earth and perhaps elsewhere? I tried to imagine what would be if the universe did not exist. . . . The more I wrestled with such problems the less I could

explain to myself, until at last I was driven to the question of questions: Why is there something? Why is there anything? Why is there not nothing? How did it all come to be?[1]

In *The Mystery of Existence: Why Is There Anything at All?*, John Leslie and Robert Lawrence Kuhn phrase the question this way: "Why does there exist *anything*? Why a world with its stars, its planets, its humans, its atoms—why these or any other such items . . . instead of utter emptiness?"[2]

The design argument arose out of wonder at the fact that the universe displays an orderly and predictable structure. The philosophical argument we are about to enter is concerned with the *existence*, rather than the order, of the material universe. But first a short detour.

CAN PHYSICS SUPPLY THE ANSWER?

In recent years, a number of prominent scientists have written popular books claiming that science has beaten philosophy to the punch and explained, in scientific terms alone, without reference to God, religion, or anything supernatural, why the universe exists and (even further) why something rather than nothing exists. Has science answered Wolfe's "question of questions" on its own?

That is what the physicist Lawrence Krauss claims in his 2012 *New York Times* best seller, *A Universe from Nothing: Why There Is Something Rather than Nothing*. Stephen Hawking, the famed cosmologist and theoretical physicist at Cambridge University, makes the same claim in his book, *The Grand Design*, coauthored with the physicist Leonard Mlodinow. Krauss and Hawking and Mlodinow promise to explain in purely scientific terms, without reference to God or the supernatural, why there is something rather than nothing, Because of such authoritative pronouncements, many believe that science has explained just about everything, making belief in God or a supreme being unnecessary. But are these scientists right?

Philosophers have been disappointed by both books. For despite the grand promises made on their dust jackets, neither book delivers. Why is there something rather than nothing? Despite his book's catchy title, *A Universe from Nothing*, Krauss answers: the universe *may* have come into existence out of a "quantum haze." What is this? It is a gigantic field of negative energy governed by the complex mathematical equations of quantum mechanics. Philosophers who reviewed the book were quick to point out that Krauss's book leaves unexplained the quantum haze, negative energy, and the mathematical laws of quantum theory.

So, why is there something rather than nothing at all? Hawking and Mlodinow answer: the universe was brought into existence by the law of gravity acting on a quantum field. "Because there is a law like gravity, the universe can and will create itself from nothing." Thus, "the beginning of the universe was governed by the laws of science and doesn't need to be set in motion by some god."[3] Critics quickly pointed out that this leaves unexplained the law of gravity as well as the quantum field.

All three physicists leave the big questions unanswered, among them:

- Why is there a law of gravity rather than no law of gravity?

- Why does the quantum haze in all its mathematical complexity exist?

- Why are there laws of physics rather than no laws at all?

- Why is there something rather than simply nothing at all?

In "A Designer Universe?" the Nobel laureate Steven Weinberg writes:

I have to admit that, even when physicists will have gone as far as they can go, when we have a final theory, we will not have a completely satisfying picture of the world, because we will still be left with the question "Why?" Why this theory, rather than some other theory? For example, why is the world described by quantum mechanics? Quantum mechanics is the one part of our present physics that is likely to survive intact in any future theory, but there is nothing logically inevitable [i.e., logically necessary] about quantum mechanics; I can imagine a universe governed by Newtonian mechanics instead. So there seems to be an irreducible mystery that science will not eliminate.[4]

Weinberg is giving expression to the sense of incompleteness and intellectual dissatisfaction that many people feel when they contemplate the prospect of a purely scientific account of the universe.

WHY SCIENCE BY ITSELF CAN'T DELIVER

I discussed this briefly in the previous chapter. Philosophers and logicians have carefully analyzed the logical structure of scientific explanations. Their analysis shows that every scientific explanation always includes, as one of its explanatory components, one or more laws of nature. Essentially, a scientific explanation explains a specific phenomenon P by showing that P is a consequence of initial physical conditions and one or more general laws of nature.

A law of nature is a general truth expressing one or more of the universe's regularities. The problem is that a law of nature is only a part of the material universe. A scientific explanation therefore always explains one *part* of the material universe in terms of another *part*, leaving the rest unexplained. It follows that no purely scientific explanation will ever account for the whole. More exactly, no purely scientific explanation will ever account for the general fact that the material universe (including the laws of nature that govern it) *exists*. Recall what Michio Kaku writes in *The God Equation*:

> Physics says nothing about where the laws of physics themselves come from. . . . The key feature of any [physical] theory of everything is likely to be its symmetry. But where does this symmetry come from? This symmetry would be a by-product of deep mathematical truths. But where does mathematics come from? On this question, [science] is again silent.[5]

This is not to say that science is invalid or that science is all wrong. Science provides acceptable explanations of many parts of the universe. For instance, it explains why water expands when it freezes, why lightning appears before thunder, and so on. This is to say, however, that some questions, including the ultimate question of existence, are too fundamental for science to answer.

INTRODUCING THE COSMOLOGICAL ARGUMENT

The question at stake is the most fundamental question of *cosmology*, the study of the universe as a systematic whole. The subject takes its name from the Greek word *kosmos*, which means the universe considered as an orderly and beautiful system. Cosmological questions have intrigued human beings since the dawn of history, and they continue to interest us today. The next argument I shall present is called the "cosmological argument for the existence of God." Wolfe's question of questions has an answer if this classic argument is on the right track—an answer reached through careful reasoning.

Although Plato, Aristotle, and most of the major philosophers throughout history presented versions of this line of thought, the argument I am about to present is a modernized rendition inspired by the cosmological arguments given by the Italian philosopher Saint Thomas Aquinas (1224–74) and the German philosopher Gottfried Leibniz (1646–1716)—two thinkers whose pathbreaking contributions rank with those of Socrates, Plato, and Aristotle. The cosmological arguments of theirs that inspired me, and the argument I am about to state, are technically called "modal" cosmological arguments, for reasons that will become apparent.

Definitions

Some definitions are required before the argument can begin. Recall that logic as an academic subject is the study of the principles of correct reasoning. *Modal* logic is the branch concerned with possibility, contingency, and necessity—sometimes called the "modes" of truth and falsity. What are these?

In ancient times, Aristotle and other logicians noticed that there is a radical difference between a truth such as 1 + 1 = 2 (understood in the standard meaning) and a more mundane proposition such as the statement that Plato has a beard on December 1, 400 BC. The mathematical statement is true in all consistently describable contexts, false in none. Put another way, it is true in all logically possible circumstances, false in none. Thus, not only is it true; it would have been true no matter how the physical world might have been, and it will remain true no matter how the world might be in the future. Logicians call this kind of truth a "necessary" truth, which is appropriate because *necessary* means "cannot be otherwise."[6]

In contrast, the proposition that Plato has a beard, although true on December 1, 400 BC, would have been false if Plato had chosen to shave it off the day before. Logicians call this kind of proposition a "contingent" truth because whether or not it is true or false depends on (is contingent on) circumstances that can change and that could have been otherwise.

In modal logic, the modes of truth are given precise definitions.

- A *necessary truth* is a proposition that is true and that could not possibly be false under any consistently describable circumstances. Thus, a necessary truth is true in all possible circumstances, false in none. The proposition that all squares have four sides (given the standard meaning of the sentence expressing the proposition) is an example.

- A *necessary falsehood* is a proposition that is false and that could not possibly be true under any consistently describable circumstances. A necessary falsehood is thus false in all possible circumstances, true in none. The proposition that 1 + 1 = 76 (given the standard meaning of the sentence expressing the proposition) is an example.

- A *contingent truth* is a proposition that is true in some consistently describable circumstances and false in others. The proposition that World War II ended in 1945 is an example. Surely that horrible war could have been ended earlier than 1945 if the opposing sides had come to their senses sooner.

- A *possible truth* is a proposition that is true in at least one consistently describable circumstance. The proposition that someone wins the New York State lottery ten times in a row in 2030 is an example.

Modal logic is the most active branch of logical theory. It is a fascinating field of thought in which all kinds of pioneering research is taking place. Modal logic is also philosophically important, for most of the great arguments in philosophy down through the centuries have been modal in nature, when analyzed closely. I offer suggestions for further study at the end of this chapter.

Modality Applied to Being

The definitions just given are from propositional modal logic. In *quantificational* modal logic, necessity, contingency, and possibility are applied to being or existence rather than to the truth and falsity of propositions. In the following definitions, the word *being* just means an entity that exists. Rocks, clouds, chemicals, and people are all "beings" in this sense.

- A being exists *necessarily* if it exists and would have existed no matter what circumstance had obtained. Furthermore, it will exist no matter what circumstances will obtain. It exists, then, in all possible circumstances. Put another way, its nonexistence is an impossibility. If such a being exists, it is a *necessary being*.

- A being exists *contingently* if it exists but would not have existed had circumstances been sufficiently different. Thus, it exists in some possible circumstances and fails to exist in other possible circumstances. Such a being is a *contingent being*. Rocks, flowers, mountains, and cakes are obvious examples.

Modality and Explanation

When we explain the existence of a contingent being such as a mountain, a flower, or a loaf of bread, we always refer to external circumstances or to the action of external beings. For example, the existence of a mountain is explained by reference to preceding geological conditions, which in turn are explained in terms of even earlier physical conditions, and so forth. The existence of a flower is explained by reference to the seed from which it grew, the soil that nourished the seed's growth, the sunlight it depended on, perhaps the actions of a gardener, and so forth. The existence of a loaf of bread is explained by reference to the action of the baker who baked it, the temperature of the oven, the flour, the yeast, and other external factors.

Our ordinary explanatory practices with respect to contingent beings make sense, for a contingent being exists at the mercy of circumstances beyond itself. It would never have existed had circumstances been sufficiently different; yet it in fact exists. It is therefore eminently reasonable to suppose that something external to it accounts for the fact of its existence. It is just as reasonable to look for an external cause.

In the case of a necessary being, if one exists, the situation is radically different. Since its existence is independent of all changing circumstances, it has always existed and always will exist. Nothing external caused it to be because it never came *into* existence.

This explanation of modality has been intuitive. The fundamental ideas are sharpened and extended systematically, in theoretical form, with axioms and theorems, in textbooks on modal logic, of which there are many.[7]

THE MODAL COSMOLOGICAL ARGUMENT

Now for the promised argument.

1. Contingent beings exist. (This is the data in need of explanation.)
2. Every existing thing is either a contingent being or a necessary being.
3. It is impossible that something comes into existence out of absolutely nothing.
4. The hypothesis that contingent beings came into existence out of nothing is not a reasonable explanation for the fact that contingent beings exist.
5. It is impossible that something caused itself to exist.
6. The hypothesis that the collection of all contingent beings caused itself to exist is not a reasonable explanation of the fact that contingent beings exist.
7. The hypothesis that a contingent being is the cause of all contingent beings is not a reasonable explanation of the fact that contingent beings exist.
8. Therefore, if there is an explanation for the general fact that contingent beings exist, that explanation refers to the causal action of something that is not contingent; in other words, it refers to the causal action of one or more necessary beings.
9. If one or more necessary beings caused the existence of all contingent beings, that would explain the existence of contingent beings.
10. If two proposed explanations explain the very same facts, the simpler of the two—the explanation making the fewest assumptions or that refers to the fewest entities—is the more reasonable of the two.

11. Therefore, the best explanation for the fact that contingent beings exist is that the contingent beings composing the material universe were caused to exist by one necessary being.

12. Therefore, a necessary being exists and is the ultimate cause of all contingent beings.

13. This we commonly call "God."

Each premise can be supported with a subargument. The crucial ones are inferences to the best explanation.

Arguments for the Premises

Argument for premise 1: Contingent beings exist. When we examine the universe, we see many things that come into and pass out of existence. Flowers, rivers, birds, and lakes are obvious examples. Even things as seemingly permanent as mountains exist contingently. Geologists, for example, tell us that the Cascade Mountains (in western North America) were formed 40 million years ago and one day will no longer exist. But if something comes into and passes out of existence, then it is a contingent being. Therefore, contingent beings exist.

Argument for premise 2: Every existing thing is either a contingent being or a necessary being. This is clearly a necessary truth—a proposition that cannot possibly be false—for there is no middle ground between contingent and necessary existence. Therefore, premise 2 is true.

Argument for premise 3: It is impossible that something comes into existence out of absolutely nothing. Medieval philosophers thought deeply about this issue. They argued *ex nihilo nihil fit*: "out of nothing comes nothing." They believed that ex nihilo nihil fit is a necessary truth as certain as any truth of pure mathematics. The following is one way to justify the ex nihilo principle on the basis of abstract reason alone.

A state of complete nothingness would contain no possibilities at all, for possibilities are somethings. Therefore, if there ever were to be, or to have been, a state of absolute nothingness, that state would contain no possibilities. But if there were a state with no possibilities at all, then it would contain no possibility that something comes into existence out of it.

Therefore, it is not possible that something comes into existence out of absolutely nothing.

The philosopher Richard Purtill suggests an empirical argument for the ex nihilo principle, that is, an argument based on observations. Here is my summary. If reality were to be such that objects as big as universes can simply pop into existence out of nothing for no reason, then we should expect to occasionally observe things of various sizes coming into existence out of sheer nothing for no reason. For instance, a green pig wearing a yellow wig just materializes out of thin air in front of you as you walk down the street. But in all of recorded history, nothing has ever been observed coming into existence out of nothing. The best explanation, Purtill argues, is that the ex nihilo principle is true.[8]

Some philosophers support the ex nihilo principle by arguing that it is a necessary presupposition of scientific investigation. They have a point. It is hard to see how science could proceed if "it just came into existence out of sheer nothing" were an acceptable scientific explanation for anything.

Argument for premise 4: The hypothesis that contingent beings came into existence out of nothing is not a reasonable explanation for the existence of contingent beings. This follows validly from the previous premise. That is, if the previous premise is true, then this premise *must* be true.

Argument for premise 5: It is impossible that something caused itself to exist. The cause exists prior to the effect: the baker (the cause of the bread) exists before the bread exists, the factory exists before the car exists, and so forth. For an entity to cause itself to exist, it would have to exist before it exists and then bring itself into existence. This is self-contradictory. But self-contradiction is the mark of the impossible. It is therefore impossible that something caused itself to exist.

Argument for premise 6: The hypothesis that the collection of all contingent beings caused itself to exist is not a reasonable explanation for the existence of contingent beings. This follows validly from the previous premise.

Argument for premise 7: The hypothesis that a contingent being is the cause of all contingent beings is not a reasonable explanation for the existence of contingent beings. In order for a contingent being, call it C, to be the cause of all contingent beings, it would have to first be the cause of itself, which as we have seen is impossible. Premise 7 seems eminently reasonable. The philosopher Michael Rota puts the point this way:

> The cause of all contingent beings can't itself be a contingent being, for the group we're considering contains all the contingent beings that ever were. If the cause were a contingent being, then it would be inside the very group that needs an explanation.
>
> That would mean that it would have to cause itself (whether directly or indirectly by causing something else that causes itself). But this is impossible; nothing can cause itself to exist, whether directly or indirectly. In order for something to cause itself to exist, it would have to be able to cause things, but in order to be able to cause things, it would have to exist. So to cause itself to exist, it would have to already exist to do the causing.[9]

Peter van Inwagen supports the point in a different way:

> If the only beings were contingent beings, could there be an explanation of the fact that there were contingent beings? Could there be an answer to the question, 'Why are there contingent beings'? It is hard to see how there could be. Any statement that was true in a world in which there were only contingent beings . . . would derive its truth from the way those contingent beings were arranged. . . . And all such statements would appear to presuppose the existence of contingent beings. It seems wholly implausible to suppose that a series of statements all of which presuppose the existence of contingent beings could add up to an explanation of the existence of contingent beings. One might as well suppose that one could explain the existence of human beings by setting out a series of statements about the properties of human beings and the relations human beings bear to one another.[10]

Argument for premise 8: If there is an explanation for the general fact that contingent beings exist, that explanation refers to the causal action of something that is not a contingent being, that is, to the causal action of one or more necessary beings. When we explain the existence of a contingent being or a collection of contingent beings, we always refer to an external condition or cause. Given premises 2, 4, and 6, the action of one or more necessary beings is the only reasonable candidate.

Argument for premise 9: If one or more necessary beings caused the existence of all contingent beings, that would explain the existence of contingent beings. Van Inwagen comments, "This is not, of course, a very detailed explanation, but it seems to be a perfectly satisfactory explanation as far as it goes."[11] Similarly, the hypothesis that a potter caused the vase to exist would explain the existence of the vase. One might have further questions, but the existence of the vase would be explained.

Argument for premise 10: If two proposed explanations explain the very same facts, the simpler of the two—the explanation making the fewest assumptions or that refers to the fewest entities—is the more reasonable choice of the two. Keep in mind that Ockham's razor is routinely employed in modern science as well as in everyday thought.

Argument for premise 11: Therefore, the best explanation for the fact that contingent beings exist is that the contingent beings composing the material universe were caused to exist by one necessary being. This follows from the previous steps, for the alternative hypotheses have all been ruled out.

Argument for premise 12: Therefore, a necessary being exists and is the ultimate cause of all contingent beings. This is reasoning to the best explanation.

Argument for 13: This being is commonly called "God." A necessary being is a being that never came into existence and that will never pass out of existence. It is a being whose nonexistence is impossible. Next, it seems clear that matter is by its nature contingent. Why? Here is one reason; further reasons will be given below. Modern astrophysics has shown that matter and all physical processes originated a finite time ago in an event called the "big bang" (we will examine this theory later in this chapter). But anything that originated at a point in time is contingent. If matter is contingent, then the necessary being that caused the existence of all contingent beings is the cause of the entire system of space, time, energy, and matter. In short, it is the Creator of the material universe.

But this is the core conception of God shared by theists of many different monotheistic religious communities around the world, including Islam,

> Michio Kaku writes in *The God Equation*:
>
> Physics says nothing about where the laws of physics themselves come from. So, the cosmological argument of Saint Thomas Aquinas concerning the ... First Cause is left relevant even today.[12]

Judaism, and Christianity. Therefore, let's call it "mere theism." The modal cosmological argument just presented is an argument for mere theism. The conclusion seems justified.

Of course, mere theism is not a detailed or complete conception of God. To go deeper, you might begin by studying philosophical theology, the branch of philosophy containing theories of God's nature. You might also study the nature of necessary existence as developed in modal logic. Both subjects offer a wealth of material for the scholar who wants to think more deeply about God. References are provided at the end of this chapter.

Objections

Why Not Suppose the Material Universe Is Itself the Necessary Being? This won't work. There are three powerful (and contemporary) reasons to suppose that matter is contingent. First, as I mentioned, physicists have shown that matter originated a finite time ago in the big bang. But for obvious reasons, anything that originated at a point in time is contingent. Therefore, matter is contingent.

Second, physicists have constructed mathematical models of matterless worlds. Therefore, there is at least one matterless *possible* world. It follows again that matter is contingent, for matter might not have existed had consistently describable conditions been sufficiently different.

Third, there is nothing self-contradictory or logically inconsistent in the notion of a possible world containing abstract objects, such as propositions and mathematical functions, but no matter, that is, no atoms, no chemical elements, no radiation, and so forth. But in logical theory and mathematics, if a state of affairs or world is consistently describable, then that is a good reason to believe that it is logically possible. Therefore, matter is logically contingent, for it might not have existed. But if matter is logically contingent, then it seems to follow that the material universe is logically contingent.[13]

Why Not Millions of Gods? The reply to this objection takes us back to Ockham's razor. Recall from the previous chapter that philosophers and scientists from the earliest times have agreed that when two hypotheses equally explain the same data, the simpler of the two (the one that makes the fewest assumptions or posits the fewest entities) is the more reasonable choice. Science cannot operate without this principle for (again) the simple reason that (a) for every set of data, an infinite number of explanations are possible, each of increasing complexity, and (b) it is impossible to settle on a best explanation without relying on Ockham's principle or one like it.

Now consider the conclusion that one ultimate cause exists. Compare this to the conclusion that two independent causes created the universe. Both hypotheses explain the same data; however, the first is simpler. Ockham's razor supports monotheism on this one.

Modern scientific cosmology gives us further reasons to posit one supreme rather than many almost supreme gods. For instance, as we have seen, astrophysicists tell us that all chains of cause and effect—throughout the entire universe—coalesce into a single, unified series that traces back to a single starting point. In *The Little Book of the Big Bang: A Cosmic Primer*, the astronomer Craig Hogan condenses the history of the material universe into one chain of causes and effects that stems from a single creation event.[14] And as we've seen, Weinberg affirms the same point when he concludes that all the evidence from modern physics indicates a "common starting point" for the universe as a whole.

Aquinas and Leibniz were more in line with modern science than they could have known when they maintained that the material universe has just one ultimate cause.

What Caused God? This is perhaps the biggest objection of all. In *Why I Am Not a Christian* (1927), Bertrand Russell sums up and quickly dismisses the cosmological argument in one often-quoted paragraph. Here is his argument in full.

> Perhaps the simplest and easiest to understand [argument for God's existence] is the argument of the First Cause. (It is maintained that everything we see in this world has a cause, and as you go back in the chain of causes further and further you must come to a First Cause, and to that First Cause you give the name of God.) . . . [The argu-

ment] that there must be a First Cause is one that cannot have any validity. I may say that when I was a young man, and was debating these questions very seriously in my mind, I for a long time accepted the argument of the First Cause, until one day, at the age of eighteen, I read John Stuart Mill's *Autobiography*, and I there found this sentence: "My father taught me that the question, Who made me? cannot be answered, since it immediately suggests the further question, Who made God?" That very simple sentence showed me, as I still think, the fallacy in the argument of the First Cause.[15]

Carl Sagan (1934–96), noted astronomer and host of the acclaimed 1980 TV series *Cosmos*, gave essentially the same objection.

If we say "God made the universe," then surely the next question is, "Who made God?" In what way, exactly, does the God hypothesis advance our knowledge of cosmology?[16]

Russell and Sagan believed that by asking one question, they had deflated the cosmological argument. What can the theist say in response?

First, the Russell-Sagan question needs to be restated so that it applies to the argument I have presented. Instead of asking, What caused God?, let's ask, What caused the necessary being's existence?

The question seems to place the theist in another logical bind. If the theist says that God, or the primal necessary being, is explained in terms of a prior necessary being (a "Godfather"), then the question arises for *that* being: To what does it owe *its* existence? On the other hand, if the theist answers that the existence of the primal necessary being has no explanation, then he is saying that God's existence is a brute (unexplained) fact. In that case, the theistic solution to the riddle of existence appears to be no better than that of the atheist who says that the existence of the material universe is a brute fact. For in this case, the theist leaves the existence of God unexplained just as the atheist leaves the existence of the material universe unexplained.

However, the philosophical notion of a necessary being points us toward a modal solution to this puzzle. In his textbook *Metaphysics*, van Inwagen, who is also a leading researcher in contemporary philosophical modal logic, writes:

> It is conceivable that someone might object to [the hypothesis of a necessary being] on the ground that it "merely pushes the problem of the existence of things back a step." The worry here is something like this: All right, the necessary being explains the existence of the contingent beings, but what explains its existence? Why does it exist? But [to ask, of God understood as a necessary being, "Why does God exist?" or "What accounts for God's existence?"] is to neglect the fact that a necessary being is one whose non-existence is impossible. Thus . . . there is by definition a sufficient reason for [God's] existence: there could hardly be a more satisfying explanation for the existence of a thing than that its non-existence was impossible.[17]

Van Inwagen identifies another attractive feature of the necessary being conclusion.

> Why should there be anything at all? . . . If we could show that there was a necessary being . . . we should have an answer to our question. For if there were a necessary being, then it would be impossible for there to be nothing. And if we could show that it was impossible for there to be nothing, that, surely, would count as an answer to our question.[18]

These thoughts on the nature of necessity explain the sense in which theism supplies a deeper explanation, a more complete answer, to the ultimate cosmological question, namely, Why is there something rather than nothing? These thoughts also show, I believe, that the modal cosmological argument can be defended rationally.

FURTHER REFLECTIONS ON NECESSARY EXISTENCE

Necessary existence is a strange but fascinating concept. It is not just an imaginary idea dreamed up by religious thinkers, as some critics might believe. Rather, it is a well-established logical concept studied in depth by contemporary logicians and mathematicians. New books on modal logic containing deep analysis of necessary existence appear every year. In its highest reaches, modal logic merges into mathematics. The thoughts suggested here on God's necessity can be quantified and formulated rigorously using the latest logic and math. They deserve to be taken seriously.

The precise definitions of *necessary* and *contingent* existence presented earlier are abstract. Here is a more visual way to approach the idea. Begin by thinking about a being whose existence depends on changing external circumstances—a specific apple sitting on a table, for instance. If the orchard had not been planted, the apple would not exist. If the water table had been too low, if the bees had not pollinated the trees, if the temperature had been too high, the seed would not have grown, and the apple would not exist. The apple, in short, exists at the mercy of circumstances beyond itself. Its existence hangs by a thread, depending as it does on the shifting sands of time and change. If circumstances had been sufficiently different, the apple would not *be*. It would not have being. If circumstances had been even more different, no apples at all would actually exist. The apple on the table exists contingently.

You and I are also contingent beings, for we owe our existence to our parents, as well as to many external conditions (the availability of food and water, the temperature of the earth, the existence of the sun, etc.). We also owe our existence to many circumstances that could have been different. If the earth had been destroyed by an asteroid a million years ago, we would not exist today. If our parents had not been born, we would not exist. All human beings exist contingently.

Now imagine a being whose existence does not depend on the shifting sands of time and change. It exists no matter what the case is, it would have existed no matter what would have been the case, and it will exist no matter what the case will be. Under no possible circumstances would it fail to exist. Its nonexistence, in other words, is logically impossible.

Unlike a contingent being that exists at the mercy of external circumstances, this being exists under its own steam, so to speak. Just as a necessary truth (e.g., the whole is greater than the part) is such that it cannot possibly be false, no matter what the circumstances, this being is such that it cannot fail to *be*, no matter what. This is all very theoretical, and surely confusing at first, but *that* would be a necessary being.

So, while a contingent being exists precariously, at the mercy of time and circumstance, always in danger of going out of existence, a necessary being, if one were to exist, would exist no matter what, serenely unaffected by chance and shifting circumstances—never in danger of going out of existence.

BACK TO OCKHAM'S RAZOR

Suppose that you find the design argument (from the previous chapter) rationally compelling, and you also find the cosmological argument reasonable. Given this, which of the following two hypotheses is more logical?

H1: The Designer and the necessary being responsible for the existence of the material universe are two different beings.

H2: The Designer and the necessary being responsible for the existence of the material universe are one and the same being.

Ockham's razor points us to H2, for H2 explains the same data explained by H1 but with fewer assumptions and fewer basic explanatory entities. The second hypothesis thus knits the design and cosmological arguments into a single intertwined inference to the best explanation favoring monotheism over polytheism.

Uniting the design and cosmological arguments brings the issue close to home: if God created the universe for a purpose, then God created *you* for a purpose. And that is an amazing thought.

REFLECTION ON THE MODAL COSMOLOGICAL ARGUMENT

Should we accept the conclusion of this historic argument? One consideration worth keeping in mind is this: when seeking to explain something, it is rational to seek the best explanation. This is the driving force behind science, the maxim of every courtroom, and the spirit of every academic subject. Seeking the best explanation is not only common sense; it is the spirit of philosophy; and it is life. If, after exploring all the available ways to make sense of a phenomenon, one hypothesis stands out as the best or the only sensible explanation, that is a good reason to accept it.

There is something elemental in all this. Children often ask strings of "why" questions. Why is the sky blue? Why does the sun move across the sky? Their natural curiosity sometimes draws their parents into an explanatory regress. It is human to ask why. People of all cultures and all times have asked the ultimate cosmological question: Why is there something rather than nothing? The cosmological argument gives expression to the universal human desire to make sense of things as a whole. If the cosmological argument is correct, the material universe was created by a being existing beyond space, time, matter, and energy—a being many naturally call God. The Christian philosopher William Lane Craig writes:

> We ought to ponder long and hard over this truly remarkable conclusion, for it means that transcending the entire universe there exists a cause which brought the universe into being. . . . [T]his conclusion ought to stagger us, ought to fill us with a sense of awe and wonder at the knowledge that our whole universe was caused to exist by something beyond it and greater than it.[19]

One final consideration. I said this with respect to the design argument. Perhaps the cosmological argument by itself doesn't take us all the way to the God of the Bible or to God as God is portrayed within Christianity. Perhaps, in this argument, reason once more elevates our minds above matter, space, energy, and time and then pauses to gesture silently toward a majestic supernatural agency who created it all, as if to say, "This is as far as I can take you, but the journey is not finished." Perhaps faith is the next step of the journey.

EINSTEIN, MODERN COSMOLOGY, AND THE EXISTENCE OF GOD

The modal cosmological argument just presented fits nicely with, and receives support from, modern big bang astrophysics. The next cosmological argument that I will present, known as the *kalam* cosmological argument, gels with the previous argument as well as with modern astrophysics. However, some scientific background is required before I start the argument.

Enormous advances in astronomy became possible with the invention of the telescope in Europe in the seventeenth century.[20] Thanks to a string of constant improvements by European opticians and telescope makers over the next one hundred years, discoveries occurred at a rapid pace. Only about four thousand stars are visible to the naked eye, but millions are visible through astronomical telescopes because they gather far more light than the human eye can gather.

By the mid-eighteenth century, astronomers in Europe were investigating smudgy specks of light called *nebulae* (Latin for "clouds"), most visible only through powerful telescopes. Were the nebulae stars? Or were they some other kind of object? At the time, no one knew for sure. Since telescopes before 1917 were not powerful enough to adequately resolve their details, nebulae were still a mystery at the start of the twentieth century.[21]

Astronomy began advancing dramatically after Albert Einstein presented his theory of general relativity in 1915. His theory changed forever our understanding of the nature of space, time, and the cosmos.

Einstein's General Theory of Relativity

At the beginning of the twentieth century, three assumptions were taken for granted by most physicists and astronomers.

1. Euclidean geometry—the geometry of a flat surface—correctly describes the spatial structure of the universe.
   Comment. In Euclidean geometry, parallel lines never meet. In a Euclidean universe, two objects traveling along exactly parallel paths could theoretically keep moving forever without ever meeting.

2. The universe is eternal: it has neither a beginning nor an end.
   Comment. This was a working assumption for most scientists, even though in the nineteenth century, the German scientist and philosopher Hermann von Helmholtz (1821–94) and the German physicist and mathematician Rudolf Clausius (1822–88) had argued, on the basis of the newly discovered second law of thermodynamics, that the universe must have had a beginning in time.[22] They also argued, on the basis of the second law, that the universe is heading inexorably toward "heat death"—a state in which all motion has stopped and the temperature of the universe is absolute zero. Their arguments were largely ignored.

3. The universe is static on the large scale.
   Comment. Most scientists did not believe the universe as a whole is, or could be, expanding or contracting or otherwise evolving in a direction.

Einstein took all three governing assumptions for granted as he was researching and developing his general theory of relativity, which he completed and published in 1915. His general theory is a theory of gravity, and it was an advance on the theory of gravity proposed by Newton in the seventeenth century. Unlike Newton's theory, which was expressed in algebraic terms, Einstein's was expressed in geometrical terms.

The new theory of gravity contained many surprises. The geometry of the universe, Einstein claimed, is not the familiar Euclidean geometry of a flat surface that we all learned in junior high or middle school. Rather, it is Riemannian geometry, the geometry of a positively curved surface such as that of a globe.

Furthermore, claimed Einstein, the presence of matter causes space to curve. Because space with matter is curved, objects move through space in curved rather than straight paths. Space isn't just an empty void through which objects move; it is flexible and has a *shape*.

Einstein thus rejected the first widely accepted assumption in physics—that the geometry of the universe is Euclidean. Since the force of gravity is universal, the differential equations of general relativity theory constituted a new blueprint for the overall structure of the universe.

In 1917, Einstein plugged the latest astronomical data into the equations of his yet-to-be-tested theory. The result troubled him greatly. His equations indicated that the universal force of gravity is causing the universe to implode like a collapsing building. Einstein immediately saw that *if* this is right, then the universe is not static on the large scale; rather it is changing in a direction. This bothered him because it contradicted the third governing assumption of physics, namely, that the universe is static on the large scale.

Moreover, and even worse, if the universe is collapsing, this suggests that it began a finite time ago, for (1) no known physical force could stop a universal gravitational collapse, and (2) the collapse has obviously not yet run its course. Einstein strongly wanted to avoid a universal beginning and a universal end, for both would violate the second assumption—that the material universe is eternal. In a moment we will see *why* he wanted to avoid a cosmic beginning.

It is noteworthy that the three guiding assumptions listed above were not derived from science or based on scientific data, as Einstein himself later admitted. They were working assumptions.

To avoid the two unwelcome conclusions—that the universe is evolving on the large scale and that it all began a finite time ago—Einstein tinkered with his equations. Specifically, he inserted a new term to the left side, which he named the "cosmological constant." Denoted by the Greek letter Λ (lambda), this constant represented a hypothetical antigravity force that, if it were to exist, would exactly oppose and balance the force of gravity, prevent a cosmic collapse, and hold the universe in equilibrium on the large scale for eternity.

So Einstein inserted lambda into his equations, even though no such antigravity force had ever been discovered and despite the fact that the natural solution to the equations of general relativity indicated an evolving universe that began a finite time ago rather than a universe that is static and eternal. The cosmological constant was inserted for one reason only: to prevent his theory from predicting a dynamic universe with a *beginning*.

Over the next dozen or so years, huge advances were made in astrophysics, culminating in the amazing discovery that the material universe is not infinitely old; rather it began to exist a finite time ago in a single event now called the "big bang." Surprisingly, this discovery, one of the greatest in twentieth-century astrophysics, owes much to the pathbreaking research of a humble Catholic priest, who was also one of the greatest mathematical physicists of the twentieth century.

Georges Lemaître, Father of the Big Bang Theory

Georges Lemaître (1894–1966) was born in Belgium into a devout Catholic family. From an early age, he showed signs of mathematical genius. As a young man, Lemaître was attracted equally to the Catholic priesthood, theology, mathematics, engineering, and physics. The life path he chose allowed him to pursue all five. While studying for the priesthood, he took courses in higher mathematics, engineering, and theoretical physics in preparation for the academic part of his vocation. In 1914, when World War I began, Lemaître and his brother left college to serve on the front lines. Georges actually carried math and physics textbooks into the trenches and studied between ferocious and bloody battles.

After the war, Lemaître was admitted to Cambridge University, where he did research in physics under Sir Arthur Eddington (1882–1944), one of Britain's greatest astrophysicists and at the time one of the most famous scientists in the world. Next came studies at Harvard and MIT, supervised by Harlow Shapely (1885–1972), one of the greatest American astronomers of the day.

Between 1920 and 1925, Lemaître earned doctorates in mathematics and physics, was ordained to the Catholic priesthood, and was appointed professor of physics at the prestigious Catholic University of Louvain, Belgium. While meeting his duties as a diocesan priest, Lemaître taught courses in physics and mathematics and conducted advanced research in general relativity theory.

Lemaître's First Scientific Paper. In 1917, the Dutch astrophysicist Willem de Sitter (1872–1934) proposed a new solution to Einstein's equations that surprised everyone. The new solution described "a static universe that was completely devoid of matter."[23] This result was anathema to Einstein: the very possibility of empty space was inconsistent with a number of assumptions embedded in his general theory.

In 1925, Lemaître published his first scientific paper. In this now historic work, he showed that de Sitter had made an error in his calculations: a de Sitter universe would indeed be empty of matter, but it would not be static: *it would be expanding*. This was an amazing result at the time, calculated by hand on paper and coming two years before the discovery by astronomers of the expansion of the universe.

Einstein was puzzled. How, he asked, could empty space *expand*? Why would it expand? How could space do anything without the presence of matter? This made no sense in the context of his general theory with lambda added.

At this point, Lemaître was still assuming an eternal universe. The model universe he derived using Einstein's equations was expanding in the future but was static (and thus eternal) in the past.

Lemaître's Second Scientific Paper. In 1927, Lemaître published his second paper. Using astronomical data received in private correspondence from the leading astronomers of the day, Edwin Hubble (1889–1953) and Harlow Shapely, and the field equations of general relativity, Lemaître proved that a model universe containing matter that starts "from a static Einstein state stretching back into the indefinite past" *must be expanding in the future*. This result was even more amazing than the result obtained in his first paper.

Astronomers had not yet proved that the universe is expanding; everyone still assumed (and wanted to believe) that the universe is static on the large scale.

Lemaître's second paper contained the first complete solution to Einstein's field equations that was based on empirical data and that *required* an expanding universe. Again, this result came two years before astronomers finally had the data to prove that the universe is indeed expanding. By solving gigantic systems of equations in differential geometry with pencil and paper, the young priest had previsioned one of the greatest astronomical discoveries of all time—a discovery that I'll turn to in a moment.

At this point, Lemaître was still assuming an eternally old cosmos. His 1927 model of the universe assumed an initial eternally static state and had the universe expanding only in the future.[24] But Lemaître had shown something remarkable: even if we posit a past-eternal static Einstein universe, the whole thing, *space-time included*, must now be expanding. In this same paper, Lemaître also derived the principle originally named "Hubble's law" but known today officially as the "Hubble-Lemaître law."[25]

This law states that the nebulae are receding from us and from each other at velocities directly proportional to their distances. Lemaître also gave the first estimate for the number known today as the "Hubble constant," a number astrophysicists use to estimate both the size and the age of the universe. Lemaître was also the first to attribute the recession of the nebulae to the actual expansion of space itself—an idea that is as mind-boggling today as it was in 1927.[26]

Lemaître's theory attracted little attention, even though it raised enormous problems for the reigning assumption of a static, eternal universe. For instance, if the universe is past eternally static, why would it wait until a recent moment to start expanding? How could a universe be static for an infinite number of years and then all of a sudden start expanding? And why, after having been static for an infinite number of years, would it do so?

A short time after his second paper was published, Lemaître met Einstein at an international physics conference in Brussels. Over a period of several days, the priest discussed his calculations with the great physicist. The two men even traveled to England together to visit Eddington's laboratory—followed everywhere they went by the world press.

Still Einstein was not convinced. He accepted Lemaître's mathematics but rejected Lemaître's physical conclusions.[27] Einstein was still wedded to the assumption of an eternally static cosmos.

The next big discovery in cosmology would come from another unlikely source, a man who had been a boxer before becoming a professional astronomer. I'll return to Father Lemaître in a moment.

Hubble Solves the Mystery of the Nebulae

In 1919, when Edwin Hubble began observing the heavens with the 100-inch Hooker telescope at Mount Wilson, near Los Angeles, the largest telescope in the world at the time, it was generally believed that the Milky Way star system is the whole universe; that is, it was believed that all the stars and objects in the heavens belong to one system of stars, the Milky Way. It was also believed, of course, that the Milky Way system is static on the large scale.[28]

By 1925, Hubble had resolved individual stars within the Andromeda nebula. When he inspected the photographic images under a magnifying glass, he discovered that the stars were Cepheid variable stars, a type known to brighten and dim periodically, with the period of variation a mathematical function of the star's intrinsic (internal) brightness. After measuring the period of variation, Hubble was able to determine the total amount of intrinsic light these stars emitted. Using this value, and the law of physics stating that light decreases with distance according to a mathematical formula first discovered by Newton, Hubble was able to calculate the actual distance to the Andromeda nebula.

To his surprise, he found that the Andromeda nebula is not a smudgy-looking star; it is a separate star system composed of millions of stars, located outside the Milky Way. The Milky Way is therefore not the whole cosmos. Within a few years, Hubble was able to show that the heavens contain millions of separate star systems, now called "galaxies." Astronomers today count more than 200 billion galaxies, each containing hundreds of billions of stars on average.

Next, on the basis of a photographic analysis of the light arriving on earth from many galaxies, Hubble discovered that other galaxies are moving away from ours and from each other at enormous speeds.[29] In 1929, he published his data and made the announcement that shook the world of science: the *best explanation* of the data is that the universe as a whole is expanding. It is expanding like a balloon being blown up. We live in a dynamic, not a static, cosmos.

However, astronomers still assumed that the universe is past-eternal. The question now became: How can the universe be both past-eternal and expanding? It was Lemaître who finally solved the problem.

The Big Bang Theory

Between 1927 and 1930, Lemaître found new problems with expanding, past-eternal Einsteinian model universes. By the end of 1930, he began to suspect that any universe that satisfies the field equations of general relativity and Hubble's galactic data *cannot have existed forever*. After verifying that the model cannot be altered to allow for an eternally old universe, Lemaître drew his momentous conclusion: the universe does not have an eternal past. The best relativistic model of the universe indicated a "beginning of all physical processes."[30] *The physical universe began to exist a finite time ago.*

When Lemaître published his findings in 1931, the scientific community immediately (and emotionally) rejected his conclusion. Eddington said in an address, "Philosophically, the notion of a beginning . . . is repugnant to me."[31] Einstein could not accept the theory "because of its metaphysical implications [a cosmic beginning]."[32] The first time Lemaître tried to speak to Einstein about the matter, Einstein said, "No, not that, that suggests too much the creation."[33] If I may propose a translation: "No, that comes too close to suggesting the opening line of the book of Genesis."[34] Most scientists rejected Lemaître's conclusion but not on the basis of scientific evidence: they rejected it on the basis of nonscientific assumptions to which they were emotionally wedded—assumptions that ruled out a universal beginning.

Despite the hostile response, in 1933, Lemaître was invited to the California Institute of Technology (Cal Tech), in Pasadena, California, one of the foremost scientific research institutes in the world, to conduct a series of seminars on his solutions to Einstein's field equations and on his theory of cosmic rays. Einstein was in the audience when Lemaître lectured on his 1927 paper. After the lecture, the great physicist stood up and called Lemaître's theory "the most beautiful and satisfying interpretation of creation to which I have ever listened."[35] Lemaître's argument had convinced the greatest physicist in the world.

Each day now, Lemaître and Einstein walked the grounds of Cal Tech discussing their theories, followed everywhere by reporters from around the world. Einstein later called his decision in 1917 to insert the cosmological constant (lambda) into his equations "the biggest blunder of my life."[36]

Lemaître's calculations indicated that all the physical processes in the universe started from an initial "super dense state" containing the entire mass-energy of the universe packed into a single point too small and dense for the equations to describe. Lemaître named this initial state the "primeval atom." As the universe burst out of this point, it expanded, and space, time, and matter all came into existence and took form.

Lemaître also derived theoretical implications that anticipated discoveries that would be made years later by others. For instance, he hypothesized that the cosmic rays that seem to pervade the universe from every direction are leftover energy from the initial "fireworks" at the birth of the universe. He also suggested that the universe expanded quickly and then slowed to its present level of expansion.

Lemaître named the initial explosion that resulted in the expanding universe the "big noise." The English astronomer Fred Hoyle (1915–2001), an atheist at the time, disliked Lemaître's hypothesis so intensely that he mockingly named it "the big bang." Although he was making fun of Lemaître's idea, the new name stuck. Astronomers now estimate that the material universe, and all physical processes, began about 13.8 billion years ago in one initial creation-like event. Lemaître received a number of prestigious awards for his work.

During the 1930s and 1940s, several competing cosmological theories were proposed by astrophysicists, each one retaining the assumption of an eternal universe, although none was adequately supported by the data. Each of these theories was proposed for one reason only: to avoid a cosmic beginning.[37]

Final Confirmation: The Cosmic Microwave Radiation

In 1965, Arnold Penzias and Robert Wilson, scientists at the Bell Telephone Laboratories in New Jersey, were using a giant radio receiver to track signals from NASA's Echo communications satellites. No matter how finely they tuned their instrument, they kept hearing static they could not explain. At first, they thought the static might be caused by pigeon droppings inside the instrument's large, horn-shaped antennas. However, this was ruled out after they cleaned the antennas and the noise remained. After checking every component, they concluded that the static they were hearing was coming not from their instruments but from deep space.

The mystery deepened when they discovered that the signal was being received from every direction in space and at exactly the same strength. They finally realized that the static could only be low temperature microwave radiation bathing the earth uniformly from every corner of the universe. The question now became: What cosmic process could possibly generate this type of universal radiation?

A colleague now recalled a prediction that had been derived from Lemaître's big bang hypothesis almost twenty years before by the physicists Ralph Alpher and Robert Herman. If the universe began in a dense state and then exploded, residual heat left over from the initial explosion would be detectable as microwave radiation at about three degrees above absolute zero, bathing the earth uniformly from every direction. A similar prediction had also been made by Lemaître. All of a sudden, *the best explanation* was clear: the microwave radiation predicted by Lemaître, Alpher, and Herman was exactly what Penzias and Wilson had detected. The two Bell scientists had discovered the heat left over from the big bang.

Their discovery disproved those theories that had been proposed during the 1930s to avoid a cosmic beginning. It also confirmed Lemaître's theory of the big bang, for the cosmic background radiation was predicted by the big bang theory but could not be explained at all on any opposing theories.

Almost overnight, the scientific community shifted to Lemaître's side. Today at least four independent lines of empirical evidence indicate that the big bang hypothesis is the best explanation of the total data, making it one of the most well-confirmed theories in all of physics.

1. The data from the redshift of the galaxies can be explained in no other way.
2. The cosmic microwave background radiation can be explained in no other way.
3. The mixture and distribution of the elements across the universe can be explained in no other way.
4. The changes in the galaxies over past time can be explained in no other way.

In sum:

1. The big bang theory is the best explanation of the redshift data, the cosmic microwave data, the data on the mix and distribution of the elements, and the data on the changes in galaxies over time.
2. This comprises virtually all the relevant data.
3. Therefore, the big bang theory is the best explanation of the totality of the data.
4. Therefore, it is reasonable to accept the big bang theory as true.

The point deserves emphasis. The scientific argument for the big bang theory takes the form of an inference to the best explanation.

Thus, in his standard textbook on the big bang, the cosmologist Joseph Silk writes that although models for exotic universes can be sketched on paper, "our preference must be for the simplest tenable cosmology. Practically all known astronomical phenomena can be understood in the context of big bang cosmology—if not completely, then at least to a greater degree than in any alternative framework that has yet been proposed. Thus, we shall accept the big bang model as providing a satisfactory description of the universe."[38]

On June 17, 1966, Father Lemaître was in a nursing home close to death when news of the discovery of the cosmic microwave radiation, which he had predicted in 1933, was presented to him. He died three days later. In his wonderful biography, John Farrell writes that the humble Belgian priest "convinced a generation of thinkers to embrace the notion of cosmic expansion and the theory that this expansion could be traced backward to a cosmic origin, a starting point for space and time that Lemaître called 'the day without yesterday.'"[39] It is an astonishing thought: *the material universe began to exist a finite time ago*. But what follows from this?

THE *KALAM* COSMOLOGICAL ARGUMENT

At the start of this chapter, I noted that philosophers have given many different versions of the cosmological argument. During the ninth century, Islamic philosophers of the *kalam* (Arabic, "science of discourse") school in Baghdad presented and defended the kalam cosmological argument. The reasoning they employed was derived from their studies of Aristotle and other ancient Greek philosophers. The kalam argument had also been stated previously by Christian philosophers, such as John Philoponus (ca. 490–ca. 570).[40] Today the most prominent advocate of the kalam cosmological argument is the American philosopher William Lane Craig, who summarizes it in three steps.

1. Whatever begins to exist has a cause.
2. The material universe began to exist a finite time ago.
3. Therefore, necessarily, the material universe has a cause.[41]

This argument is obviously valid; that is, if the premises are true, then the conclusion *must* be true. It follows that if you don't accept the conclusion, it is incumbent on you as a critical thinker to provide an argument against one of the premises. And if you accept the premises, then you logically ought to accept the conclusion. Now, if the conclusion is true, then *something* caused the entire material universe to come into existence.

Let's think about this for a moment. *Something* caused the entire material universe to come into existence. Since the cause precedes the effect in some distinct way, this "something" must be a being whose existence transcends space, time, energy, and all matter—the whole works. The cause of the material universe is therefore not a material being, and it exists in some sense outside space and time.

If we employ Ockham's razor and if we keep in mind insights from the design argument, then the cause of the universe is a supernatural being of unimaginable power, unimaginable knowledge, and supreme majesty, existing in some sense beyond space, time, energy, and all matter. As Aquinas, Leibniz, and the many other famous proponents of the cosmological argument would say, this we naturally call "God."

But are the premises reasonable? The ex nihilo principle and common sense provide solid support for the first premise ("Whatever begins to exist has a cause"). Big bang astrophysics provides solid support for the second premise ("The material universe began to exist a finite time ago"). The conclusion logically follows, in the sense that if the premises are true, then the conclusion clearly must be true.

The conclusion of the kalam cosmological argument thus has direct support from logic, common sense, and big bang astrophysics—a tough combination to beat. A powerful argument indeed for an astonishingly existential conclusion.

THE "GOD OF THE GAPS" OBJECTION TO ALL THEISTIC ARGUMENTS

I have presented and defended updated versions of four classic arguments for God's existence—two design arguments and two cosmological arguments. Some critics will undoubtedly object in the following way. "Your arguments," they will say, "are all 'God of the gaps' fallacies and therefore prove nothing." What does the critic mean? A fallacy is an error in reasoning. A "God of the gaps fallacy" is an argument for God's existence that reduces to the following form. Phenomenon p has not been explained by science. Therefore, p must have been caused by God. Thus, God exists.

Now, everyone agrees that any argument that reduces to this form is fallacious and therefore proves nothing. The obvious reply to a God of the gaps fallacy argument is this: "Just wait. Science will explain the phenomenon in due time. There's no good reason to infer God's existence here."

However, the four classic theistic arguments that I presented are not God of the gaps arguments. Rather, the first three argue that the phenomenon in question is something that *in principle* cannot be explained by science. And after a number of reasoned steps, each concludes that mere theism offers the best explanation. As noted, inference to the best explanation is the bread-and-butter reasoning of everyday life—most of what we know about the world is derived from this kind of thinking. There is no good reason to employ inference to the best explanation in everything we do and then drop it when it comes to the big questions of life, such as whether or not God exists. The fourth argument I presented—the kalam argument—is not an inference to the best explanation. However, both of its premises are supported with best explanation reasoning. And as we have seen, the fact in question, that the material universe began to exist a finite time ago, is one science cannot in principle explain.

We have now examined four classic arguments for God's existence and the most common objections to those arguments. However, some people believe that this leaves out the most powerful positive argument for atheism, namely, the so-called argument from evil. The two design arguments and the two cosmological arguments, some people might say, give us strong reasons to believe that God exists. However, they might add, the fact that the world contains massive quantities of evil or suffering makes it more reasonable overall to reject belief. Are these critics right? This is the topic of the next chapter.

FOR FURTHER STUDY

Craig, William Lane, and J. P. Moreland, eds. *The Blackwell Companion to Natural Theology.* Oxford: Wiley-Blackwell, 2012. For Craig's full presentation of his kalam argument, see chap. 3, "The Kalam Cosmological Argument," 101–201.

Craig, William Lane, and Quentin Smith. *Theism, Atheism, and Big Bang Cosmology.* Oxford: Oxford University Press, 1993.

Craig, William Lane, Kevin Meeker, J. P. Moreland, Michael Murray, and Timothy O'Conner, eds. *Philosophy of Religion: A Reader and Guide.* New Brunswick, NJ: Rutgers University Press, 2002.

Feser, Edward. *Five Proofs of the Existence of God.* San Francisco: Ignatius Press, 2017.

Herrick, Paul. *Philosophy, Reasoned Belief, and Faith: An Introduction.* Notre Dame, IN: University of Notre Dame Press, 2022.

Koperski, Jeffrey, *The Physics of Theism: God, Physics, and the Philosophy of Science.* Oxford: Wiley-Blackwell, 2014.

Pasnau, Robert, and Christopher Shields. *The Philosophy of Aquinas.* New York: Westview Press, 2004.

Rasmussen, Joshua. *How Reason Can Lead to God: A Philosopher's Bridge to Faith.* Downers Grove, IL: InterVarsity Press Academic, 2019.

For contemporary criticisms of the cosmological argument

Mackie, J. L. *The Miracle of Theism: Arguments for and against the Existence of God.* New York: Oxford University Press, 1983.

Martin, Michael. *Atheism: A Philosophical Justification.* Philadelphia: Temple University Press, 1992.

For the reader interested in modern scientific cosmology

Farrell, John. *The Day without Yesterday: Lemaître, Einstein, and the Birth of Modern Cosmology.* New York: Thunder's Mouth Press, 2005.

Hogan, Craig J. *The Little Book of the Big Bang: A Cosmic Primer*. New York: Springer Verlag, 1998.
Trefil, James. *The Moment of Creation*. New York: Charles Scribner's Sons, 1983.
Weinberg, Steven. *The First Three Minutes: A Modern View of the Origin of the Universe*. New York: Basic Books, 1993.

For the reader interested in philosophical theology

Flint, Thomas P., and Michael Rea, eds., *The Oxford Handbook of Philosophical Theology*. New York: Oxford University Press, 2011.
Morris, Thomas V. *Our Idea of God: An Introduction to Philosophical Theology*. Notre Dame, IN: University of Notre Dame Press, 1991.
Murray, Michael J., and Michael Rea. *An Introduction to the Philosophy of Religion*. Cambridge: Cambridge University Press, 2008.

For the reader interested in modal logic and necessary existence

O'Conner, Timothy. *Theism and Ultimate Explanation: The Necessary Shape of Contingency*. Oxford: Wiley-Blackwell, 2012.
Plantinga, Alvin. *The Nature of Necessity*. Oxford: Clarendon Press, 1974.

For an introduction to modal logic

Herrick, Paul. *Introduction to Logic*, chap. 35. New York: Oxford University Press, 2012.

Advanced works in modal logic

Cresswell, M. J., and G. E. Hughes. *Modal Logic: A New Introduction*. New York: Routledge, 1996.
Garson, James. *Modal Logic for Philosophers*. 2nd ed. Cambridge: Cambridge University Press, 2013.
Konyndyk, Kenneth. *Introductory Modal Logic*. South Bend, IN: University of Notre Dame Press, 1986.

interlude two

Christianity's Contributions to World Culture

In chapters 2 and 3, I relied on the results of modern experimental science and modern mathematics. It is seldom noted today, but both subjects were born in Europe during the sixteenth and seventeenth centuries in institutions of higher education that had been founded by the Catholic Church and that were staffed with faculty who were all believing Christians.

MODERN SCIENCE

Turning to modern experimental science first, the sociologist and historian Rodney Stark (1934–2022) constructed a list of every working scientist active during the birth of modern science in the sixteenth and seventeenth centuries. Next he researched the religious beliefs of this group of fifty-two, each a pioneer in his field. Fifty of the fifty-two were either devout or conventional Christians; only two were skeptics. Both skeptics, however, like the others, had been educated at Christian universities and had conducted their research in institutions reflecting Christian theological beliefs.[1]

Indeed, the pioneers in nearly every branch of modern experimental science as it emerged were actually monks and priests who combined scientific research with their religious duties. The historian Thomas Woods writes:

> For example, Father Nicolaus Steno . . . is often identified as the father of geology. The father of Egyptology was Father Athanasius Kircher. The first person to measure the rate of acceleration of a freely falling body was yet another priest, Father Giambattista Riccioli. Father Roger Boscovich is often credited as the father of modern atomic theory. Jesuits so dominated the study of earthquakes that seismology became known as "the Jesuit science." Even though some thirty-five craters on the moon are named for Jesuit scientists and mathematicians, the Church's contributions to astronomy are all but unknown to the average educated American.[2]

Thus, "the Catholic contribution to science," writes Woods, "went well beyond ideas—including theological ideas—to accomplished practicing scientists, many of whom were priests."[3]

The size of the church's contribution to science is also seldom noted today. The historian Charles Homer Hoskins wrote the following in his now-classic work, *The Rise of Universities*: "Between 1200 and 1500 at least 80 universities were founded in Europe, many starting out on church property."[4]

The Christian origin of modern experimental science is hard to deny. The first modern scientific laboratories, scientific research institutes, scientific societies, scientific libraries, and science journals were all founded by churchmen and Christian scholars educated in and associated with church institutions.

Stark argues that there is a conceptual link between (a) the Christian conception of a rational God who created an intelligible universe fit to be probed by the human mind and (b) the birth of modern experimental science in Europe. Other scholars have argued the same point, including the great mathematician and philosopher Alfred North Whitehead (1861–1947), a founder of modern symbolic logic. In a famous lecture delivered at Harvard University in 1925, Whitehead argued that medieval Christianity and the Christian conception of God and God's relation to the world provided "the soil, the climate, the seeds" for the birth of modern science.[5]

In *Religion and Science: Historical and Contemporary Issues*, Ian Barbour (1923–2013), distinguished historian of the relation between science and religion, asked: "Why was it in Western civilization alone, among all the cultures of the world, that science in its modern form developed? [Premodern] Arabic science was more advanced than Western science in the thirteenth century, especially in astronomy, optics, and medicine, but it fell far behind in subsequent centuries."[6]

Barbour concluded that during the Middle Ages Christianity supplied the necessary "intellectual presuppositions" and worldview framework, including an "interest in nature for its own sake," that led to the birth of modern experimental science.[7] This is a deep subject that I will not enter into further here.[8]

FROM THE MONASTERY TO THE LABORATORY

The eighty or more universities of medieval Europe that gave the world modern experimental science during the sixteenth and seventeenth centuries grew out of monasteries and cathedral schools scattered across the continent from Ireland to Italy. Each of these institutions was originally a small Christian community of monks, students, and spiritual individuals seeking God in communion with others through a life of physical labor, private and communal prayer, charity, humility, study, and spiritual meditation.

Going further back, the French historian Pierre Hadot has shown that the spiritual exercises practiced in the early monasteries of medieval Europe were influenced by modes of spirituality taught in the Stoic schools of ancient Rome and ultimately trace back to spiritual practices associated with Plato and Socrates.[9] A continuous line of development can therefore be traced from ancient Greek and Roman philosophy to Christian spirituality to the birth of modern experimental science.

The monastic institutions of early medieval Europe are often looked down on by modern secular scholars who consider them centers of crude thought and superstition. To the contrary, most were centers of learning where knowledge was valued both for its own sake and because true learning, it was believed, elevates the soul toward the source of all truth, God. The point deserves a moment of attention.

The intellectual milieu in the medieval monasteries of Europe has been described as a "theocentric humanism" in which truth is sought in all areas of thought and all knowledge is unified by being related ultimately to God, the source of all truth. Scholars were encouraged to explore and apply logical reasoning to every aspect of the natural world. Learning was actually considered a form of worship, for the study of the natural world was thought to be the study of God's handiwork and, as such, expressed respect and reverence for the Creator. Within this cultural matrix, all knowledge was valued, and disciplined logic and rational debate were prized.

The spirit of medieval scholarship is exemplified in the work of Saint Albert the Great (ca. 1200–1280), the teacher of Saint Thomas Aquinas. Albert taught his students that no topic is off limits to the Christian scholar; all truth is to be sought, in every area, for God is to be sought, and since God is the source of all truth, the search for truth in any area ultimately leads us to God.

Albert was so interested in the natural world and observational science that he once had himself lowered over the edge of a cliff in a rickety basket just to watch eagle eggs hatching. Contrary to the way they are sometimes portrayed by their modern critics, medieval scholars such as Albert and Thomas Aquinas were not all ivory tower dreamers wasting time wondering how many angels can dance on the head of a pin.[10]

The philosopher and historian Steven Marrone writes that in the medieval monasteries can be seen "the birth of a society in which the learned were free to turn their efforts to analysis and speculation for their own sakes, and eventually to that use of pure reason on which philosophy prides itself today."[11] New "habits of mind" were giving birth to a new "literate culture." The monastic scholars, he argues, were the intellectual pioneers of the rationalist movement that paved the way for the birth of the modern university system.[12] Thus, in the monastic system, "the major disciplines of high medieval learning started to take shape, crystalizing around the seed of newly composed and soon universally adopted textbooks that were structured as collections of debating points touching on all significant aspects of the subject field. At the heart of all stood logic, now the paradigm for investigation and summary in all fields."[13] Monastic scholars saw no conflict between their Christian religious faith and the scientific study of nature; they considered them concordant.[14]

MODERN MATHEMATICS

Since modern science makes heavy use of mathematics, it should not be surprising to learn that modern mathematics was also born in the same intellectual milieu, within European universities and institutions established by the Catholic Church and staffed by Christian scholars. Although elementary algebra was founded by Persian and Arab mathematicians during the early medieval period, the big advances that ushered in modern algebra occurred in Europe during the Renaissance and after. For example, during the seventeenth century, John Napier (1550–1617) published the first book on logarithms, Blaise Pascal (1623–62) discovered probability theory, René Descartes (1596–1650) discovered analytic geometry, and Gottfried Leibniz (1646–1716) and Isaac Newton (1641–1727) independently discovered differential and integral calculus.[15] The process grew from there to the magnificent structure of mathematics and mathematical logic that led to the birth of the digital computer in the twentieth century in England and America and the extraordinary advances that have followed.

THE FIRST MODERN POLITICAL PHILOSOPHY

Science and math as we know them today are not the only products of the first modern university system. The same intellectual matrix that gave birth to modern science and modern math also gave birth to the first modern theory of universal human rights, the first modern theory of international law, and (underlying both) the first modern political philosophy.

Although it is true that political theory as we know it today builds on philosophical ideas going back to ancient Greece and Rome, as well as to wisdom recorded in the Hebrew scriptures, *modern* political philosophy was born in Europe during the fifteenth, sixteenth, and seventeenth centuries, as Christian theologians, preachers, scholars, and philosophers discussed the following set of interconnected ideals circulating throughout the continent.

- All human beings, by virtue of their humanity alone, regardless of age, wealth, religion, income, socioeconomic status, gender, or nationality, reflect the image of God in their soul. This is the biblical doctrine of the *imago Dei*.

Comment. The *imago Dei* is called a Judeo-Christian moral principle because it appears in both the Hebrew scriptures and the Christian New Testament.[16]

- By virtue of this image of divinity, each human being possesses an intrinsic and equal value that is independent of social status, income, nationality, and so forth—a sacredness that even the highest authorities must respect.

- By virtue of this intrinsic value, each human being possesses inalienable rights that can be asserted against every other person and even against the highest authorities, including the state.

- The most basic of these rights are rights to life and liberty and the right to own property.

- The primary purpose of any legitimate government is to serve the people by protecting their human rights—rights they received not from the state but from God at birth.

- The rights of the individual are most secure when they are protected by an elected government whose power is strictly limited by written constitutional law endorsed by the people on the basis of reasonable considerations and regarded by all as the highest law of the land.

I hasten to add that these principles are ideals: they are not descriptions of present reality. Ideals are aspirational rather than descriptive: they guide us as we seek to improve the society in which we live.

The philosophy underlying and connecting these ideals was originally called "liberalism" because it championed the liberty of the individual against the power of the state. As new ideas on liberty developed during the

---

The Oxford University historian J. M. Roberts writes:

At the heart of Christianity ... there always lay the concept of the supreme, infinite value of the individual soul. This was the taproot of respect for the individual in the here-and-now, a respect buttressed by Roman concepts of law and legal rights, and by the emphasis on moral autonomy which went back to ancient Greece.[17]

nineteenth and twentieth centuries, the original set of ideals became known as "classical liberalism," and the later ideals became known as "modern liberalism."

If the six classical liberal ideals listed above sound familiar, that is because so much of our contemporary thought on government, human rights, and politics reflects the ideas of the first modern political thinkers—all Christian scholars inspired by biblical teachings and writing within a Christian intellectual milieu rooted in the universities, churches, and salons of early modern Europe.[18] Although classical liberal ideas sound commonplace today, they were revolutionary when they were first proposed and debated in the sixteenth and seventeenth centuries. Classical liberal ideas were anathema to kings possessing nearly absolute power and their defenders.

POLITICAL AND SOCIAL REFORM MOVEMENTS

As Richard Weaver noted, ideas have consequences.[19] Motivated by classical liberal ideas—with a heavy emphasis on the doctrine of the *imago Dei*—Christian activists launched programs of political and social reform, including efforts to make governments more accountable to the people, programs to aid the poor and marginalized, the world's first antislavery crusade, and the first movements for the rights of workers, women, and children. Some of the first modern political thinkers even stated the first *moral* critique of the actions of some of the sixteenth-century European conquistadors and colonizers in the New World.

Critique of the Conquistadors

The Indigenous peoples of the Americas are fully human beings whose souls bear the image of God. As sacred creations of God, they deserve to be treated with the same respect and concern as any other human being on earth. Therefore, any exploitation, abuse, or enslavement of them by European conquerors and colonizers is morally wrong. So argued the sixteenth-century Spanish missionary and Dominican friar Bartolomé de Las Casas (ca. 1474–1566). Catholic theologians and philosophers at the Spanish University of Salamanca, founded in the thirteenth century, produced theological arguments for the same conclusion, also with appeal to the doctrine of the *imago Dei*.[20]

The World's First Antislavery Crusade

Slavery was a worldwide institution, existing and accepted as natural on every continent, when Christian writers and activists in Europe and the American colonies launched the world's first antislavery movements during the seventeenth century. For example, as early as 1644, the Reformed Presbyterian Church in Scotland condemned slavery on biblical and philosophical grounds. Faith Martin writes this of the Reformed Presbyterians, known as "Covenanters":

> Most remarkable was their fearless and relentless condemnation of slavery.... In 1644, the formidable Covenanter theologian Samuel Rutherford had declared that all men were made in the image of God and as such could not be bought or sold. "A man being created according to God's image, he is *res sacra*, a sacred thing, and can no more, by nature's law, be sold or bought than a religious and sacred thing dedicated to God.... Every man by nature is a freeman born, that is, by nature no man comes out of the womb under any civil subjection to King, Prince, or Judge to master, captain, conqueror, teacher."[21]

Furthermore:

> Covenanters in America honed and expanded the case against slavery. Slavery is shown to be sinful by direct scripture testimony and by conclusions justly derived from the great principles of Christian equity laid down in the sacred volume.... God, the creator, has given to man certain rights of which he cannot be lawfully deprived, except as a punishment for crime.... The Creator has not bestowed on one class the chartered privilege of lordship over another.... "God has made of one blood all men to dwell upon the earth."... The national disgrace of slave-holding must be wiped off by letting the oppressed go free. Sin must be forsaken or the avenging justice of God shall overtake us.[22]

Martin's research is worth quoting at further length:

> Reformed Presbyterian ministers published articles and pamphlets, had their anti-slavery sermons printed in the *New York Times*, and were

sought after as speakers at abolitionist rallies. They were "mobbed, stoned, egged and burned in effigy." . . . In 1800, when other Christian churches were merely passing resolutions condemning slavery, Reformed Presbyterians ruled that no member of the church who owned a slave could take communion. . . . Two Reformed Presbyterian ministers met with Abraham Lincoln in the weeks leading up to the Emancipation Proclamation, encouraging him to take the step. . . . Reformed Presbyterian homes were important stops on the Underground Railroad.[23]

We consider it painfully obvious today that slavery is morally wrong. However, the antislavery movement appears remarkable when you consider that it formed at a time in world history when human slavery was entrenched and considered right on every continent.

Duty to the Poor

The English philosopher John Locke (1632–1704) wrote one of the first systematic philosophical arguments supporting and unifying the nascent classical liberal ideals and the associated capitalist economic institutions emerging in the Europe of his day. In the first volume of his *Two Treatises on Government* (1689), Locke reminded his readers of their common duties toward the poor and marginalized:

> God has given no one of His children such a property in his peculiar portion of the things of this world, but that he has given his needy brother a right to the surplusage of his goods . . . when his pressing wants call for it. . . . Charity gives every man a title to so much out of another's plenty as will keep him from extreme want, where he has no means to subsist otherwise.[24]

Put another way, those with a surplus have a moral duty to help those in need. For Locke, this duty served as a rider on the right to own property. Left unanswered by Locke was the question of whether charity should be a matter of individual conscience exercised solely within the private sector or whether the duty to aid those in need should be administered by the state and funded by taxes as a *supplement* to the charitable work of individuals, churches, social entrepreneurs, and various (voluntary) benevolence organizations.

Rights of Workers, Women, and Children

During the early years of the Industrial Revolution, inspired by the doctrine of the *imago Dei* and other classical liberal ideals, Christian activists launched the world's first movements championing the rights of workers, women, and children. The British philosopher A. C. Grayling tells the story in his fascinating history of freedom, *Toward the Light of Liberty: The Struggles for Freedom and Rights That Made the Modern Western World*.[25]

A survey of world history, I believe, reveals that most revolutionary changes begin with transformative ideas in the minds of human beings. Many transformative ideas and whole fields of thought arose out of the intellectual culture that was born within the academic institutions of medieval and early modern European Christianity. In addition to the ideas and subjects already noted, a partial list includes the social sciences, modern medicine, modern public health, modern machine technology, the first modern hospitals, the first schools of social work, the first international humanitarian agencies, and the first private institutions serving the poor and the marginalized, such as the settlement houses that opened across America during the nineteenth century.

Ironically, the modern academic world, as secular as it has become, has its roots in an intellectually inclined monastic culture where humble monks, priests, and spiritual seekers searched for God and deep knowledge in harmony with faith, love, hope, and charity.

FOUR

Why Would God Permit Evil?

Christians and people of faith within other religious traditions believe, on the basis of reason and religious experience, that God exists and that God is personal, omnipotent (all-powerful), omniscient (all-knowing), omnibenevolent (all-good), and infinitely loving. Many people of traditional faiths also believe that God loves us like loving parents love their children. But the world is full of suffering, both human and animal. Why would God, traditionally understood as infinitely loving, omnipotent, and so forth, create a world containing *natural* evils, such as earthquakes, hurricanes, floods, birth defects, and diseases, as well as *moral* evils, such as murder, theft, armed robbery, assault, war, genocide, and slavery?

And why would God, as traditionally conceived, create human beings who become mass murderers, such as Hitler, Stalin, and Mao Zedong?[1] Wouldn't a God of infinite love, power, and knowledge have simply not created such moral monsters? In short, wouldn't God have created a world with much less natural and moral evil than this one contains?

These questions about God and suffering have traditionally been grouped together and called "the problem of evil" since it is puzzling or problematic why God, as traditionally conceived, would create a world containing terrible evils, both natural and moral.

In what follows, let's define *evil* broadly as diseases, natural disasters, crimes, war, and other things that introduce suffering into the world. And by *God*, let's mean the all-powerful, all-knowing, all-good, and infinitely loving Creator and designer of the universe. In my experiences discussing the question of God's existence with people over many years, the problem of evil is the biggest barrier to belief. Understandably, the heart-wrenching questions it raises predispose them to doubt the existence of a loving God before any positive evidence has been given.

THE TRADITIONAL ARGUMENT FROM EVIL

The problem of evil, in turn, has given rise to a philosophical argument against the existence of God (as traditionally conceived), which I will call the traditional argument from evil because the idea goes back to ancient times. Here is an initial statement of the problem and the corresponding argument.

The Problem of Evil (Initial Statement)

Why would God, being all-good, all-powerful, infinitely loving, and so forth, allow evil (suffering) to exist? It seems that God, understood in this way, would not allow *any* evil. Yet evil obviously exists.

Argument from evil (initial statement)

1. If God exists, then evil (suffering) does not exist.
2. But evil obviously exists.
3. Therefore, necessarily, God does not exist.

The argument is clearly valid. That is, if its premises are true, then its conclusion *must* be true. The only question, then, is this: Are the premises true?

Argument for premise 1: If God exists, then evil does not exist. Just as loving parents do not want their children to suffer, God—being all-loving—

would not want any creature to suffer. God would therefore be opposed to all suffering. Being all-good, all-powerful, all-knowing, and all-loving, God would therefore not allow any suffering to exist. Therefore, premise 1 is true.

Argument for premise 2: Evil obviously exists. Hospitals are full of people suffering from terrible illnesses, the world is full of violence, and many die every year from horrible natural disasters. Therefore, premise 2 is true.

THE TRADITIONAL ARGUMENT IN MORE DETAIL

Having presented the basic ideas, it is time for a more in-depth analysis. Pulling all the threads together:

1. If a being is all-good, it is completely opposed to all evil (suffering).
2. If a being is all-knowing, it is aware of every evil that exists.
3. If a being is all-powerful, it has the power to prevent any evil.
4. Therefore, an all-good, all-knowing, all-powerful God would not allow *any* evil to exist.
5. Therefore, God (as traditionally defined) would not allow *any* evil to exist.
6. Evil obviously exists.
7. Therefore, God (as traditionally defined) certainly does not exist.

The argument appears airtight at first glance; however, there is actually a logical gap between premises 3 and 4. Step 4 follows logically from the previous steps only if the following assumption is inserted.

Assumption. Necessarily, an all-powerful, all-good, all-knowing being will always eliminate every bit of evil it can possibly eliminate.

With this assumption added, the argument looks invincible. But is the assumption true? To some people, the assumption seems self-evident. Others disagree. They point out that if an all-powerful being were to have a *morally sufficient reason* to permit an instance of suffering S—in other words, a reason that would morally justify permitting S—then that being might permit S, and its permitting S would not be morally wrong.

Here is an analogy from everyday life. A child does not want to go to the doctor. But the parents know that the appointment is necessary if the child is to become well again. Although the child is crying and frightened, the parents take the child to the doctor, and the child soon becomes healthy again. The parents had a morally sufficient reason to take the child to the doctor, even though the trip caused the child some suffering before the happy ending.

Similarly, *if* God were to have a morally sufficient reason for permitting some instance of suffering S, then God might allow S to occur, and there would be nothing morally wrong with God allowing S to occur. God would be justified in allowing S to occur. This much is common sense. Now, it certainly seems *possible* that God has a morally sufficient reason— perhaps one we have not yet thought of—to allow the evils we observe. Therefore, it is possible that God would not eliminate every evil we see, and the needed assumption (that necessarily, an all-powerful, all-good, all-knowing being will always eliminate every bit of evil it can possibly eliminate) is false. But are we talking about real possibilities here?

Are there logical reasons God *might have or might have had* for permitting a preventable instance of suffering? What reason could God possibly have had for not preventing some of the horrible evils of the twentieth century, such as the Nazi Holocaust or the Communist-run forced famine in Ukraine that killed approximately six million poor farmers during the 1930s? Christian philosophers have suggested several; the possible reasons they propose are called "theodicies."

THEODICIES

A *theodicy* is a reason God *might have had* to permit suffering. Keep in mind as we proceed that theodicists do not claim to have identified the reasons God actually had. They are only suggesting reasons God might have had for permitting some of the evils we observe. If at least one theodicy seems sensible, then it is logically *possible* that God exists and has a morally sufficient reason to permit some evils. In which case, the assumption (that necessarily, an all-powerful, all-good, all-knowing being will always eliminate every bit of evil it can possibly eliminate) is simply false. But that assumption is needed if the traditional argument from evil as stated above is to go through. The assumption is false if at least one theodicy is sensible because if at least one theodicy is sensible, then it is *possible*, for all we know, that there are some evils God could eliminate but for a morally sufficient reason does not eliminate.

Theodicies are thus defensive in nature: they are offered to rebut the assumption in the traditional argument from evil that "necessarily, an all-powerful, all-knowing, all-good being will always eliminate every bit of evil it can possibly eliminate."

The Free Will Theodicy

This theodicy goes back to ancient times. According to this proposal, God, being supremely good, is infinitely loving, since love is obviously an intrinsic good.[2] God's act of creation therefore must have been an act of love: God created us to be loved by him and to love him in return. But love is an act of will. More deeply, it is an act of a *free* will. For real love, by its inherent nature, is freely given; it is not coerced, nor is it determined by external circumstances or forces.[3] It follows that God freely chose to create us. It also follows that God gave us free rather than predetermined wills, since God created us to love and to be loved, and real love requires freedom. Furthermore, the possession of free will must itself be a good thing since it is a necessary condition for an act of genuine love.

However, a truly free will has a dual nature. It can be used for good, but it can also be used for bad. For if our wills are capable only of doing good, then they are not truly free. Thus, if a person truly has free will, then the person has the power to love God and also the power to reject God; the power to do good things and the power to cause suffering. Only if we have free will in this sense are we capable of real love.[4]

So, in the very beginning, free will must have been a purely good thing, for, given that love is good and is always something freely given, the freedom of the will was necessary if human beings were to one day enter into a loving relationship with God, the ultimate source of love and goodness. However, this original freedom—pure in the beginning—included the power to rebel against God, since (again) real freedom includes the power to do bad and to do good. And life experience shows that when we turn from God, the result is usually suffering and disorder.

Thus, on this theodicy, evil entered the world after the Creation, when free creatures misused their gift of free will by rebelling against their Creator. This is one possible explanation of how evil might have arisen in a world that was originally created in a state of complete goodness. It also explains how suffering might have entered the world *without God having been its cause*.

So the morally sufficient reason God might have had for permitting the suffering we see around us is this: God allows suffering caused by the creaturely misuse of free will because the gift of free will is a necessary condition for God's ultimate goal, which, scripture assures us, is that human beings will one day freely enter into an eternal and loving relationship with their Creator in the next life, in heaven. Without free will, a loving response to God would be impossible, for creatures would be robots incapable of real love.

Freedom, including the freedom to misuse freedom, then, was a necessary precondition for God's ultimate goal: a heavenly reunion so great that its value will one day outweigh, justify, and redeem all the suffering that led up to it. Wouldn't *that* be a morally sufficient justification for God allowing evil?

The impact on the traditional argument from evil should be apparent. The mere *possibility* that the free will theodicy is true is a reason to reject the crucial assumption needed by that argument, namely, that "necessarily an all-powerful, all-good, and all-knowing being will always eliminate every bit of evil it can possibly eliminate." For if it is even possible that the free will theodicy is true, then that assumption is false. And as we have seen, if that hidden assumption is false, then the traditional argument from evil has an unsupported premise.[5]

Incomplete Lives

Some ask, What about people whose lives on earth are wrecked or cut short by the evil actions of others? Or those whose lives are ruined by accidents, diseases, and destructive acts of nature? Christian philosophers, such as C. Stephen Layman, argue that the following corollary fits logically within a traditional theistic worldview.

> If there is an almighty and perfectly good entity who has purposes for its creatures and the creatures die before those purposes are fulfilled, then the purposes will be fulfilled (insofar as possible) after the death of those creatures [in heaven].... [For] love will not accept tragedies and horrors as final if there is any alternative.... A God of love would seek the fulfillment of his creatures and therefore would not allow wickedness to have the last word in the long run. Being omnipotent, God would have the power to raise creatures from the dead and make a future life after death possible.[6]

The Rug Maker Theodicy as an Addendum

Many traditional theists find the free will theodicy inadequate because they believe it implies that God does not intervene in the natural order. They reject this implication because of four beliefs they consider certain: (1) being omnipotent and omniscient, God is ultimately in control of the universe; (2) God has the power and knowledge to intervene in the natural order to bring good out of evil; (3) given the mess we human beings have made of things, God has good reason to intervene; (4) being all-good, God will intervene to bring good out of evil in the end.

Taking these beliefs into consideration, some philosophers maintain that the free will theodicy is stronger when it is supplemented with the rug maker theodicy suggested by the philosopher J. R. Lucas.[7] According to this theory, God is like a master Persian rug maker who teaches his children by letting them weave the rug from one end while he weaves from the other. When his children make mistakes, as they inevitably will because they are novices, he adjusts the weave from his side so that his plan from the beginning—a beautiful rug—is accomplished in the end. Like the rug maker, God will intervene to bring good out of bad and beauty out of ugliness to complete his plan for humankind in the end. On this theodicy, God enters into human history and into individual human lives to offer help; God does not remain aloof.

The rug maker analogy suggests another kind of theodicy. If we look at only one tiny spot on a beautiful rug or a beautiful painting, we will miss the overall beauty of the whole. Some small spots up close may even look ugly. God, being omniscient, sees the whole of creation; we see only a fraction of the whole. Many traditional theists argue that the evil we see in the world is only a small part of a whole that will one day be redeemed and made good by God in the fulfillment of time. Theories that portray God bringing good out of evil and beauty out of ugliness in the end are sometimes called "aesthetic" theodicies.

Saint Augustine may have had a similar idea in mind when he wrote that "God did not deprive man of the power of free will because he at the same time foresaw what good he himself would draw out of evil."[8] This complement to the free will theodicy can be found in the writings of Saint Thomas Aquinas and many other philosophers. It can also be found in the Hebrew scriptures.[9]

The Frankenstein Objection

Even if a good deal of evil is due to human free choice, a problem remains. According to theism, God is the Creator of human nature. Isn't there a flaw in human nature if many humans keep doing bad things over and over again and never seem to learn? If so, isn't this flaw at least partly the fault of the Creator of human nature? Doesn't Dr. Frankenstein bear some responsibility when the monster he created keeps doing monstrous things? Doesn't the Creator of a flawed nature bear at least some responsibility for the bad actions of the creature? If so, then the vast amount of human wrongdoing implies a flaw in God. But God is thought to be morally perfect. Surely God could have made better creatures than us, or at least the worst of us. Why didn't God make a world populated only by saints? How might a traditional theist answer this objection?

Although the free will theodicy as stated here offers a reason God might have for allowing moral evil, it does not offer a reason for God allowing *natural* evil. The next theodicy offers an explanation of both kinds of evil.

The Moral Qualities Theodicy

On this theodicy, first proposed by Bishop Irenaeus (130–202), God is not like a master sculptor who makes perfectly formed and completed statues from scratch. Rather we human beings begin our existence in an imperfect, immature, and incomplete state. Furthermore, the world we enter at birth is full of hardships, temptations, and other hurdles. However, the challenges of this world exist for a purpose: imperfect, immature creatures will only develop and mature morally and spiritually by overcoming challenges, resisting temptations, and persevering through other hardships. This, Irenaeus hypothesized, is the morally sufficient reason why God created the hurdles, temptations, and other challenges of this world. Our assignment, if we will accept it, is to meet and overcome life's many difficulties and thereby to grow morally, and spiritually, in small steps over a lifetime.

Our world, then, is like a military boot camp for moral and spiritual growth. God filled the world with hurdles and temptations to test us and help us develop our spiritual capacity. Life is a struggle, with many lessons to be learned. But it is not a meaningless struggle, for it is all growth toward something higher—toward a state of being in the next life that, scripture assures us, will be so magnificent as to redeem and justify all the suffering that came before.[10]

Different religious outlooks characterize this future life in different ways. As a Christian, Irenaeus believed that life on earth is a preparation for an eternal union with God in heaven, in a realm that will be so filled with love, goodness, and beauty as to make the process of growth leading up to it—as painful and difficult as it was—worth the cost.

But is overcoming challenges, enduring hardships, and resisting temptations actually required for moral and spiritual growth? To test the idea, imagine a world devoid of all suffering, hardships, temptations, and moral challenges. In this Edenic paradise, there is no war, crime, poverty, loneliness, hunger, pain, disease, or natural disasters. There are no temptations of any kind. Suffering is not even possible. Every need is instantly satisfied. Everyone is taken care of by nature like pampered pets. No sacrifice is ever required. Now, given these conditions, what would the inhabitants of this pampered world be like?

Irenaeus would argue that many moral and spiritual character traits we value would not exist. For instance, no one would ever have felt, or expressed, sympathy or compassion for another person. For you can't possibly feel or express sympathy or compassion for another person if no one is suffering or in need. But someone who has never felt or expressed sympathy or compassion in the face of someone in need cannot possibly develop the corresponding character traits (being sympathetic or compassionate). Compassion and sympathy would not exist.

In a pampered world, no one would ever have helped another person, for no one would ever need any help. But a person cannot be genuinely charitable without ever having performed an act of charity. The character trait of charity would not exist.

Other examples come quickly to mind. It seems that no one in a pampered world would ever have faced danger or trouble. Consequently, no one would ever have the opportunity to be courageous or brave, for courage and bravery only develop as we confront dangers. The character traits of courage and bravery would also be missing.

Similar arguments can be made for such moral and spiritual qualities as self-discipline, perseverance, responsibility, generosity, and the work ethic. Would love exist in such a world? That's a question worth pondering. The philosopher John Hick, a contemporary defender of the Irenaean theodicy, writes:

> We can at least begin to imagine a world custom-made for the avoidance of all suffering. But the daunting fact that emerges is that in such a world, moral qualities would no longer have any point or value. . . . It would be a world without need for the virtues of self-sacrifice, care for others, devotion to the public good, courage, perseverance, skill, or honesty. It would indeed be a world in which such qualities, having no function to perform, would never come into existence. . . . Perhaps most important of all, the capacity to love would never be developed; except in a very limited sense of the word, in a world in which there was no suffering.[11]

Again, the claim is not that the moral qualities theodicy identifies God's actual reasons for allowing the hardships we confront. The claim is only that it is *possible* God allows hardships for the reasons outlined. But if this theodicy is plausible, we have another reason to reject the crucial assumption in the traditional argument from evil that, "necessarily, an all-powerful, all-good, and all-knowing being will always eliminate every bit of evil it can possibly eliminate." For God might not eliminate a hardship if it is a necessary condition for magnificent moral and spiritual growth leading to redemption and an ending that outweighs the costs that led up to it. And God's decision not to eliminate the hardship and the suffering that results would seem to be morally justified.[12]

The Birthright Objection

But if God is all-powerful, then it seems that God must have the power to build moral and spiritual qualities into us before we are born, just as God builds eye color or musical talent into a person before birth. If God were to build moral and spiritual traits into each person at birth, then no one would need to confront actual hardship, suffering, or temptation. The world would then contain no evil and no hardships, yet it would still contain the moral and spiritual character traits. And a world like that would be morally better. Therefore, that is what God would have done. Since the world contains evils, hardships, and temptations, it follows that the traditional argument from evil succeeds, and God doesn't exist.

Defenders of Irenaeus's theodicy reply that moral and spiritual qualities simply can't be built in or programmed at birth, even by an omnipotent God. In support of this claim, they argue that a person can't possess moral and spiritual qualities without actually having experienced and freely responded to real challenges. In other words, the moral and spiritual qualities are logically dependent on actual lived experiences coupled with the exercise of real free will; they cannot simply be built in before birth. Is this right? Could a person be compassionate, or even know what compassion is, without having ever experienced and freely responded to someone in need? Could a person come to be brave without ever having experienced and freely responded to real danger? Could a person be born fully compassionate, brave, and charitable prior to any lived experiences? Can moral character traits be conferred on us before birth, like hair or eye color? Or do they only develop over time as a person freely confronts real perils, temptations, and suffering? If this reply is sound, the objection fails.

The Quantity of Evil Objection

Let's grant that some challenges are necessary for moral and spiritual growth. But this many? Did God have to permit the Holocaust? The mass killings ordered by Lenin, Stalin, Mao Zedong, Ho Chi Minh, and Pol Pot? The many wars of history? Cancer? Couldn't God have created an environment for moral and spiritual growth that contains a lot less suffering? In the end, it is the vast amount of evil, not the mere existence of some evil, that deeply troubles many critics of both traditional theodicies. This thought leads us to the *evidential* problem of evil and the response known as "skeptical theism."

A SECOND INFLUENTIAL ARGUMENT FROM EVIL: THE "EVIDENTIAL ARGUMENT"

The most talked about argument from evil in philosophy today is no longer the traditional one. Rather it is an argument first presented by the philosopher William L. Rowe during the 1970s. Known as the "evidential argument from evil," this argument focuses on the *kind* of evil (suffering) that we see around us, not the mere fact that evil exists.

Rowe's argument from evil grew out of the evidential problem of evil, which I'll summarize in the following terms. It is logically *possible* that God and evil both exist. So the special assumption needed by the traditional argument from evil is false and the traditional argument fails. However, the world appears to contain a good deal of *gratuitous* evil, defined as evil that God (if God were to exist) would have no morally sufficient reason to permit. We can't be completely certain that the world contains gratuitous evil, but a great deal of evil surely *looks* gratuitous, for (1) it seems that the world would have been a morally better place if evils such as the Holocaust, World Wars I and II, and Stalin's crimes against humanity had never occurred; and (2) there appears to be no morally sufficient reason why a good God would permit these and other terrible tragedies. Since God certainly would not permit gratuitous evil, it follows that very probably God does not exist.

Rowe organizes these thoughts into an argument that runs about like this:

1. An instance of evil is "gratuitous" if God would have no morally sufficient reason to permit it.

2. In some cases of suffering, we cannot think of any morally sufficient reason God might have had for permitting that suffering.

3. Therefore, in some cases of suffering, it appears that there is no morally sufficient reason that would have justified God permitting that suffering.

4. Therefore, in some cases of suffering, there is very probably no morally sufficient reason that would have justified God permitting that suffering.

5. Thus, it is very probable that some gratuitous evil exists.

6. If God were to exist, there would be no gratuitous evil at all.

7. So it is very probable that God does not exist.

8. The most reasonable conclusion to draw is, therefore, that God does not exist.[13]

Rowe supports the premises with subarguments. In partial support of premise 2, he gives an example of suffering that at least appears to be gratuitous.

> Suppose in some distant forest lightning strikes a dead tree, resulting in a forest fire. In the fire, a fawn is trapped, horribly burned, and lies in terrible agony for several days before death relieves its suffering. So far as we can see, the fawn's intense suffering is pointless, for there does not appear to be any greater good such that the prevention of the fawn's suffering would require either the loss of that good or the occurrence of an evil equally bad or worse. Nor does there seem to be an equally bad or worse evil so connected to the fawn's suffering that it would have had to occur had the fawn's suffering been prevented.[14]

However, we cannot be completely certain that no morally sufficient reason exists that would justify God allowing the fawn to suffer, for we

> are often surprised by how things we thought to be unconnected turn out to be intimately connected. Perhaps, for all we know, there is some familiar good outweighing the fawn's suffering to which that suffering is connected in a way we do not see. Furthermore, there may be unfamiliar goods, goods we haven't dreamed of, to which the fawn's suffering is inextricably connected. Indeed, it would seem to require something like omniscience on our part before we should lay claim to knowing that there is no greater good [justifying the fawn's suffering].[15]

Nevertheless, even if an investigation were to show that the fawn's suffering was not pointless because it led to some (unseen) greater good that outweighed the suffering and thus justified God permitting it to happen, it seems extremely unlikely that *all* instances of suffering all around the world lead to either some greater good that justifies permitting the suffering or to the prevention of evils at least as bad that morally justify God permitting the suffering.

In support of premise 6, Rowe argues that God, being loving to the highest degree, would certainly prevent any instance of suffering unless he could not do so without thereby losing some greater good or permitting some evil equally bad or worse. In other words, God would prevent any instance of evil unless he had a morally sufficient or overriding reason to allow it. If God has no morally sufficient reason to permit an evil, he will not permit it. Therefore, premise 6 is true.

Rowe's novel argument stimulated an avalanche of replies from theistic philosophers around the world. One group of theistic critics of Rowe's argument became known as the skeptical theists.

THE SKEPTICAL THEIST RESPONSE TO THE EVIDENTIAL ARGUMENT

William Alston (1921–2009) was one of the first Christian philosophers to respond to Rowe's argument. A pioneer of contemporary epistemology and one of the greats of twentieth-century philosophy, Alston taught for many years at the University of Michigan. For reasons that will become apparent, his general line of response was named "skeptical theism." Alston asked, How could we ever *know* that some particular evil E is gratuitous? That is, how could we ever know that there is absolutely *no* morally sufficient reason that would justify God permitting some particular evil E? For to be sure that an instance of suffering E is gratuitous, we would have to accomplish two things:

1. Grasp all the reasons God could possibly have had for permitting E.
2. Find reasons to rule out as morally insufficient each of these reasons.

How, Alston asks, could we—with our limited cognitive abilities—possibly accomplish both tasks? Wouldn't we have to know as much as God knows or would know? Wouldn't we have to have minds as big as God's mind? Is it plausible to suppose that *if God did have a sufficient reason for permitting some instance of suffering E, we would have thought of it*? But why believe that this is true? Given the limited nature of the human intellect compared to God's, isn't it highly likely that many of the reasons God would have for creating the world this way would be beyond our cognitive grasp?[16]

Of course, God's reasons would not contradict sound human reasoning or true morality, for traditional theism holds that God's eternal nature is the source of both reason and morality and thus cannot stand in contradiction to either one. God's reasons could be beyond our present human comprehension without standing in contradiction to our deepest and most rational and moral considerations.[17]

It follows, Alston argues, that our intellectual powers are "radically insufficient" to allow us to know that the fourth premise of Rowe's argument is true (that in some cases of suffering, there is very probably no morally sufficient reason that would have justified God permitting that suffering).[18] Skepticism (lack of belief) with respect to premise 4 is thus the correct response to Rowe's argument.

Put another way, because of our human limits, we can never have a good reason to believe that some particular evil E is probably gratuitous.[19] The philosophers C. Stephen Evans and R. Zachary Manis put the point this way:

> Given that God is both omniscient and transcendent, there is every reason to believe that God is privy to a vast amount of knowledge about the relations between good and evil of which we are ignorant. We have every reason to believe, then, that for any allegedly pointless evil, if there were some justifying reason that God had for allowing it, we very likely would not be in a position to perceive it. If God exists, it is virtually certain that many of his reasons are inscrutable to us.[20]

A skeptical theist is therefore someone who maintains that (1) traditional theism is true; (2) our human cognitive faculties are far too limited to allow us to know all the reasons God might have had or might have for permitting any specific evil; and therefore (3) we ought to be skeptical regarding any claim, such as Rowe's, that gratuitous or unjustified evils probably exist. If the skeptical theists are right, we have no good reason to accept at least one of Rowe's premises, and his argument fails.

Does skeptical theism defeat Rowe's evidential argument from evil and save traditional theism from refutation?

CONCLUDING REFLECTION

The argument from evil, in either its traditional or evidential form, certainly gives us some reason to doubt that God, as conceived within traditional theism, exists. On the other hand, as we have seen, there are serious philosophical responses to the arguments from evil—responses that call into question in a deep way the key premises of those arguments.

Clearly the existence of many evils can be explained on the basis of the free will theodicy. Surely many other evils can be explained on the basis of the moral qualities theodicy. Can the remainder be explained on the basis of skeptical theism?

In addition, as we have seen, there are many profound reasons to believe in the existence of God. Many philosophers contend that although the argument from evil is some evidence against theism, the many compelling arguments in favor of God's existence radically outweigh it, so that after we balance the total evidence, it remains eminently reasonable to believe in God. This is the conclusion the philosopher Richard Swinburne draws after examining many of the major arguments for and against God's existence in his pathbreaking book, *The Existence of God*.[21]

The free will theodicy and the moral qualities theodicy suggest reasons God might have had for permitting some of the evils of this world. And with respect to a particularly troubling evil, how can anyone really *know* that God would have had no morally sufficient reason to permit it? Given the theodicies and the case made by the skeptical theists, and the parallel argument suggested in the book of Job, chapters 38–40, is it reasonable to hold on to faith in the face of the enormous amount of suffering the world contains?

However, if God doesn't exist and there is no such thing as a life after death in heaven, then all this talk about God bringing good out of evil and redeeming all things in the end is foolish. Is it illogical to believe in heaven and life after death? That is the topic of the next chapter.

FOR FURTHER STUDY

Adams, Marilyn McCord, and Robert Merrihew Adams, eds. *The Problem of Evil*. New York: Oxford University Press, 1990.
Howard-Snyder, Daniel, ed. *The Evidential Argument from Evil*. Indianapolis: Indiana University Press, 1996.
Lucas, J. R. *Freedom and Grace*. Grand Rapids, MI: Eerdmans, 1976.
Peterson, Michael, ed. *The Problem of Evil: Selected Readings*. Notre Dame, IN: University of Notre Dame Press, 1992.
Plantinga, Alvin. *God, Freedom, and Evil*. Grand Rapids, MI: Eerdmans, 1974.
———. *The Nature of Necessity*, chap. 9. New York: Oxford University Press, 1974.

FIVE

Hasn't Science Proved That Life after Death Is Impossible?

FRANKLIN'S EPITAPH

When he was a young man, Benjamin Franklin (1706–90) wrote his own epitaph. His words can be found inscribed on a sign over his grave in Christ Church Cemetery, Philadelphia, just two blocks from the Pennsylvania State House, where he and the other Founders drafted the Declaration of Independence in 1776 and the United States Constitution in 1787.

> The body of B. Franklin, Printer, Like the Cover of an old Book, Its Contents torn out, and stript of its Lettering and Gilding, Lies here, Food for Worms. But the Work shall not be lost; For it will, as he believ'd, appear once more in a new and more elegant Edition, Corrected and improved By the Author.[1]

Dr. Franklin's epitaph expresses his belief that he—the person known as Ben Franklin—is an immaterial soul inhabiting a physical body. At death, although his physical body will turn to dust, he himself will live again in heaven, "corrected and improved."

Most people throughout history have believed, like Franklin, that each person is an immaterial soul temporarily inhabiting a material body and that the soul survives bodily death to live again in a heavenly realm beyond space, time, and matter.[2] Socrates and Plato are only two of the many great philosophers to argue deeply for the view movingly expressed by Franklin.

Although belief in the soul and in life after death has been declining over the past century, polls show that the majority of people today still hold to both beliefs. And a CBS News poll found that 66 percent of Americans believe in both heaven and hell. Surprisingly, a Pew poll found that 27 percent of agnostics and 13 percent of atheists believe in an afterlife.[3]

In philosophy, the view that a human being is an embodied soul—an immaterial soul joined to a material body—is called "mind-body dualism" ("dualism" for short). Most dualists claim that (1) the soul, also called the "mind," rather than the body, is the true self and thus the bearer of moral responsibility and personal identity; and (2) the mind or soul, though immaterial, affects (causes changes in) the physical brain, and the brain in turn causes changes in the mind. In other words, the immaterial mind and the material brain causally interact. The brain, dualists believe, is the interface between the soul and the material world.[4] For this reason, mind-body dualism is also called "mind-body interactionism," or just "interactionism." On the dualist view, mind and body, though separate and distinct entities, are intimately connected.

Since ancient times, the main alternative to mind-body dualism has been the materialist view of the mind. Materialism is the general view of reality according to which nothing exists but matter in motion. *Matter* may be defined as that which physics studies: subatomic particles, atoms, molecules, quanta of energy, fields, and so forth, and things composed of such stuff. On a materialist view of consciousness, the mind or self is nothing more than the physical brain, or (as some materialists put it) the functioning of the brain.

In my experience, the majority of college students enrolled in public institutions today believe that the mind is nothing more than the physical brain. Thoughts, they say, are simply physical events occurring physically within the brain. The materialist theory of the mind was uncommon in ancient times; it did not rise to prominence until after the birth of modern experimental science, for reasons that will become apparent in this chapter.

We all know that the brain (along with the rest of the body) disintegrates and turns to dust after death. If materialism is true and the mind is nothing but the physical brain, then it is very hard to see how life after bodily death is possible.[5] On the other hand, if dualism is true, it is at least *possible* that we live on after the death of our physical bodies, for if dualism is true, the soul or mind is not the brain or any other physical part of the degradable physical body.[6]

As a teacher at a public community college, I have found that many if not most students reject traditional beliefs in the immaterial soul and personal immortality because they believe that both beliefs have been disproved by modern science. Of course, people change their minds over the span of a lifetime, and many who reject traditional religious beliefs in their youth become believers later in life. But has science proved that dualism is false and that materialism is true? Has science proved that your mind is nothing more than your physical brain? Has science proved that there is no such thing as a soul and no such thing as life after bodily death? These are among the questions we will investigate in this chapter.

However, even if science has not disproved survival after death, it does not follow that we *do* live on after bodily death. The last section of this chapter turns to philosophical reasons to believe, with Franklin and with many other philosophers, that each of us is an immaterial soul temporarily housed in a physical body and destined for a future life beyond this material world.

HAS SCIENCE PROVED THAT MATERIALISM IS TRUE AND SURVIVAL AFTER DEATH IS IMPOSSIBLE?

The answer is no. To prove that, scientists would first have to refute the strongest arguments for dualism, for again, if dualism is true, then life after death is certainly possible. But they have not. Second, they would have to give a scientific proof that survival is impossible. But they have not.

Socrates, Plato, and Aristotle gave arguments for mind-body dualism, as have many eminent philosophers since their time. But the modern conversation begins with arguments developed by the French philosopher René Descartes (1596–1650), the founder of modern philosophy, who was also one of the greatest mathematicians of all time and a founder of modern science.[7]

DESCARTES'S DIVISIBILITY ARGUMENT

In his *Meditations on First Philosophy, in Which Is Proved the Existence of God and the Immortality of the Soul*—the book that broke radically with past philosophical styles to launch the modern era in philosophy—Descartes observes:

> There is a great difference between a mind and a body, because the body, by its very nature, is something divisible, whereas the mind is plainly indivisible. For in truth, when I consider the mind, that is, when I consider myself in so far only as I am a thinking thing, I can distinguish in myself no parts, but I very clearly discern that I am somewhat absolutely one and entire; and although the whole mind seems to be united to the whole body, yet, when a foot, an arm, or any other part is cut off, I am conscious that nothing has been taken from my mind; nor can the faculties of willing, perceiving, conceiving, etc., properly be called its parts, for it is the same mind that is exercised in willing, in perceiving, and in conceiving, etc. But quite the opposite holds in corporeal or extended things; for I cannot imagine any one of them which I cannot easily sunder in thought. This would be sufficient to teach me that the mind, or soul, of man is entirely different from the body, if I had not already been apprised of it on other grounds.[8]

This famous line of reasoning, known today as Descartes's divisibility argument, makes more sense once it has been slightly fleshed out in more exact contemporary terms. Here is my suggestion.

1. The human mind has a property (an attribute or characteristic) that the human brain—and any other material object—lacks.
2. Necessarily, for any x and for any y, if x has a property that y lacks, then x and y are not one and the same entity; rather, they must be two distinct entities.[9]
3. Therefore, the human mind and the human brain are not one and the same entity; rather, they must be two distinct entities.
4. It also logically follows that the human mind is not identical to any purely material object—the brain, a part of the body, or any part of the material world.
5. Therefore, mind-body dualism is certainly true.

This is what logicians call a *deductive* argument, one claiming that the conclusion *must* be true if the premises are true. The argument is clearly *deductively valid*, which is to say that its conclusion must indeed be true if all its premises are true. The only way to attack Descartes's argument, then, is to give an argument against one of its premises. But before we proceed, each premise can be supported by a subargument.

Arguments for the Premises

Argument for premise 1. In what follows, I am assuming that by *part* Descartes means a "substantial" part—a part of a whole that can be detached so as to stand alone, on its own apart from the whole.

1a. Every macroscopic part of the human body—including every part of the human brain—is divisible into stand-alone parts.

1b. The human mind is not divisible into stand-alone parts.

1c. Therefore, premise 1 is true.

Argument for premise 2.

2a. Necessarily, for any x and for any y, if x and y are numerically identical (are one and the same entity), then every property of x is a property of y, and every property of y is a property of x.

2b. Therefore, premise 2 is true.

Argument for premise 1a. Each cell in the brain, like every cell in the rest of the body, can be surgically removed and placed on a microscope slide to stand alone and to be viewed at high magnification. The same can be said for each subcellular part of the brain and each subcellular part of the rest of the body. Therefore, premise 1a is true. This premise is not controversial.

Argument for premise 1b. The ordinary parts of the mind—the parts known and experienced directly, such as thoughts, beliefs, hopes, images, ideas, wishes, and sensations—have never been surgically removed from the mind and placed on a laboratory bench or microscope slide to be viewed apart from the mind. No scientist has ever claimed to have removed a part of a patient's mind, such as a belief (e.g., a belief that 1 + 1 = 2), and placed it on a microscope slide by itself. No scientist has ever removed a patient's hope (e.g., a hope that tomorrow will be sunny), and placed it in a test tube. Indeed, such a thing is conceptually incoherent. Therefore, conscious mental states cannot be physically removed from the mind, mounted, and studied standing alone using scientific instruments. The mind's parts (hopes, beliefs, and such) are not stand-alone parts.

Before we assess this part of the argument, the term *numerical identity* needs to be clarified, and the second premise needs an explanation. As many people know, Bob Dylan (born in Duluth, Minnesota, on May 24, 1941) and Robert Zimmerman (born in Duluth, Minnesota, on May 24, 1941) are one and the same person; they are not two different people. In logic, x and y are *numerically* (or *quantitatively*) identical if they are one and the same entity and not two different entities. Bob Dylan and Robert Zimmerman are thus numerically identical; that is, they are one and the same entity.

Contrasts are always important when learning an abstract concept. One must not confuse numerical identity with *qualitative identity*. Two things x and y are qualitatively identical if they have exactly the same properties, or qualities. Two separate whiteboard markers that look exactly alike (same color, same shape, same brand, etc.) are qualitatively identical. However, they are not *numerically* identical (because they are two distinct markers, not one and the same marker).

Now to premise 2 (necessarily, for any x and for any y, if x has a property that y lacks, then x and y are not one and the same entity; rather they must be two distinct entities). This premise is a theorem of formal logic. An application will help make the premise clear. Suppose that the police claim that Joe Doakes robbed the local bank, and they offer video surveillance footage to prove it. Now suppose that on further investigation, the police determine that the robber in the video is six feet tall, while Joe Doakes is only five feet tall. In this case, Doakes has a property or attribute that the robber lacks, namely, the property of being five feet tall. Common sense says that if the robber has an attribute (being six feet tall) that Joe Doakes lacks (he is only five feet tall), the robber and Joe Doakes must be two different people, not one and the same. Despite its technical appearance, premise 2 is simply a formal logical expression of a commonsense idea employed in everyday life.

The supporting premise 2a is an axiom of formal logic known to specialists as "Leibniz's law" (also known as the "principle of the indiscernibility of identicals"). The name sounds forbidding, but the principle is actually common sense. In plain terms, Leibniz's law states that (necessarily) if x and y are numerically identical (are one and the same thing), then any property possessed by x is also possessed by y, and vice versa.

The law sounds self-evident, doesn't it? To give a fictional example, since Clark Kent and Superman are numerically identical (one and the same person), any property or attribute possessed by one is possessed by the other. So if Clark Kent is standing, then Superman is standing; if Clark Kent has black hair, then Superman has black hair; and so forth. It can be proved using modern symbolic logic that premise 2 is logically implied by Leibniz's law. The second premise is on very solid logical ground. Descartes's argument is complete.

HAS SCIENCE REFUTED DESCARTES?

Some cognitive scientists challenge the supporting premise 1b, the claim that the mind cannot be divided into stand-alone parts. Their argument goes like this:

1. The mind contains ideas, memories, thoughts, hopes, sensations, and such.

2. Each of these can be thought of or imagined (and then studied) in some sense apart from the mind itself.

3. Therefore, the mind, too, contains stand-alone parts, and 1b is false.

4. But if 1b is false, then premise 1 lacks support.

5. Therefore, Descartes's first premise lacks support, and his argument fails.

This line of reasoning sounds promising until it is examined closely. It is true that the parts of the mind cited—ideas, memories, thoughts, hopes, sensations, and the like—can be thought of and studied analytically within psychology. However, it remains the case that thoughts, hopes, memories, and such cannot be surgically removed from a mind and *physically* placed on microscope slides to be physically viewed outside of and apart from that mind. Your memory of last Christmas cannot be surgically removed from your mind and placed by itself on a scale or in a test tube. The very idea of a hope or a belief separated from a mind and sitting all by itself on a laboratory bench or mounted on a microscope slide is conceptually incoherent.

The reason is intriguing. *It makes no sense at all to imagine an unowned thought standing completely on its own on a lab bench apart from the mind currently thinking it.* A thought that is not part of a mind, in other words, one that is not being thought by a mind, standing alone by itself on a table, makes no sense.

So, if the mind has parts, then the *way* in which it has parts is radically different from the way in which the brain has parts, in which case it still follows that the mind has properties the brain lacks, which entails that the mind and the brain must be two distinct entities. It also follows that the mind is not numerically identical to any other part of the body or to any material, natural, or physical object.

Descartes's central claim — that the mind cannot be divided into stand-alone parts — has also been challenged by scientists who put forward dissociative identity disorder (multiple personality disorder) and split-brain syndrome as counterexamples. They argue that in these cases, the mind appears to split into separate parts that can be studied individually. Does this imply that 1b is false? Let's examine this question.

Split-brain syndrome occurs when the corpus collosum (a bundle of nerve fibers connecting the two hemispheres of a person's brain) is damaged or severed, and the individual experiences what seem to be two separate streams of consciousness, each wholly or partly unaware of the other. In a case of dissociative identity disorder, the mind appears to divide into two or more separate personalities, or streams of consciousness, each wholly or partly unaware of the other. According to these critics, both disorders are cases in which the mind breaks down into stand-alone parts — contrary to Descartes's claim. Their argument goes about like this:

1. In cases of dissociative identity disorder, the mind appears to divide into two or more separate personalities, or streams of consciousness, each wholly or partly unaware of the other.

2. In cases of split-brain syndrome, the mind appears to divide into two separate streams of consciousness.

3. Both disorders are cases in which the mind breaks down into stand-alone parts.

4. If the mind can break down into stand-alone parts, then Descartes's premise 1b is false.

5. Therefore, Descartes's premise 1b is false.

Not so fast, Descartes's defenders reply. In the split-brain cases, the two streams of consciousness cannot be physically removed, separated, stained, and physically placed on different microscope slides to be physically viewed apart from each other. Indeed, it makes no sense to think of a stream of consciousness physically sitting by itself on a microscope slide like a laboratory specimen, apart from a mind. If there are two separate streams of consciousness within one mind, they cannot physically stand alone in isolation from the mind they belong to. Likewise, for cases of multiple personality disorder: the different personalities cannot be physically removed from the mind they belong to and placed side by side in separate test tubes on a lab bench for separate viewing and testing. The very idea of a personality, or even a part of a personality, physically sitting on a table *apart from a mind* simply makes no sense.

It follows, again, that the way in which the mind has parts is radically different from the way in which a material object such as the brain has parts. If so, then the mind has properties the brain lacks, and mind-body dualism must be true.

The Argument from Neuroscience

Some materialists have argued as follows:

1. Brain scientists have discovered correlations between reported mental events and observed brain events. For instance, every time a patient reports feeling a pain in the arm, neurons x, y, and z light up at the same moment, at a certain spot in the brain. Every time a patient reports seeing red, neurons x', y' and z' activate at the same moment at a certain spot in the brain, and so forth.

2. In addition, when one specific part of the brain is damaged, at the same time, a specific mental function is lost.

3. If reported mental events can be correlated with observed brain events occurring at the same time and if the loss of a mental function can be correlated with the loss of a brain function at the same time, then it follows that each mental event is (numerically) identical to a brain event, and the mind simply is the physical brain.

4. Therefore, materialism with respect to the mind is true and mind-body dualism is false. The mind is nothing more than the brain or the brain in action.

This argument may seem compelling at first glance; however, it has severe problems. To begin with, the third premise begs the question against dualism. Why? First, correlation is not the same as, and does not prove, numerical identity. The mere fact that A and B occur at the same time within a complex system does not prove that A and B are one and the same thing!

Second, the two sides of the correlation—reported mental events and observed brain events—have radically different properties, as we have seen. But if the two sides of a correlation have radically different properties, then the correlation by itself does not establish numerical identity.

Thus, brain studies that correlate reported mental states and observed brain states happening at the same time do not rule out the possibility that the mental state and the physical state are separate and distinct entities. These brain studies, in other words, are logically consistent with the truth of dualism.

Furthermore, the correlations discovered in the laboratory do not disprove dualism or prove materialism because *mind-body dualism actually predicts the same experimental result*, namely, that reported mental events will be found to correlate with observed brain states. The point is so important, and so often overlooked, that some elaboration is called for.

Mind-body dualism claims that the brain and the mind or soul—though distinct—causally interact: minds cause changes in brains, and brains cause changes in minds. The brain, according to dualism, is the interface between the soul and the material world. Therefore, if mind-body dualism is true, we should expect that each time an observable brain event occurs, a reported mental event occurs, and vice versa.

The upshot is that the correlations between reported mental events and observed brain events discovered in the laboratory are expected if materialism (with respect to the mind) is true, and they are also expected if dualism is true. If the correlations are predicted equally by both theories, then they neither prove nor disprove either theory. This popular argument for materialism with respect to the mind fails. The next popular argument is no improvement.

The Causal Closure Argument

If you read books by materialists, sooner or later you will come across this argument in one form or another. First, a system is said to be "causally closed" if the objects within the system are never influenced by anything outside the system. Now some physicists claim that the material universe is causally closed. By this they mean that no immaterial or supernatural causes enter into and affect the workings of anything within the material universe. But mind-body dualism claims that the material brain is influenced by the immaterial mind. If mind-body dualism is true, the material universe is *not* causally closed, for the brain is affected by immaterial mental causes each time the mind acts on the brain. Thus:

1. The material universe is causally closed.

2. If mind-body dualism is true, the material universe is not causally closed.

3. Therefore, mind-body dualism is false.

This argument faces two devastating criticisms. First, it is circular. The material universe is causally closed only if dualism is false. If dualism is true, the universe is not causally closed. Thus, the very first premise presupposes the falsity of dualism. Therefore, no one would accept the first premise without *already* having accepted the conclusion! The argument commits the fallacy of circular reasoning.

Second, although it sounds scientific, premise 1, "the causal closure principle," has *not* been proved scientifically. Furthermore, there are good reasons to believe that it never will be. Critics of materialism, such as the philosopher Laurence BonJour, ask how scientists could ever prove the principle true. No empirical investigation, BonJour argues, "that is at all feasible (practically or morally), could ever establish that human bodies, the most likely focus of such external influence, are in fact never affected, even in small and subtle ways, by non-material causes." [10] Many scientists accept the causal closure principle, BonJour notes; however, no one has yet given a compelling reason to believe it is true.[11] This popular argument for materialism with respect to the mind fails. The next argument is a slight improvement.

The Identity Theory Argument and Ockham's Razor

During the 1960s, a philosophical theory of the mind emerged that, it was claimed, explains consciousness in purely material terms consistent with the latest results of brain science. According to the mind-brain identity theory (the "identity theory" for short), thoughts, sensations, beliefs, and such are nothing more than physical events, states, and processes of the brain. (From here on, mental events will be shorthand for mental events, states, and processes; and brain events will refer to brain events, states, and processes.) The mind, in other words, is numerically identical with the physical brain.[12] My experience in the college classroom indicates that this is the most popular view on the college campus today.

So, the philosopher J. J. C. Smart, one of the first prominent defenders of the theory, wrote, "Why do I wish to resist [dualism] and [accept the identity theory]? Mainly because of Ockham's razor."[13] His argument went about like this:

1. Both mind-body dualism and the mind-brain identity theory explain exactly the same data.

2. But the identity theory is theoretically simpler than dualism.

3. Ockham's razor recommends adopting the simpler of two theories when both explain the same data.

4. Therefore, the identity theory is likely true.

Smart didn't give an argument for premise 1; he simply assumed it. We'll see in a moment why this is problematic. Here is his subargument for premise 2:

2a. The identity theory explains consciousness in terms of one ultimate kind of substance (matter), while dualism posits two radically different kinds of substances (an immaterial mind and a physical brain).

2b. Therefore, premise 2 is true.

Smart was right: the identity theory is theoretically simpler than dualism, in the sense he defined. However, dualists are not without a response. They claim that dualism explains many aspects of consciousness left unexplained by the identity theory, including the subjective nature of consciousness, intentionality, qualia, and the privacy of the mental. (We'll examine all four in a moment.) The upshot is this: if dualists are right and their theory explains aspects of consciousness left unexplained by the identity theory, then Smart's first premise is false. But if so, then Ockham's razor does not favor the identity theory, for Ockham's razor only points to the simpler of two theories when both theories explain the very same data. What aspects of consciousness are left unexplained by the identity theory (and by materialism in general)? Here are four.

FOUR MORE ASPECTS OF CONSCIOUSNESS THAT MATERIALISM CANNOT EXPLAIN

Qualia

Close your eyes and imagine a stop sign. What color is the experienced image? If you imagined an ordinary stop sign, the image in your mind is experienced as red (and white). You are aware of its color directly from inside your consciousness. Philosophers call experienced mental states, such as the experienced color of a sunset, the taste of chocolate, the smell of a rose, the sound of a bell, and the feel of velvet, "qualia" (sing. quale). Now, as you experience this red image in your mind—this quale—certain physical things are occurring in your brain at the same time.

For instance, brain scientists say that when we experience the color red, certain electrical activity occurs among the cells in a particular part of the brain. However, if brain surgeons were to open your brain at the moment you are experiencing the red image, they would not see a red spot shaped like a stop sign physically in, or on, some part of your brain like a physical image on a movie screen. Your brain is normally gray. Nothing in your brain turns from gray to red when you form and directly experience a red image in your mind.

It follows, by the theorem of logic that states that if x has a property that y does not have, then x and y are two different entities, that the quale— the red image you directly experience inside your consciousness—is not numerically identical to any physical part of your brain. The quale is a part of your mind but not a part of your brain. Therefore, your mind has a property that your brain lacks. It follows that the identity theory is false and mind-body dualism is true.

The Qualia Argument

1. When I form an image in my mind of a red stop sign, I directly experience within my consciousness an image of a red stop sign—a sign experienced as red.

2. But a red stop sign cannot be observed anywhere on my brain; an image of a red stop sign does not appear visibly on the surface of my brain or anywhere inside my brain.

3. Therefore, when I form an image in my mind of a red stop sign, the quale (my experienced mental image) has properties that no part of my brain possesses and that no other part of my body possesses, namely, the experienced redness and the experienced shape of a stop sign.

4. Therefore, my mind has properties that my brain lacks and that any other part of my body lacks.

5. If x has a property that y lacks, then x and y are two different entities and not one and the same thing.

6. Therefore, my mind and my brain must be two distinct entities.

7. Furthermore, it also follows that my mind is not identical to any other physical part of my body.

8. If so, then mind-body dualism is true, and the identity theory (along with materialism in general) is false.

9. Therefore, mind-body dualism is certainly true.

In *What Does It All Mean?*, Thomas Nagel, a leading researcher today in the philosophy of mind, argues that science will never show, and cannot possibly show, that mental images and other experienced mental states are numerically identical to brain states, or that the mind simply is the physical brain.

When we discover the chemical composition of water, for instance, we are dealing with something that is clearly out there in the physical world. . . . When we find out it is made up of hydrogen and oxygen atoms, we're just breaking down an external physical substance into smaller physical parts. It is an essential feature of this kind of analysis that we are *not* giving a chemical breakdown of the way water *looks*, *feels*, and *tastes* to us. Those things go on in our inner experience, not in the water that we have broken down into atoms. The physical or chemical analysis of water leaves them aside. But to discover that tasting chocolate was really just a brain process, we would have to analyze something mental—not an externally observed physical substance but an inner taste sensation—in terms of parts that are physical. And there is no way that a large number of physical events in the brain, however complicated, could be the parts out of which a taste sensation was composed. A physical whole can be analyzed into smaller *physical* parts, but a mental process can't be. Physical parts just can't add up to a mental whole.[14]

Intentionality

Some kinds of mental states possess a property that philosophers of mind call "intentionality." (This property is also called "aboutness.") A mental state is intentional if it is inherently or in itself *about* something. That which an intentional mental state is *about* is called that state's "intentional object." For instance, my belief that Sir Paul McCartney plays bass guitar is *about* Paul McCartney, and Sir Paul is the intentional object of my belief. My hope that tomorrow will be sunny is *about* tomorrow's weather, and so forth.

The aboutness of thought is a directly experienced mental property that is hard to deny. However, a word of caution is called for here. The word *intentional* in the philosophy of mind has nothing to do with "intending" to do something or with having a "purpose." The intentionality of the mental is merely the property of being about something.

The problem for materialists is that it seems clear that intentionality, or aboutness, cannot possibly be a property possessed inherently by a purely material, or physical, object. Why?

First, the aboutness of a thought is not a property recognized in current physics. (Aboutness does not appear in any physics or chemistry handbooks listing measured physical properties.) Furthermore, the latest science indicates that the physical nature of any material object will one day be fully explained in terms of standard physical properties without mentioning intentionality at all or anything remotely like it. An atom, or a clump of atoms, or a quantum of energy, considered merely as a physical object, isn't *about* anything; it just *is*.

The question dualists put to materialists is therefore this: How can an atom or a neuron, or a chemical in someone's brain, or a clump of nerve fibers in a person's frontal lobe, be inherently *about* Paul McCartney? Or about tomorrow? Or about anything? Which physical properties would make a bundle of neurons a belief about McCartney rather than about Ringo Starr? About tomorrow rather than about next week? No one in neuroscience has satisfactorily explained how intentionality can be reduced to (explained solely in terms of) neurons, electrochemical brain signals, molecules, chemicals, or any other purely physical objects. BonJour writes, "There is no reason at all to think that the internal structure of my physical and neurophysiological states could somehow by itself determine that I am thinking about the weather rather than about the Middle East or the stock market."[15]

The Intentionality Argument

1. Some mental states possess intentionality inherently, but nothing in the physical brain or body possesses intentionality inherently.

2. If x has a property not possessed by y, then x and y are not numerically identical.

3. Therefore, the mind is not the brain or any part of the brain or body.

4. If so, then mind-body dualism is true, and the identity theory (along with materialism in general) is false.

5. Therefore, mind-body dualism is certainly true, and materialism is false.

Argument for premise 1

1a. Many kinds of mental states are inherently intentional; they are essentially about something.

1b. No purely physical states are inherently intentional.

1c. Therefore, premise 1 is true.

Some have proposed books as counterexamples to the dualist's claim that no physical objects are inherently intentional. However, although the physical pages, ink marks, and cardboard cover making up a physical book may be "about" philosophy or "about" John Lennon, and so on, the paper and ink are not in themselves or *inherently* about the subject matter. The aboutness of the physical book is a property read into it by a mind that knows the relevant language.

Subjectivity

In recent years, Nagel and other prominent philosophers specializing in the study of consciousness have put forward a new argument for dualism. Their case begins with the claim that mental states have a directly experienced, subjective quality that cannot be fully expressed objectively in the quantitative language of any of the physical sciences. In the case of any conscious mental state, they argue, *there is something it is like* to be in that state. For instance, there is something it is like to feel nostalgic, to taste chocolate, to remember last summer fondly, to hope for snow, to be in love. And this "something it is like" cannot be defined mathematically or in the language of any of the physical sciences. Nagel calls this subjective aspect of consciousness the "what it is like" quality of the mental.

In addition, it is very unlikely that this subjective quality will ever be reduced to (explained without remainder in terms of) particles of matter and quanta of energy moving in space and time under the governance of the laws of physics and chemistry alone. For all materialist attempts to reduce consciousness to purely physical events and objects—attempts that go back centuries—have failed. It follows, these dualists argue, that subjective consciousness and the physical brain are not one and the same thing. It also follows that the mind is not identical to any physical object.

How can a physical pile of atoms or a quark or an electromagnetic field have a subjective, qualitative awareness? How can there possibly be "something it is like" to be a proton, an atom, or a potassium ion? Scientists haven't the foggiest idea. The subjective aspect of consciousness appears to be yet another mental property that cannot be reduced to matter in motion governed by the laws of physics and chemistry as they apply to the brain.

The Subjectivity Argument

1. Conscious mental states have a subjective, qualitative aspect.
2. No atom, clump of atoms, or any other purely material object has this subjective or qualitative aspect.
3. If *x* has a property not possessed by *y*, then *x* and *y* are not quantitatively identical.
4. Therefore, the mind is not the brain or any part of the body.
5. If so, then the identity theory (and materialism in general) is false and mind-body dualism is certainly true.
6. Therefore, mind-body dualism is true, and the identity theory (along with materialism in general) is false.

Privacy

The last argument in this series begins with the claim that our mental states are private, whereas our brain states are publicly observable. It is obvious that your brain is publicly observable. Surgeons can operate on and inspect any part of your brain. Every part of the brain can be fully described publicly, in the third-person languages of science and mathematics—without using the word *I*.

Not so with the mind. No one but I can literally have my thoughts, although others can ask me what I am thinking. If I take a bite of a Hershey bar, no one else can literally have or experience *my* taste of chocolate. Of course, others can take a bite of my candy bar and have their own experience of the taste of chocolate. Likewise, no one but you can literally have your thoughts. And just as I am the only one who has immediate access to my thoughts, feelings, sensations, and other mental states, you are the only one who has immediate access to your thoughts and other mental states.

Some philosophers sum up the point this way: each of us has private access to the directly experienced contents of our mind. Brain scientists can ask us what we are thinking about, but they must take our word for it; they cannot literally experience or "have" our thoughts and sensations. If you look closely, you will find that in every scientific experiment where neuroscientists claim to have tapped into someone's mental states, they had to ask the person which mental state they were experiencing at the time. This is the privacy of the mental.

Now if the mind is private, in the sense defined, while the brain is public, in the sense defined, then the mind and the brain have differing properties. It follows again that the mind and the brain must be two distinct substances, and dualism in one form or another is true.

The Privacy Argument

1. The brain (like every material object and physical part of the body) is publicly accessible.

2. The mind is private; it is not publicly accessible.

3. If x has a property not possessed by y, then x and y are not quantitatively identical.

4. Therefore, the mind is not the brain or any part of the body.

5. If so, then the identity theory (and materialism in general) is false, and mind-body dualism is certainly true.

6. Therefore, mind-body dualism is certainly true, and the identity theory (along with materialism in general) is false.

Philosophers who endorse materialism have never satisfactorily explained how a purely material entity can possess intentionality, qualitative content, subjectivity, or privacy. And the arguments we have examined explain why. Dualism offers the best explanation of these very obvious facts of consciousness.[16] Thus, one could argue:

1. Mental states possess the properties of intentionality, qualitative content, subjectivity, and privacy. This is the data in need of explanation.

2. Despite centuries of trying, researchers have not produced a theory that satisfactorily explains these properties of the mind in material or physical terms alone.

3. Mind-body dualism explains the data reasonably well and points to further research.

4. Therefore, mind-body dualism is the best explanation of the data.

5. Therefore, it is most reasonable to believe that a human being is a hybrid creature composed of a material body joined to an immaterial mind.

ARISTOTLE'S VERSION OF MIND-BODY DUALISM

Not all mind-body dualists agree with Descartes. Many favor a theory first developed by Aristotle (384–322 BC), Plato's most famous student. Aristotle argued that every material substance is a hybrid composed of matter and form. The form is the organizational structure; the matter is the underlying stuff structured by the form. For example, a penny is round, and it is composed of copper. Its roundness is part of its form; its copper is the matter structured by the form.

Next, the "substantial form" of a material object is the organizational structure that makes it the kind of substance it is. Every horse has a substantial form that makes it a horse rather than a cat or a tree; every human being has a substantial form that makes it a human being rather than a dog or a flower, and so forth. Thus, forms are abstract and immaterial, not to be identified with any particular bit of matter. Forms exist "in" the substances they structure, not outside them or above them, and they are active entities, for they impart powers to the underlying matter. A material substance is thus not just a collection of atoms of matter; it is a combination of matter and form. The human soul, Aristotle argued, is the substantial form, and the material body is the matter, of a living human being.

Aristotle's dualistic theory has significant implications regarding life after death. Both Aristotle and Descartes believed in a life to come after death. However, in Descartes's view, the human soul is a complete person on its own. After bodily death, it is the complete person that survives. On Aristotle's view, a soul without a body to structure and animate is not a complete person. The soul, as an active but nonphysical form, can continue to exist after the physical body dies, but lacking a body to animate, the soul exists in an incomplete and "unnatural" state, for it is the nature of the soul to be the form of a complete human person by animating a body.

Cartesian dualists who argue for immortality do not see bodily death as the death of a person, for they identify the person with the immaterial soul and argue that the soul lives on in a higher realm after the death of the body. On the Aristotelian account, however, bodily death is the death of the person, even though the soul can live on in a diminished and incomplete state after earthly death. On the Aristotelian view, body and soul are both essential for full personhood. In the next life, argue Christians influenced by Aristotle, the whole person begins to exist again only when God joins a resurrected body—related in some way to the person's earthly body—to the person's form or soul. Although numerous Christian philosophers have defended Descartes's view of the soul, the traditional Christian view is closer to Aristotle's: our souls continue to exist in an incomplete and diminished state after bodily death; the full person returns to life only after the soul is joined to a resurrected body.[17]

Although materialism in one form or another is in fashion today in the academic world, arguments for dualism in one form or another have been presented and defended rigorously by some of the most eminent philosophers and logicians of the twentieth century, including Saul Kripke, Roderick Chisholm, Sir Karl Popper, Thomas Nagel, and Alvin Plantinga. The list of important scholars who have defended mind-body dualism also includes pathbreaking neuroscientists such as Wilder Penfield and the recipient of the 1963 Nobel Prize in physiology or medicine, Sir John Eccles.

CHRISTIAN MATERIALISM

Not everyone will be convinced by the philosophical arguments for mind-body dualism that form part of my case for survival. Indeed, some Christian philosophers today reject dualism and actually argue for a materialist theory of the mind. Christian materialists, as they are called, also argue that Christianity is compatible with a materialist view of consciousness. (Of course, they do not argue that Christianity is consistent with a materialist theory of reality in general, for materialism as a general theory holds that matter is all that exists, and Christians believe that God is not a material being.) On the Christian materialist view, then, there is no such thing as an immaterial human soul that lives on after the death of the body. However, philosophers in this school of thought, such as Peter van Inwagen,

Lynn Rudder Baker, Trenton Merricks, Dean Zimmerman, and Kevin Corcoran, offer materialistic accounts of the resurrection of the dead, life after death, and other central doctrines of the Christian faith.

If these scholars are right, life after death and personal resurrection can be defended philosophically whether one is a materialist or a dualist. This strengthens the case for immortality, for the main argument against survival is that materialism is true and that materialism rules out survival. This is one debate I am not entering in this book. No book can cover everything. For the scholar who wishes to pursue this issue, I offer suggestions at the end of the chapter.

CONCLUDING REFLECTIONS ON DUALISM

During the twentieth century, many philosophers, psychologists, and brain scientists rejected the traditional belief in the soul and the afterlife and attempted to explain the mind (and everything else about us) in scientific terms consistent with materialism. However, defenders of dualism pushed back, arguing that no materialist theory proposed adequately explains the subjective nature of consciousness that we experience privately and directly from the inside, the privacy of the mental, the directly experienced, subjective mental states called qualia, or the intentionality (aboutness) of many of our conscious states. And no scientific experiment, or series of experiments, has ever disproved dualism, historically the most common view of humanity.

Why do so many philosophers, scientists, and psychologists advocate materialism? It took me a long time to realize the answer. They are not materialists because they have proved dualism false, for they have not. Nor are they materialists because they have proved materialism true. Rather, they are engaged in a research program based on hope: they hope to one day explain everything in terms of matter alone, without reference to anything immaterial or supernatural. Of course, the fact that they hope that materialism will one day be shown to be true does not prove that materialism is indeed true.

Science has not disproved dualism and therefore has not proved that life ends at bodily death.[18] But are there any good reasons to believe that the traditional doctrine of immortality or survival after death is true?

POSITIVE REASONS TO BELIEVE IN LIFE AFTER BODILY DEATH

I'll now present two positive arguments for survival. The first general line of reasoning can be found in the writings of philosophers and literary figures from Plato to C. S. Lewis. The second is an argument from the transcendent nature of the human spiritual capacity.

C. S. Lewis's Argument from Joy

Down through the ages, poets, artists, and philosophers have written of an unusual feeling they have experienced from time to time, a sensation they have described as a faint but persistent longing for a reality that, although it cannot be put into words, seems to transcend ordinary experience.

Some have described this feeling as a longing for an unknown object that is attracting them from beyond the visible world. Some have described it as a yearning for eternal and unconditional love. Others have spoken of a heartfelt desire for union with God or a longing for a perfect home in the universe. The common factor in all these accounts is that the unusual feeling is a longing for a radically transcendent reality that would, if found, permanently fulfill our deepest nature.

In his autobiography, *Surprised by Joy*, and in his first book of Christian apologetics, *The Pilgrim's Regress*, C. S. Lewis (1898–1963), tutor of medieval literature at Oxford University and later chair of medieval and Renaissance literature at Cambridge University, used the language of the Romantic movement to describe this experience of longing and named it "joy."[19] Joy, he stated, is felt as a "stab," a "pang," and an "inconsolable longing" in the heart for an unknown object calling from beyond; something that draws us yet remains hidden; something that cannot be described in words. Joy, he said, "is distinct not only from pleasure in general but even from aesthetic pleasure."[20]

As a teen and as a young adult, Lewis was an atheist. He converted to theism and then journeyed from theism to Christianity in his thirties, after years spent trying to prove to himself that God does not exist and (not coincidentally) after years searching unsuccessfully for an earthly object that would satisfy the mysterious and inconsolable longing that he sometimes felt.

Of course, Lewis could have dismissed joy by concluding that it is an irrational Freudian complex aimed at nothing or that it is some other irrational psychological condition. However, he found that he could not shut off joy, nor could he explain it away as nonsense, illness, or irrationality. After he found that many sensitive souls throughout the ages had reported the same experience, he reasoned that joy must be a natural desire existing within human nature, in the depths of the human soul. However, because earthly objects evoke the feeling but never satisfy it, this peculiar desire, he concluded, must in the final analysis be a desire for a transcendent object calling us from beyond the material world.

In "The Weight of Glory," Lewis turned his thoughts on this desire for the transcendent into a philosophical argument for the existence of God and of heaven, known today as the "argument from joy" but also as the "argument from nostalgia." Lewis wrote:

> We remain conscious of a desire which no natural happiness will satisfy. But is there any reason to suppose that reality offers any satisfaction to it? "Nor does being hungry prove that we have bread." But I think it may be urged that this [objection] misses the point. A man's physical hunger does not prove that that man will get any bread; he may die of starvation on a raft in the Atlantic. But surely a man's hunger does prove that he comes of a race which repairs its body by eating and inhabits a world where eatable substances exist. In the same way, though I do not believe (I wish I did) that my desire for Paradise proves that I shall enjoy it, I think it a pretty good indication that such a thing exists and that some [people] will.[21]

In *Mere Christianity*, Lewis put the argument this way, with some spiritual advice added at the end.

> Creatures are not born with desires unless satisfaction for those desires exists. A baby feels hunger: well, there is such a thing as food. A duckling wants to swim: well, there is such a thing as water. Men feel sexual desire: well, there is such a thing as sex. If I find in myself a desire which no experience in this world can satisfy, the most probable explanation is that I was made for another world. If none of my earthly pleasures satisfy it, that does not prove that the universe is a fraud.

Probably earthly pleasures were never meant to satisfy it, but only to arouse it, to suggest the real thing. If that is so, I must take care, on the one hand, never to despise, or be unthankful for, these earthly blessings, and on the other hand, never to mistake them for the something else of which they are only a kind of copy, or echo, or mirage. I must keep alive in myself the desire for my true country, which I shall not find till after death; I must never let it get snowed under or turned aside; I must make it the main object of life to press on to that other country and to help others to do the same.[22]

Here is one way to reconstruct Lewis's famous argument in step-by-step form.

1. An object exists corresponding to every one of our basic, natural desires.
   Gloss. For instance, the desire called "hunger" has food as its object, and food exists; the desire called "thirst" has water as its object, and water exists, and so forth.

2. Joy is not an irrational psychological complex, an illness, or an illusion; it is a natural desire existing deep within human nature.

3. It is therefore reasonable to suppose that joy, like the other natural desires, is aimed at an actually existing object, for there is no good reason to think that joy is an exception.

4. Thus, it is likely that the object at which joy is directed truly exists.

5. Experience and self-reflection reveal that joy is a desire for an eternal, transcendent reality beyond space and time that will satisfy our deepest longings, a supernatural reality that will allow for the completion of our nature.

6. No material object or place on earth satisfies this description.

7. God in heaven is the best candidate for this transcendent reality.

8. Therefore, it is reasonable to believe that God exists and that we will find our ultimate completion not on earth but in union with God in heaven after bodily death.

Parts and hints of Lewis's argument from joy can be found throughout many of his writings, including his *Chronicles of Narnia* and his space trilogy (*Out of the Silent Planet*, *Perelandra*, and *That Hideous Strength*).

However, questions arise. Does joy really point to something real beyond this world? Is it an indicator of God? Of heaven? Or is it just a quirky feeling unique to Lewis and a few neurotic romantics and artists? Is it an irrational complex that can be cured with drugs or by the proper therapy?

One reason to take joy seriously as an indicator of something beyond this earthly realm is that many gifted and wise philosophers, poets, artists, and sensitive souls over the centuries and across many cultures, East and West, who were not mentally ill, have written about it, testified to its existence, and taken it seriously. The romantic theme of a transcendent longing deep within the human soul, of a desire pointing to something beyond this material world, if we will listen to it, can be found in the writings of many great thinkers and artists.

Saint Augustine identified the longing for transcendence with a yearning for God when he placed the following passage at the beginning of his greatest work, *Confessions*:

> *Great are you, O Lord.* . . . *[W]e* . . . who are a due part of your creation, long to praise you. You arouse us so that praising you may bring us joy, because you have made us and drawn us to yourself, and our heart is restless until it rests in you.

Saint Bonaventure (1217–74), a philosopher who taught with Thomas Aquinas at the University of Paris during the thirteenth century, also interpreted our longing for transcendence as a longing for God. He titled his greatest work, *The Soul's Ascent to God*.

In the twentieth century, the "hobo poet" Harry Kemp (1883–1960) wrote:

> Who Thou art I know not
> But this much I know;
> Thou hast set the Pleiades
> In a silver row;
>
> Thou hast sent the trackless winds
> Loose upon their way,

Thou hast reared a coloured wall
Twixt the night and day:

Thou hast made the flowers to bloom
And the stars to shine;
Hid rare gems of richest ore
In the tunnelled mine.

But chief of all Thy wondrous works,
Supreme of all Thy plan,
Thou hast put an upward reach
Into the heart of man.[23]

Father Edward Flanagan (1886–1948), founder of Boys Town (a village and school for homeless children) in Omaha, Nebraska, often said, when counseling teachers of youth, "The simple fact is that nothing earthly can fill the void in the human heart."[24]

George Harrison wrote a song expressing the Lewisian theme of life as one long search for God driven by a desire for transcendence. His song "Long, Long, Long" can be found on the Beatles' *White Album*. Many profound spiritual thinkers have given expression, in one way or another, to the romantic theme at the center of Lewis's life.

The Excess Spiritual Capacity Argument

Once, after a class discussion of God's existence, a student who had been defending atheism came up to me and expressed his feeling that, from an atheist point of view, the death of a beloved friend is "such a waste" — a waste of something wonderful and intrinsically valuable. Isn't there something terribly *wrong* with a universe so wasteful of value? His heartfelt lament serves as an introduction to the next argument.

No matter how long a person lives, no matter how varied their life, a potential for further spiritual development and further love remains unactualized at death. This is a potential for becoming more of what one is, at the deepest level.

Thus, no matter how long we live on earth, in the end we are incomplete, unfinished creatures. At death, our souls are like a song that has only partly been sung; like a flower that has only just begun to bloom.

The question arises: Why do we human beings possess a spiritual capacity far greater than anything we can use up in this earthly life? If we were made for this life only, why do we possess a transcendent capacity within our souls that can only be partially tapped during our brief time on earth? These thoughts lead to the excess spiritual capacity argument.

1. Human beings possess a spiritual capacity that cannot be fully actualized in the course of any earthly life. This is the data to be explained.

2. This excess spiritual capacity is not expected on the atheist assumption that God does not exist and there is no such thing as life after death.

3. This excess capacity makes sense on the traditional theistic view that we are souls created by God not just for a life on this planet but also for a future life of continued growth in a heaven beyond this material world.

4. Traditional theism, with its belief in life after death, and atheism, with its denial of life after death, are the two great worldviews competing for our allegiance today.

5. Of the two major views, traditional theism offers the best explanation of the data.

6. This is a strong reason to believe that we survive bodily death and that life continues in a supernatural realm.

Can Naturalistic Evolutionary Theory Explain Joy and Our Excess Spiritual Capacity?

Most human beings throughout history have believed in God or a supreme being. And anthropologists have not found a single society lacking religious practices. Scholars in the cognitive science of religion, a branch of the broader field of the evolutionary science of religion, seek to explain our religious tendencies in terms of naturalistic evolutionary theory alone, that is, in terms of natural selection operating on random mutations, without reference to God or to anything supernatural.[25] Keep in mind that the evolutionary process, according to modern naturalism and materialism, is blind in the sense that it is not aimed at a goal, and it is not guided by God or by any other supernatural force or intelligence.

If you venture into the cognitive science of religion, you will find researchers who argue that our inclinations to believe in God and to engage in religious ceremonies are nothing more than evolutionary adaptations built into us by a blind process of Darwinian natural selection. As traits conferred by a blind process of evolution, they signify nothing beyond this world. Religious tendencies, these researchers argue, were "selected" by the evolutionary process merely because they conferred a reproductive advantage on those possessing them. The advantage? The claim is that religious traits fostered human cooperation within the groups of individuals possessing them. This in turn gave those groups a reproductive edge in the struggle for survival. In other words, the possession of religious traits raised the rate of reproduction for their possessors above the rates of their competitors.

I'm not convinced by this evolutionary explanation, however, for the following reason. It is very possible that religious tendencies spread among a population might increase group cooperation while at the same time draining energy and attention from purely reproductive activities, thus reducing rather than increasing the group's rate of reproduction. I have not seen this possibility dealt with quantitatively.

Other researchers claim that our religious tendencies are merely unintended by-products of other, nonreligious traits selected (blindly) by the evolutionary process. And then there are "exaptation" theorists who claim that our tendencies to believe in God and to engage in religious practices are evolutionary traits that served a different, nonreligious purpose when first selected; they took their present (religious) form only after a long period of (unguided) evolutionary change.

All such theories can be used to call belief in God and our other religious tendencies into question by suggesting that our religious tendencies can be explained as unintended products of the evolutionary process—traits signifying nothing beyond this world—rather than as products of sound reasoning. If our religious tendencies can be explained away as mere products of a blind process of evolution, then Lewis's joy and our excess spiritual capacity can likewise be explained away with the same evolutionary arguments.

And if joy and our excess spiritual capacity can be explained away as mere evolutionary traits signifying nothing beyond the evolutionary process, then Lewis's argument from joy is in trouble.[26]

This is not the place to venture into the details of modern evolutionary theory as it bears on religious belief. Instead, I will offer an argument that I believe undercuts all arguments that claim to explain away our religious tendencies as mere products of evolution, including the experience Lewis named joy and our excess spiritual capacity. My argument relies on the fine-tuning argument presented and defended in chapter 2.

1. The fine-tuning argument refutes purely naturalistic evolutionary theory by showing that the evolutionary process is the intended result of the precise arrangement of the fundamental constants of physics, an arrangement that is itself the product of divine design.

2. It follows that the evolutionary process was God's way of bringing intelligent human life and its general traits into existence.

3. Therefore, our religious tendencies, including joy and our excess spiritual capacity, ultimately come from God and are reflections of divine providence.

4. Therefore, on reflection, joy and our excess spiritual capacity are best explained not as products of a blind process of evolution but as parts of God's overall strategy of leading us to himself.

5. Understood this way, joy and our excess spiritual capacity are two of many pointers toward God and toward a future life beyond bodily death, as Lewis claimed.

I contend that this argument undercuts those evolutionary arguments claiming that our religious tendencies, including joy and our excess spiritual capacity, point to nothing beyond our life on earth.

Naturalistic evolutionary theory is the subject of vexed debate today. The theistic view of human nature is not inconsistent with modern evolutionary science if we reject naturalism and understand the evolutionary process as God's way of creating human beings. This is the view known as "theistic evolutionary theory"—the union of theism, rather than naturalism, with standard evolutionary science. Not all Christians accept theistic evolution; however, many do. The issue remains a matter of debate within the Christian community—a debate I will not enter here.

CONCLUDING REFLECTION

We've looked at philosophical reasons to believe that each person is an embodied soul—an immaterial soul only temporarily inhabiting a physical body in this earthly life. If dualism is true, then life after death is possible. We considered the major attempts to show that mind-body dualism is false and that life after death is impossible. We also looked at arguments for the claim that life after bodily death is a reasonable hope. What conclusion should a thoughtful person draw? What is the best explanation of all the data? Which hope should reasonable people base their lives on?

APPENDIX: THE ARGUMENT FROM MIND-BODY DUALISM TO THEISM

Once you accept mind-body dualism, the following question arises: Who or what creates an immaterial soul and unites it to a physical body the moment a new human being comes into existence? The answer cannot be a purely material process or agent, for material processes and agents are mindless. The answer cannot be supplied by science, for the laws of science refer only to material objects. Theism offers what seems to be the only possible explanation. God creates each immaterial soul and unites it to a physical body each time a new human being comes into existence. The union of mind and body is thus one more area where theism helps us make sense of a phenomenon that would otherwise be unexplained. This suggests a best explanation argument from mind-body dualism to theism:

1. Mind-body dualism is true.

2. Some agent or process creates an immaterial soul and unites it to a physical body each time a new human being comes into existence.

3. This agent or process cannot possibly be a purely material agent or process.

4. Therefore, an immaterial agent or process creates a soul and unites it to a body when a new human being comes into existence.

5. God is the most plausible candidate for this role.

6. Therefore, theism is the best explanation of the data.
7. It is therefore reasonable to believe that God or a supreme being exists.

Theism and dualism are related in many different ways, as you probably imagined.[27]

FOR FURTHER STUDY

Bagget, David, Gary R. Habermas, and Jerry L. Walls, eds. *C. S. Lewis as Philosopher: Truth, Goodness, and Beauty*. Downers Grove, IL: InterVarsity Press Academic, 2008.

Feser, Edward. *Philosophy of Mind: A Beginner's Guide*. Oxford: OneWorld, 2005.

Foster, John. *The Immaterial Self: A Defense of the Cartesian Dualist Conception of the Mind*. New York: Routledge, 1991.

Koons, Robert C., and George Bealer, eds. *The Waning of Materialism*. New York: Oxford University Press, 2010.

Lavazza, Andrea, and Howard Robinson, eds. *Contemporary Dualism: A Defense*. Routledge Studies in Contemporary Philosophy. New York: Routledge, 2016.

Lewis, C. S. *The Pilgrim's Regress*. Reissue ed. Grand Rapids, MI: Eerdmans, 2014.

———. *Surprised by Joy: The Shape of My Early Life*. Reissue ed. New York: Harper One, 2017.

Loose, Jonathan J., Angus J. L. Menuge, and J. P. Moreland, eds. *The Blackwell Companion to Substance Dualism*. Blackwell Companions to Philosophy. Oxford: Wiley-Blackwell, 2018.

Moreland, J. P. *Consciousness and the Existence of God: A Theistic Argument*. New York: Routledge, 2010.

Popper, Karl, and John C. Eccles. *The Self and Its Brain: An Argument for Interactionism*. New York: Routledge, 1984.

Purtill, Richard, L. *C. S. Lewis's Case for the Christian Faith*. San Francisco: Harper and Row, 1985.

Rickabaugh, Brandon, and J. P. Moreland. *The Substance of Consciousness: A Comprehensive Defense of Contemporary Substance Dualism*. New York: Wiley-Blackwell, 2023.

Spitzer, Robert J. *Science at the Doorstep to God: Science and Reason in Support of God, the Soul, and Life after Death*. San Francisco: Ignatius Press, 2023.

On Christian materialism

Baker, Lynne Rudder. *Persons and Bodies: A Constitution View*. Cambridge: Cambridge University Press, 2000.

Corcoran, Kevin J. *Rethinking Human Nature: A Christian Materialist Alternative to the Soul*. Grand Rapids, MI: Baker Academic, 2006.

———, ed. *Soul, Body, and Survival: Essays on the Metaphysics of Human Persons*. Ithaca, NY: Cornell University Press, 2001.

van Inwagen, Peter, and Dean Zimmerman, eds. *Persons: Human and Divine*. Oxford: Clarendon, 2007.

For a collection of arguments against the prospect of life after death

Martin, Michael, and Keith Augustine. *The Myth of an Afterlife: The Case against Life after Death*. Lanham, MD: Rowman & Littlefield, 2015.

SIX

Isn't It Illogical to Believe That a Miracle Occurred?

On the basis of the books of the New Testament, Christians believe that Jesus of Nazareth was crucified, died, and rose miraculously from the dead three days later. They also believe that the miracle of the Resurrection confirms his unique claim to divinity—his claim to be the Son of God. However, many people today maintain that no amount of evidence, historical or otherwise, can ever make it reasonable to believe that a miracle caused by God ever actually occurred. In reply to the central Christian miracle claim, they say, "All of human experience shows that men who have been dead for three days stay dead, and that is the end of the matter." On their view, although the ordinary historical claims made in the New Testament might be believable, the miracle claims are just not rationally credible.

The Scottish philosopher David Hume (1711–76) was the first major thinker to give a philosophical argument for the claim that although miracles might be theoretically possible, it is never, under any circumstances, reasonable to believe that a miracle actually occurred. Of course, if Hume was right, then the New Testament is not a historically reliable document, for it contains many reports of miraculous events.

Hume's argument is the most talked-about argument ever given against belief in miracles, and it remains influential today. If his argument is correct, then it is not reasonable to accept the Christian faith, for as Saint Paul said, "If Christ has not been raised, then our preaching is in vain, your faith is in vain" (1 Corinthians 15:14). For many people today, Hume's argument against belief in miracles remains a major barrier to all religious beliefs. His argument is therefore one more hurdle that any rational case for Christianity must overcome.

HUME'S FAMOUS ARGUMENT AGAINST BELIEF IN MIRACLES

When looking back on history, context is important. Before the eighteenth century, nearly all philosophers and scientists in the universities of Europe were Christians who believed that miracles had occurred, including the miracles reported in the Bible. These scholars maintained that there are good reasons to believe that God exists and that God has in the past intervened miraculously in the course of history, perhaps to disclose his existence, to send a needed message, or to help a struggling humankind by initiating a change in the direction of history.

The scholarly consensus began to erode after the publication in 1748 of Hume's treatise on epistemology, *Enquiry concerning Human Understanding*. In this now-classic work, Hume defines the word *miracle* and gives his famous argument against belief in miracles. One qualification is important: Hume does *not* argue that miracles have never occurred or that miracles are impossible. He only argues that under all circumstances, it is irrational to *believe* that miracles have occurred. Hume begins his argument with these words:

> A miracle is a violation of the laws of nature; and as a firm and unalterable experience has established these laws, the proof against a miracle, from the very nature of the fact, is as entire as any argument from experience can possibly be imagined. There [is] a uniform experience against every miraculous event, otherwise the event would not merit

Isn't It Illogical to Believe That a Miracle Occurred? 153

the appellation. And as a uniform experience amounts to a proof, there is here a direct and full proof, from the very nature of the fact, against the existence of any miracle.[1]

The wording is mine, but the rest of his argument, once fleshed out, goes about like this:

1. A *miracle* is a "violation of a law of nature" caused by God.

2. A *law of nature* represents a regularity in nature, that is, a way matter regularly behaves. Laws of nature can be expressed as mathematical equations or (in logical terms) as universal generalizations of the form, "An event of kind A is always followed by an event of kind B." For instance, dropped objects always fall; dead men always stay dead; water always freezes at 32°F under standard conditions.[2]

3. A sequence of regularly associated events is considered a law of nature only after millions of people from all around the world have repeatedly observed the regularity occurring over and over again for a long period of time, without exception.

4. Our knowledge of the laws of nature is justified on the basis of diverse observations made by millions of people all around the world over thousands of years who have repeatedly seen that dropped objects always fall, that people who have been dead for three days always remain dead, that water always flows downhill (unless it is pumped or interfered with), and so on.

5. Thus, if it is a law of nature that a certain kind of event is always followed by another kind of event—that events of kind A are always followed by events of kind B—then the likelihood that an event of kind A is *not* followed by an event of kind B is very, very close to zero.

6. It follows that if a miracle were to occur, it would be an almost infinitely improbable event.

7. The evidence that a miracle occurred will be the testimony of one or a small number of people at a specific moment in time.

8. In contrast, the evidence for the exceptionless constancy of the laws of nature will be the testimony of millions of people around the world over thousands of years.

9. Reasonable people confronted with the claim that an extremely unlikely event has occurred should weigh the evidence for the claim and the evidence against the claim. After the evidence from both sides has been compared, they should proportion their belief to the weight of the evidence by accepting the claim with the strongest support.

10. The testimonial evidence of a few people that a certain miracle occurred at a certain time will never come close to equaling the enormous weight of the testimony of millions of observers over thousands of years indicating that the laws of nature remain constant without exception.

11. Therefore, it can never, under any circumstances, be reasonable to believe that a miracle occurred.

Hume offers a second argument that supplements his first. The testimony for miracles always comes from rude, "uneducated people" living "difficult lives" in "barbarous societies." Such people tend to hanker after the miraculous because the belief comforts them by giving them hope of a future heavenly reward. But comfort and hope, Hume argues, are never evidence that a belief is true.

Furthermore, Hume adds, uneducated and barbarous people—since they are not trained in critical thinking—are easily fooled by pranksters and by their own overly vivid imaginations. And because they are not critical thinkers, they tend to believe what they want to believe rather than what the evidence indicates.

If Hume's arguments are right, then the miracle accounts recorded in the New Testament are about as believable as fairy tales. Today Hume's argument is obligatory reading in most philosophy classes in secular universities (at least in those covering the question of miracles), and students are almost invariably taught that Hume proved that it is never, under any conditions, reasonable to believe that a miracle has occurred.

It is surprising that Hume's argument against belief in miracles has so much authority today in academic philosophy, for shortly after his argument was published, William Paley and other well-known philosophers of the day raised devastating objections. It is also surprising that while Hume's argument is widely available to undergraduates, the objections raised at the time are not.

In the 1960s, a number of Christian philosophers took a fresh look at Hume's argument in light of the latest techniques of logical analysis and found large, unbridged gaps in his reasoning. Nevertheless, ideas have consequences. Hume's argument became a major support for the deism of his day. (Deism is the view that there is a God, but God takes no interest in human affairs and does not intervene in any way in human history or in individual lives.) If deism is true, Christianity, along with any other religion based on revelation and miracles, is a fraud.

HUME'S DEFINITION OF *MIRACLE*

Theistic philosophers argue that Hume's definition of the word *miracle* as "a violation of a law of nature caused by God" is mischievous. The very idea of a miracle has more initial plausibility, they argue, if we think of a miraculous event not as a *violation* of a law of nature by God or a supernatural being but as a *superseding* or an *overriding* of a law of nature by God or a divine being. The theologian Gerald O'Collins argues that we should reject Hume's definition because the word *violate* has "four meanings, all of them negative and even ugly," to wit: (1) disregard or fail to comply with; (2) treat with disrespect; (3) disturb or break in on; and (4) assault. As the Creator of the laws of nature, God "is surely better described as suspending or overriding the normal working of natural laws" rather than as "violating" them.[3]

The Purdue University philosopher Jan Cover adds an interesting point by noting that a miracle doesn't technically "violate" or contradict a law of nature, for a law of nature merely states what happens when only *natural* causes are at work. A scientific statement of a law of nature does not say what happens when God or a supernatural being intervenes in the natural order from the outside, for instance, when the Creator of the natural order temporarily overrides a law of nature and causes something to happen that otherwise would not have. If God exists, God would certainly have the power to supersede a law of nature and cause something to happen, and that action would not technically be a "violation." For many reasons, then, miracles are more plausibly thought of as "supersessions" or "overridings" rather than as "violations" of the laws of physics or the laws of nature by God.[4]

RICHARD SWINBURNE'S REPLY TO HUME

One of the foremost specialists in philosophy of religion today, Richard Swinburne, professor emeritus of philosophy at Oxford University, argues that Hume's case against miracles fails because Hume leaves out at least three relevant classes of information when he explains how we should weigh the evidence for and against a specific miracle claim. Once the missing information is added to the balance, it becomes reasonable to believe that miracles have occurred. Indeed, argues Swinburne, miracles are expected, given this additional information. This will require a short explanation.

Suppose that someone claims to have seen a four-foot-tall professional basketball player. Most people would immediately doubt the claim, and for good reason. We all know that most professional basketball players are very tall. We also know that professional basketball is a highly competitive sport and that a team with a four-foot-tall player would be at a competitive disadvantage. These propositions are part of what philosophers call our "background knowledge." This is the large body of already verified information that we rely on when we evaluate a new claim. Claims that conflict with our general background knowledge have a low degree of probability from the start—before any evidence is even considered.

My background knowledge is the reason I will immediately reply "no" if someone offers to sell me the Brooklyn Bridge. I won't even bother checking the person's credentials because I already know that public bridges are not for sale. In contrast, claims that are consistent with our background information are at least worth investigating. If someone tells me that Ringo Starr is signing albums at the music store down the street, I will check it out because the claim is at least logically consistent with my background knowledge. (For all I know, he might be.) However, if someone tells me that Bob Dylan is signing records at the local record store, I will be very doubtful because I already know that he doesn't do that sort of thing.

Furthermore, claims that are expected (given our background knowledge) have a relatively high degree of probability before the evidence is even considered, in which case less evidence is needed before they become credible or convincing. The reverse is also true: claims that are unlikely, given our background knowledge, have a low degree of probability before the evidence is considered, and more evidence than normal is needed before they become credible.

Now for Swinburne's main charge: Hume begs the question against belief in miracles when he assumes—without any argument—that the *only* background knowledge that should count when we evaluate a miracle claim is (1) our general knowledge of the exceptionless constancy of the laws of nature and (2) our knowledge of human nature. This leaves out three important subsets of background knowledge that (he claims) also ought to count when judging a miracle claim.

1. The deep philosophical reasons we have to believe that God or a supreme being exists. We examined six theistic arguments in chapters 2, 3, and 5.

2. What we have learned in the field known as philosophical theology—philosophical thought on the nature of God. Swinburne is one of many philosophers who have argued in depth, not only that God is all-knowing, all-powerful, and all-loving but also that God cares about us and desires our salvation.

3. Observations regarding the distressed state of the human condition that would give God a reason to intervene in the natural order and to mark that intervention with a surprising miracle, to get our attention, send a message, or place a stamp of approval on an event (or perhaps all three).

These three sets of information, Swinburne argues, are legitimate parts of our background knowledge because each is solidly grounded in compelling philosophical arguments. This is no idle claim. As I have noted, in *The Existence of God*, Swinburne presents and defends many of the classic arguments for God's existence. In *The Coherence of Theism*, he presents and defends the classic conception of God as omnipotent (all-powerful), omniscient (all-knowing), and omnibenevolent (all-good). And in *The Resurrection of God Incarnate* and in *Was Jesus God?*, he defends the claim that God has good reason to intervene in human affairs.[5]

So, if we follow Hume and assume that the *only* background knowledge that counts when we evaluate a miracle claim is (1) our general knowledge of the constancy of the laws of nature and (2) the facts he cites about how gullible and ignorant some people can be, then *any* miracle claim is highly unlikely before any empirical evidence is even considered. Relying only on this thin veneer of background information, no miracle claim will ever be rationally acceptable since the evidence for the unbroken constancy of the laws of nature will outweigh the usual testimony offered for a miracle.

However, Swinburne argues, suppose that our background knowledge includes the classic arguments for God's existence presented and defended by philosophers—arguments that offer solid and undefeated (he argues) reasons to believe in God. Suppose it also includes strong reasons to believe that God is a supreme and loving being who gave his creatures a high degree of freedom and who also cares about them and facts about the fallen state of the human condition that would give God a reason to intervene miraculously in human history and also in individual human lives.

With this more realistic background knowledge, Swinburne argues, we should expect that miracles have happened—and are happening today—before any empirical (observable) evidence for a specific miracle has even been examined. Miracles are now no longer ruled out from the start; they are *expected*. In this case, the sum total of *all* the evidence, evaluated in the context of all our background information, may make it very likely that a specific miracle occurred.

To see the difference an expanded set of background knowledge can make, consider an analogy suggested by Swinburne.[6] The German philosopher Immanuel Kant (1724–1804) was famous for going on an afternoon walk at exactly the same time each day—3:00 p.m.—in his native city of Konigsberg. His habit was apparently so strict that people set their clocks by his walk. Now imagine that one day three ordinary townspeople testify that the famous philosopher started his walk an hour late. Using Hume's method of evaluation, this testimony from just three people that Kant started his walk at 4:00 p.m. would immediately be outweighed by the background information that Kant had been seen by hundreds of people over many years starting his walk at exactly 3:00 every day. That is, when we balance (1) the large number of testimonies to the effect that he always walked at 3:00 against (2) the three testimonies stating that he walked at a different time on one particular day, the weight of all the evidence will overcome the claim that he changed his walk *one time*. Following Hume, using only the stated background information, we would have to conclude that the three people testifying that he walked at 4:00 once are either liars or mistaken.

Now imagine that the citizens of Konigsberg have new background information. Suppose that they learn that Kant has a very sick friend, that Kant is compassionate, and that on the day in question he had a good reason to walk later than usual: he needed to vary his time in order to visit his sick friend. On the basis of this thicker background information, it becomes more likely that the testimony from just three people is true and that one time he started his famous walk at 4:00 instead of at 3:00. It is easy to imagine other information that, if added to the background knowledge possessed by the citizens of Konigsberg, would make the testimony of the three witnesses even more credible from the start. Background information matters.

The lesson is that the background knowledge we rely on can make a big difference when we evaluate an unlikely claim. The point is so important that another example is called for, this one from the philosopher Richard Purtill.[7]

Someone tells you that the president just pardoned a convicted felon. Under the impression that the US Constitution does not allow this kind of legal action, you reply, "I don't believe it." The person answers, "But I watched the proceeding on TV." You reply, "This must be fake news because the law does not allow the president to do such a thing." The person's claim seems bogus from the start when weighed against your existing background information.

However, a few days later, you read the Constitution and learn that it does give the president the power to pardon felons. You also do some research and discover that the president had a good reason to pardon this particular individual. In light of your expanded background information, it now becomes reasonable to believe the person's testimony (that the president pardoned a felon).

To return to Swinburne's point, if the classic theistic arguments are part of our background knowledge, and if we add to this knowledge of the mess humanity has gotten itself into—a mess that gives God a good reason to intervene in history and in human lives—it becomes reasonable to expect that God has intervened in history and caused a miracle to put a stamp of authority on his message or action. This, combined with direct and specific testimony, might make it very reasonable to believe that a miracle has occurred. Hume is being unfair to theism when he restricts our background knowledge to (a) the laws of nature understood as unbreakable regularities and (b) facts about human gullibility.

COVER'S COUNTER TO HUME

Jan Cover argues that Hume overlooks another kind of evidence when he assumes without argument that the only knowledge we may appeal to when we evaluate a miracle claim is the laws of nature, facts about human gullibility, and direct testimony. Hume ignores the possibility that indirect (circumstantial) evidence might add weight to any testimony that a specific miracle occurred.[8]

Cover asks us to consider the following example: Jones has unexpectedly been found dead, and an eyewitness claims he saw Jones commit suicide. No trained detective, Cover claims, would conclude the investigation with only this direct testimony in hand—especially if the suicide was unexpected. A good detective would probe deeper by looking for indirect, or corroborating, evidence. This might include Jones's fingerprints on the gun, a suicide note, antidepressants in the medicine cabinet, interviews with close friends, Jones's behavior over the past few months, possible motives, and so forth.[9] The point is that circumstantial evidence, in addition to background information and personal testimony, plays a role when we investigate a surprising claim. In chapter 8, we will delve into the Christian claim that Jesus Christ rose from the dead three days after his Crucifixion. Circumstantial evidence will play a role in the investigation.

WILLIAM LANE CRAIG'S REPLY TO HUME

William Lane Craig is another philosopher who has challenged Hume's argument (for the conclusion that it is never reasonable to believe that a miracle has occurred). Craig begins with Paley's eighteenth-century counterargument, which he updates and summarizes this way:

Suppose twelve men, whom I know to be honest and reasonable people, were to assert that they saw personally a miraculous event in which it was impossible for them to have been tricked; furthermore, the governor called them before him for an inquiry and sentenced them all to death unless they were to admit the hoax; and they all went to their deaths rather than say they were lying. According to Hume, we should still not believe such men.[10]

Wouldn't it be reasonable, Craig asks, to believe the twelve individuals who testified at great risk to themselves? It might be possible that one sincere person is tricked by his senses or deceived by a hoaxer; it might be possible that two are tricked. One might be mentally unstable. But it is extremely unlikely, Craig argues, that twelve sincere, rational people are all fooled at once. As the number of witnesses testifying to an event rises, the likelihood that they are all deluded or that they are lying in concert declines rapidly (and the probability that they are truthful increases rapidly). The testimonies in this case are made even more credible by the fact that they were given at great personal cost and at the risk of death.

Contrary to Hume, Craig concludes that in some cases, the sum total of all the circumstantial evidence, combined with testimony from multiple witnesses who have no motive to lie and who testify at great personal cost or at great risk, can outweigh the case against an improbable claim, thereby making it reasonable to believe that a highly improbable event, such as a miracle, actually did occur.

CONCLUDING REFLECTION

If these responses to Hume's argument are correct, it follows that if someone claims that a miracle occurred, we need to look at the total evidence and not just at the laws of nature and facts about human naïveté. It also follows that if a sane person claims that a miracle occurred, it is irrational to just throw up our hands and refuse to even look at the total evidence. Notice also that when we evaluate a miracle claim, the reasoning to employ will be inference to the best explanation.

So, suppose that we have sensible reasons to believe that God exists and that God loves us and cares about us. Suppose further that we human beings have misused our freedom and messed things up terribly, giving God a good reason to intervene in the natural order and send us a message in the form of a miracle (perhaps to get our attention or as a sign of authenticity, etc.). If our background knowledge includes these general theistic beliefs (each based on arguments), then in some cases the corroborated testimony of a few sane people who have no motive to lie, combined with circumstantial evidence, may make it eminently reasonable to believe that a miracle occurred. And if those giving the testimony maintain their claims even in the face of persecution and threats of death, that could be further reason to take their claims seriously.

We'll apply these reasonable principles of evidence in chapter 8 when we investigate the Christian claim that Jesus Christ rose from the dead three days after his Crucifixion.

FOR FURTHER STUDY

Cover, J. A. "Miracles and Christian Theism." In *Reason for the Hope Within*, ed. Michael Murray, 345–74. Grand Rapids, MI: Eerdmans, 1999.

Earman, John. *Hume's Abject Failure: The Argument against Miracles*. New York: Oxford University Press, 2000.

Hume, David. *Of Miracles*. Introduction by Antony Flew. La Salle, IL: Open Court Classic, 1985.

Johnson, David. *Hume, Holism, and Miracles*. Ithaca, NY: Cornell University Press, 1999.

Keener, Craig S. *Miracles: The Credibility of the New Testament Accounts*. Grand Rapids, MI: Baker Academic, 2011.

———. *Miracles Today: The Supernatural Work of God in the Modern World*. Grand Rapids, MI: Baker Academic, 2021.

Swinburne, Richard. *The Concept of Miracle*. New York: Palgrave Macmillan, 2017.

———. *Miracles*. New York: Macmillan, 1989.

For those who want to research the case against *belief in miracles*

Fogelin, Robert J. *A Defense of Hume on Miracles*. Princeton, NJ: Princeton University Press, 2003.

Shapiro, Larry. *The Miracle Myth: Why Belief in the Resurrection and the Supernatural Is Unjustified*. New York: Columbia University Press, 2016.

SEVEN

Is the New Testament Historically Reliable?

Many people today do not believe that God or a supreme being exists. But if God does not exist, then the Christian New Testament is not historically reliable, for it contains many accounts of miracles said to be performed by God. And of course, if God does not exist, then it is never reasonable to believe that a miracle caused by God occurred anyway. However, if the classic arguments for God's existence make the most sense of our world, our lives, our experiences, then it is eminently reasonable to believe that God exists. And if God is powerful enough to have created time, space, and matter out of nothing and to have imposed a magnificent order on nature, then surely God is powerful enough to override a law of nature and cause a miracle to occur. Indeed, if God is powerful enough to have created the entire universe, then God has the power to cause a young Jewish woman living in the village of Nazareth during the first century, known to Christians as the Blessed Virgin Mary, to bear a child. And as I argued in chapter 6, if God as traditionally conceived exists, then given the mess we humans have made of things, divine interventions of a miraculous kind are actually *expected*.

So, given what has been argued so far in this book, a reasonable person should at least be open to the possibility that miracles have occurred, are occurring, and will occur in the future. The books of the New Testament contain many stories of miracles, most identifying specific people, places, and events. But why suppose that those stories are true? Why not regard the New Testament as a collection of fairy tales, as many today assume? Why suppose that it is historically reliable? Let's begin with some everyday reasoning.

HOW DO WE KNOW THAT THE BATTLE OF THE SOMME OCCURRED?

I like to read historical accounts of battles that took place during World Wars I and II. But when I open a new book of military history, how do I know that the account I am reading is accurate and truthful? It seems to me that there are six commonsense criteria, each one adding a reason to trust the report.

1. The account of the battle is an eyewitness report or is based directly on an eyewitness report.

2. The account was written close in time to the events it describes.

3. The author or source had no known motive to fabricate.

4. The author or source would have expected to face serious negative repercussions if caught lying.

5. The report was published while many eyewitnesses to the events were still alive and in a position to object publicly if the report were fallacious.

6. Many of the historical details mentioned in the account have been independently confirmed by objective research.

So, there are reasonable ways to evaluate and confirm the historicity of a book, even an old book, containing accounts of events in the distant past. Note that if a historical account satisfies just one of these six criteria, that alone does not prove the account accurate. If an account satisfies just two of these criteria, that also does not prove the account accurate. However, as an account satisfies one criterion after another, its reliability rises. If a historical account passes all six tests, we may have very good reason to believe that it is truthful. Our reasoning in this case can be cast in the form of an inference to the best explanation.[1]

Now another problem arises. If the book I hold in my hands is a reprint of an older book, how can I know that the book I am reading now was accurately copied from the original edition? If I am reading a copy of a copy of a copy of a very old book or historical document, then in addition to the test of the six criteria, I need solid evidence that the original book or document was copied accurately and transmitted faithfully to the present. These tests will serve as a commonsense background as we proceed.

Many people today reject the New Testament on the basis of two assumptions or claims:

1. The historical details contained in the books of the New Testament cannot be independently verified.

2. We do not possess the original documents and therefore cannot be sure that the books we are now reading are accurate copies of the originals.

Surprisingly, though widely believed today, both propositions are demonstrably false. Regarding the first claim, numerous respected secular historians who specialize in ancient history and many New Testament scholars at major universities have independently verified scores of specific historical claims in the New Testament using standard methods of historical research. In addition, many archaeologists, using the latest scientific techniques, have verified a large number of specific historical claims appearing in the New Testament. Compared to other widely accepted works of ancient history, the number of specific historical claims in the New Testament that have been verified is actually very large.

Regarding the second claim, scholars who specialize in the historical transmission of ancient documents have made an equally impressive case for the claim that the books of the New Testament that we read today are extremely accurate copies of the originals. Indeed, these scholars state that, based on extensive investigation, they have more confidence in the accuracy of the New Testament books than in the accuracy of *any* other famous documents of the ancient period.

The combined research of these scholars makes an impressive case for the overall historical reliability of the books of the New Testament. Their scholarship indicates that the New Testament is not a collection of fairy tales or myths; rather it is a generally reliable set of historical documents written to convey to people at the time and to future generations a number of exciting events surrounding the life and death of Jesus Christ of Nazareth.

Unfortunately, the arguments these scholars present are quite complex, and a full understanding requires a background in ancient history, textual analysis, ancient languages, archaeology, historiography, and the huge field of New Testament studies—subjects for graduate students and specialists to tackle. My field is academic philosophy. I am an amateur in the fields of biblical scholarship, ancient history, ancient languages, archaeology, and the like.

Nevertheless, it is possible for amateurs and beginning students to use common sense and the methods of critical thinking to evaluate the evidence and to make reasonable judgments on the fundamental issues. This should not be surprising: the books of the New Testament were written to be read by ordinary people employing common sense; they were not intended only for those with college degrees and time to study piles of thick books.

WERE THE NEW TESTAMENT BOOKS ACCURATELY COPIED AND TRANSMITTED TO THE PRESENT?

In high school and college, I read (parts of) the works of many ancient authors: Homer, Hesiod, Caesar, Cicero, Plato, Aristotle, and others. I don't remember a single teacher ever questioning the accuracy of any of the texts we were reading, even though the texts we possess today are copies of copies of copies in a series stretching back more than 2,000 years to the originals in some cases. The working assumption was that the copies we read today are accurate reproductions of the original works. The consensus was that the words in Caesar's *War Commentaries* are the words Caesar himself wrote 2,000 years ago—translated into English, of course. The lines in Plato's dialogues are considered the very lines Plato himself wrote 2,350 years ago, translated from the ancient Greek. Scholars agree that the Greek and Roman classics we possess today are very accurate copies of the original documents.

Can we be as confident with respect to the books of the New Testament? The philosopher and biblical scholar Norman Geisler argues that the same tests that establish the accuracy of all other ancient documents also establish the fidelity, or copying accuracy, of the books of the New Testament. Geisler summarizes the complex arguments in *A Popular Survey of the New Testament*.[2] His clear and accessible presentation is representative of a voluminous literature; it is therefore a good place to start. My presentation follows his lead, with some supplements added along the way.

Handwritten copies of the New Testament books that date from the second to the nineteenth century are called manuscript copies. Geisler notes that "we have more manuscripts, earlier manuscripts, and more accurately copied manuscripts of the [original] New Testament than of any other book from the ancient world."[3] According to Geisler, while we have only ten to twenty manuscripts for most ancient books, we have more than 5,700 surviving manuscripts of the New Testament. One of the most well-attested ancient manuscripts, Homer's *Iliad*, has 643 manuscripts. "Thus," Geisler writes, "the New Testament has an overwhelming advantage in the number of manuscripts to support the integrity of the text it is transmitting."[4]

Furthermore, Geisler argues, "The [oldest existing] New Testament manuscripts are much earlier than those for other books from antiquity. Most other [ancient] books survive on the basis of manuscripts created 1,000 years after the [original] book was composed, there being no known original manuscripts. The New Testament, by contrast, has [partial copies] that date from within about twenty-five years from the time the book was written."[5]

The New Testament scholar Gary Habermas adds this comparison: "For most of the ancient classical works, a gap of only 700 years [between the original manuscript and the earliest surviving copy] would be excellent, while 1000–1400 years is not at all uncommon."[6] Thus, Sir Frederic Kenyon, a noted expert on ancient manuscripts, writes:

> The interval between the dates of original composition and the earliest extant evidence becomes so small [in the case of the New Testament documents] as to be in fact negligible, and the last foundation for any doubt that the Scriptures have come down substantially as they were written has now been removed. Both the authenticity and the general integrity of the books of the New Testament may be regarded as firmly established.[7]

Another consideration cited by Kenyon is also important.

> While we have the entire New Testament text, this is not the case with every ancient work. For example, of the 142 books of Roman History written by Livy, 107 books have been lost. Only four and a half of Tacitus's original fourteen books of Roman *Histories* remain in existence and only ten full and two partial books from the sixteen books of Tacitus's *Annals*. In contrast, each New Testament book is complete, which is also a factor in establishing [its] authenticity.[8]

In addition, according to Geisler, "the number of manuscripts of the New Testament, of early transmissions, and of quotations from it in the oldest writers of the church, is so large that it is practically certain that the true reading of every doubtful passage is preserved in some one or the other of these ancient authorities. This can be said of no other book in the world."[9]

The philosopher J. P. Moreland notes that "there are 8,000 manuscript copies of the Vulgate (a Latin translation of the Bible completed by Jerome between 382–405) and more than 350 copies of Syriac (Christian Aramaic) versions of the New Testament (originating from 150–250)."[10]

And then there are the church fathers of the first four centuries AD. Geisler observes that almost the entire New Testament can be reconstructed from their writings, which quote from the New Testament about 36,000 times.

These are just a few of many considerations indicating that the New Testament documents were copied and transmitted to the present with an unusually high degree of accuracy. Again, when students today read Plato's *Dialogues*, Aristotle's treatises, the *War Commentaries* of Caesar, and hundreds of other ancient texts, their teachers assure them that they are reading accurate copies of the originals. By the accepted standards of historical research, the books of the New Testament we possess today are even more accurate reproductions of the original texts.

DID THE ALLEGED EVENTS REALLY HAPPEN? WERE THEY RECORDED ACCURATELY?

Geisler responds at length to this question. First, in the case of the New Testament, "We have more books written by more authors who were closer to

> The Roman general and statesman Julius Caesar (100–44 BC) wrote his *War Commentaries* between 58 and 50 BC. The oldest manuscript we possess was produced nine hundred years later. We have about 251 manuscript copies of the original document.[11]
>
> The Roman historian Livy (ca. 64 BC–AD 12) wrote his great *History of Rome* between 27 and 9 BC. The oldest manuscript we possess was copied five centuries later. We have about 473 manuscript copies of the original document.[12]
>
> The Roman senator Tacitus (AD 56–ca. 120) wrote his *Annals* in the early second century. The oldest manuscript we possess was copied six centuries later and we have 36 manuscript copies of the original document.[13]
>
> The Greek historian Herodotus (ca. 484–ca. 420 BC) wrote his *History of the Greco-Persian Wars*—the first systematic, critical-thinking-based work of history produced in the ancient world—during the fifth century BC. The earliest manuscripts we possess go back to approximately the first century AD, and in total we have 106 manuscript copies of the original document.[14]

the events and whose record has been confirmed in more ways than for any other book from the ancient world."[15] For example, "most events of the ancient world are known on the basis of one or two writers from the time period or sometime after it. By contrast, the New Testament has nine writers, and the New Testament writers were closer to the events than most other writers from the ancient world were to the events about which they wrote."[16]

Josh McDowell and Sean McDowell note that the New Testament documents "were written by eyewitnesses or from eyewitness accounts" very close to the events they describe.[17] On this last point, a good deal of serious scholarship indicates that the Gospels of Matthew, Mark, and Luke were probably written during the AD 60s, but at least during the 70s. John's gospel was probably completed by the end of the 90s.[18] All four gospels were therefore written within a lifetime of the events they describe. And the authors of the three synoptic Gospels (Matthew, Mark, and Luke) were recording eyewitness testimony related by persons approximately in their fifties and sixties who were recounting events from approximately their twenties. Many people in their sixties remember in great detail dramatic events from their twenties. For that matter, many in their nineties remember in accurate detail dramatic events from their youth. Think of World War II veterans recalling battles they fought in seventy years before.[19]

Why do these considerations matter? It is common sense that the more writers corroborating an event, the more reasonable it is to believe that the event occurred. It is also common sense that the closer to a historical event the original reports are, the more reasonable it is to believe that they are accurate. So, when we compare the New Testament with ancient documents, such as the *War Commentaries* of Caesar—accounts that are widely considered trustworthy—these considerations suggest that we should place at least as much trust in the books of the New Testament.

Human psychology provides further evidence of historical reliability. It is a historical fact that "the apostles refused to renounce their beliefs regarding the resurrected Christ even though they faced harsh persecution and martyrdom for believing."[20] Let's pause and consider this for a moment.

Scholars who study the New Testament manuscripts agree on the following:

- Even when threatened with ruin, torture, and death, the apostles refused to recant their claim to have witnessed the amazing events they reported, for instance, that Jesus claimed to be the uniquely divine Son of God, that he performed numerous miracles, and that three days after his Crucifixion he rose from the dead and appeared to his followers in bodily form.

- At least three of the apostles went to their deaths rather than retract their claims about Jesus. Peter, for example, was martyred in Rome.

But it is common sense that rational people do not usually give up their careers, suffer torments, risk great personal costs, and even death for the sake of something they *know* to be false. From a purely secular viewpoint, it is theoretically possible that one or two of Jesus's apostles were deranged, mentally ill, or dishonest. But given what we know of them, it is simply not reasonable to believe that they were all mentally ill, delusional, or dishonest.

Then there is the archaeological evidence. As mentioned, the New Testament documents contain a large number of historical details, including many specifically identified people, places, and events. As McDowell and McDowell write, "Where the [historical claims made in the Gospels] can be tested, archeological discoveries have constantly proven the documents to be remarkably reliable."[21] The Christian archaeologist Donald J. Wiseman claims that between the Old and New Testaments, more than twenty-five thousand biblical references to cities, customs, names, and events have been confirmed.[22] For example, David Turek writes:

> Roman historian Colin Hemer verified through archeology and other historical sources . . . eighty-four historical and eyewitness details from Acts 13 to the end of the book. Many are obscure details that only an eyewitness could know, such as the names of small-town politicians, local slang, topographical features, special weather patterns and water depths, etc. . . . Famed archeologist Sir William Ramsey began his research skeptical of Luke [the author of the Acts of the Apostles]. But after twenty years of study, Ramsey concluded that Luke "should be placed along with the greatest of historians." . . . [His words] stand the keenest scrutiny and the hardest treatment. . . . Luke references thirty-two countries, fifty-four cities, and nine islands without making a single mistake. . . . [A]nd he did all that without the benefit of modern-day maps, charts, and Google Earth. . . . John includes fifty-nine historically verified or historically probable eyewitness details in his Gospel.[23]

To this, scholars of ancient documents add the testimony of non-Christian sources. Habermas writes that "ancient extra-biblical sources do present a surprisingly large amount of detail concerning both the life of Jesus and the nature of early Christianity. . . . Overall, at least seventeen non-Christian writings record [and confirm] more than fifty details concerning the life, teachings, death, and resurrection of Jesus."[24]

I was once in an audience listening to an archaeologist describe a secular excavation that he worked on in the biblical lands. You might be surprised to learn what the secular archaeologists used as their main historical reference or guidebook as they planned their fieldwork: the books of the New Testament.

FROM ANOTHER ANGLE

The historicity of the New Testament can be approached from another perspective. As you read the books of the New Testament, the impression you get is that the authors at least claim to be writing serious history. For

> If you discuss the history of Christianity with enough people, you will eventually hear the counterargument that the stories in the Gospels were all copied from pre-Christian Greek stories about a gnostic redeemer who works miracles.[25] However, during the 1970s, in-depth scholarship established that Christianity predated the gnostic redeemer stories. Habermas quotes James D. C. Dunn: "The problem with all this has been that the full-blown Gnostic redeemer myth ... is nowhere clearly attested before the second century.... [T]he first redeemer figures as such do not appear till the second century, probably Christianity's contribution to syncretist Gnosticism."[26]

instance, they pay careful attention to historical details, their writing is sober and matter of fact, and they include what they claim is eyewitness testimony. The Gospels certainly read like real history. In addition—and it seems to me this is an extremely important point—the authors were followers of someone universally acknowledged to be one of the greatest ethical teachers in history, and they placed his beautiful moral principles at the center of the gospel message. It is very hard to believe that students and advocates of such high moral teachings were liars engaged in a conspiracy and deviously making things up as they went. McDowell and McDowell ask, "Are we to believe that some of the world's greatest ethical teachings came from unethical people? While possible, this hardly seems the most reasonable conclusion. Furthermore, there's no reason to suggest that they had motives for material or societal gain."[27]

Furthermore, as many commentators have observed, the gospel writers included embarrassing and counterproductive details in their accounts—elements no one in their right mind making up a phony religion would include. Examples are Peter's three denials of Jesus (Mark 14:66–72), James's initial negative reaction to Jesus (Mark 3:20; John 7:5), the frightened behavior of the apostles immediately after the Crucifixion (Mark 14:50), and the fact that women are presented in all four Gospels as the first witnesses to the empty tomb—at a time in world history when women were not considered reliable witnesses in courts of law. If you are a liar making up a fake religion, there are much better ways to make your story believable. You could have Roman guards actually see the Resurrection occur and be the first to testify; you could have Jesus appear after the Crucifixion to Pontius Pilate himself, who then becomes a secret follower.

The possibilities are almost endless (if you are a lying conspirator making up a false religion from scratch). Yet the gospel accounts do not sound gimmicked up.

Another reason to take the Gospels as serious history has already been suggested: the complete lack of evidence suggesting that even one of the apostles did anything for profit. To the contrary, they all faced cruel persecution, ridicule, and possible death for their actions. At least three and probably more died as martyrs, and the rest knew that they ran the same risk. Yet they never gave up, and no one ever recanted. Isn't it common sense that liars concocting a fake story just don't behave this way?

CONCLUDING REFLECTION

Simon Greenleaf, one of the great legal scholars of the nineteenth century, taught at Harvard for many years and wrote one of the standard textbooks on the evaluation of evidence in the courtroom. He ended his argument for the historical reliability of the Christian Gospels with this thought:

> All that Christianity asks of [people] is that they would be consistent with themselves, that they would treat its evidences as they treat the evidence of other things, and that they would try and judge its actors and witnesses, as they deal with their fellow men. Let the witnesses be compared with themselves, with each other, and with surrounding facts and circumstances, and let their testimony be sifted, as if it were given in a court of justice.[28]

The historicity of the New Testament cannot be proved with the certainty of mathematics. But no ancient text can be proved historically reliable with that kind of certainty. However, the evidence examined in this chapter indicates that the books of the New Testament are at least as historically reliable as any other books transmitted from ancient times to the present and taken seriously by historians.

Let's return now to the six commonsense criteria regarding the trustworthiness of historical documents listed at the start of this chapter, criteria I use when I read accounts of World War I and II battles. Does the evidence presented in this chapter satisfy the criteria? Do the books of the New Testament pass the test of common sense?

Let's look at this yet another way. What is the best explanation of the totality of the facts at hand? Is it that the New Testament is a book of fairy tales created by ignorant or deceitful actors? Is it that the books of the New Testament that we hold in our hands today cannot be trusted because they are probably inaccurate copies of the original documents? Or is it that the books of the New Testament are what Christians claim they are, namely, unusually accurate copies of documents authored two thousand years ago by serious individuals who had no motive to lie about the amazing things they were reporting?

APPENDIX: ON THE ALLEGED CONTRADICTIONS IN THE NEW TESTAMENT

Some critics argue that the books of the New Testament contain contradictions that call their credibility into question. They argue further that the large number of these (alleged) contradictions undermines the historical reliability of the entire New Testament and constitutes a sufficient reason to reject what the Christian scriptures claim. This is an extremely complex subject. I am not going to delve into it except to offer some food for thought and references for further study. Craig Blomberg writes:

> From at least the second century onward Christians have been well aware of the similarities and differences among the four Gospels and have offered a variety of explanations for both minute apparent discrepancies and broad, varying emphases. The same is true for the seeming dissonance within a wide variety of passages in both Testaments, either with each other or with information from outside Scripture. Not a single supposed contradiction has gone without someone offering a reasonably plausible resolution.[29]

Indeed, many scholarly books offer logical resolutions to the alleged contradictions in both the Old and New Testaments. These accounts touch on semantics, textual analysis, and the study of ancient languages. Blomberg also notes that nearly every scholarly edition of the New Testament published today contains footnotes explaining each alleged contradiction. The reader who wants to investigate would do well to study specialized books on the topic. Blomberg recommends for a start Gleason Archer's *The Encyclopedia of Bible Difficulties*.[30]

On Variations among the New Testament Manuscripts

As I mentioned earlier, handwritten copies of the New Testament books that date from the second to the nineteenth century are referred to as manuscript copies. Thousands exist. The problem is that there are many variations among the different copies. One manuscript has "Lord Jesus" where another simply has "Jesus," and so forth. The New Testament scholar Bart Ehrman wrote a best seller on the topic titled *Misquoting Jesus*. According to Ehrman, "Scholars differ significantly in their estimates—some say there are 200,000 variants known, some say 300,000, some say 400,000 or more! We do not know for sure because, despite impressive developments in computer technology, no one has yet been able to count them all."[31] From this fact, some critics argue that we have no good reason to believe that the books of the New Testament that we read today are accurate copies of the originals.

Blomberg replies that the number of known variants among the manuscript copies is not a new discovery: Christian scholars have been studying the matter for centuries.

> Nothing in all of this is new. Readers of almost any English-language translation of the Bible . . . can look at the footnotes, or marginal notes[,] . . . and see mention of a broad cross-section of the most important and interesting of these variants. Unfortunately, many readers don't consult these notes often enough.[32]

Furthermore, even if there are as many as 400,000 variants, they

> are spread across more than 25,000 manuscripts in Greek or other ancient languages. Suddenly, the picture looks quite different. This is an average of only 16 variants per manuscript, and only 8 if the estimate of 200,000 variants is the more accurate one. Nor are the variants spread evenly across a given text, they tend to cluster in places where some kind of ambiguity has stimulated them.[33]

And:

> The vast majority of textual variants are wholly uninteresting except to specialists. . . . A large percentage . . . cluster around the same verses or passages. Less than 3 percent . . . are significant enough to be presented in one of the two standard critical editions of the Greek New Testament. Only about a tenth of 1 percent are interesting enough to make their way into footnotes in most English translations. It cannot be emphasized strongly enough that no orthodox doctrine or ethical practice of Christianity depends solely on any disputed wording. There are always undisputed passages one can consult that teach the same truths. Tellingly, in the appendix to the paperback edition of *Misquoting Jesus*, Ehrman himself concedes that "essential Christian beliefs are not affected by textual variants in the manuscript tradition of the New Testament." It is too bad that this admission appears in an appendix and comes only after repeated criticism![34]

Book Note

Blomberg, Craig. *The Historical Reliability of the New Testament: Countering the Challenges to Evangelical Christian Beliefs*. City B & H Studies in Christian Apologetics. Nashville, TN: B & H Academic, 2016. This 782-page treasure offers reasoned answers to just about every criticism currently circulating. Blomberg is a distinguished professor of the New Testament at Denver Seminary. From the book's Amazon page:

> Drawing on decades of research, Craig Blomberg addresses all of the major objections to the historicity of the New Testament in one comprehensive volume. Topics addressed include the formation of the Gospels, the transmission of the text, the formation of the canon, alleged contradictions, the relationship between Jesus and Paul, supposed Pauline forgeries, other gospels, miracles, and many more. Historical corroborations of details from all parts of the New Testament are also presented throughout.

FOR FURTHER STUDY

On the historical reliability of the New Testament

Bauckham, Richard. *Jesus and the Eyewitnesses: The Gospels as Eyewitness Testimony*. 2nd ed. Grand Rapids, MI: Eerdmans, 2017.
Blomberg, Craig. *Can We Still Believe the Bible? An Evangelical Engagement with Contemporary Questions*. Grand Rapids, MI: Brazos Press, 2014.
———. *The Historical Reliability of the Gospels*. Downers Grove, IL: InterVarsity Press, 2014.
Bruce, F. F. *The New Testament Documents: Are They Reliable?* Foreword by N. T. Wright. Nashville TN: Kingsley Books, [1943] 1981. This is the sixth edition.
Cowen, Steven B., and Terry L. Wilder, eds. *In Defense of the Bible: A Comprehensive Apologetic for the Authority of Scripture*. Nashville, TN: B & H Publishing Group, 2013.
Evans, C. Stephen. *The Historical Christ and the Jesus of Faith: The Incarnational Narrative as History*. New York: Oxford University Press, 1996.
Evans, Craig. *Fabricating Jesus: How Modern Scholars Distort the Gospels*. Downers Grove, IL: InterVarsity Press, 2009.
Geisler, Norman L. *A Popular Survey of the New Testament*. Grand Rapids, MI: Baker Books, 2007.
Habermas, Gary. *The Historical Jesus: Ancient Evidence for the Life of Christ*. Joplin, MO: College Press, 1996.
Hays, J. Daniel. *A Christian's Guide to Evidence for the Bible: 101 Proofs from History and Archeology*. Grand Rapids, MI: Baker Books, 2022.
Holden, Joseph, and Norman Geisler. *The Popular Handbook of Archeology and the Bible: Discoveries That Confirm the Reliability of Scripture*. Eugene, OR: Harvest House, 2013.
Kennedy, Titus. *Excavating the Evidence for Jesus*. Eugene, OR: Harvest House, 2022. The author is a professional field archaeologist who has directed research in the biblical lands.
Kruger, Michael J. *The Question of Canon*. Downers Grove, IL: InterVarsityPress, 2013.
McDowell, Josh, and Sean McDowell. *The Bible Handbook of Difficult Verses*. Eugene, OR: Harvest House, 2013.
———. *Evidence That Demands a Verdict: Life-Changing Truth for a Skeptical World*. Updated and exp. ed. Nashville, TN: Thomas Nelson, 2017.
McDowell, Sean. *The Fate of the Apostles*. New York: Routledge, 2016.

For general study of the New Testament

Achtemeier, Paul J., Joel B. Green, and Marianne Meye Thompson. *Introducing the New Testament: Its Literature and Theology*. Grand Rapids, MI: Eerdmans, 2001.

Barton, Stephen C., and Todd Brewer. *The Cambridge Companion to the Gospels*. 2nd ed. Cambridge: Cambridge University Press, 2021.

Elwell, Walter, and Robert Yarbrough. *Encountering the New Testament: A Historical and Theological Survey*. 3rd ed. Grand Rapids, MI: Baker Books, 2013.

Klein, William W., Craig L. Blomberg, and Robert L. Hubbard. *Introduction to Biblical Interpretation*. Rev. ed. Nashville, TN: Thomas Nelson, 2004.

Metzger, Bruce. *The New Testament: Its Background, Growth, and Content*. 3rd ed. Nashville, TN: Abingdon Press, 2003.

Wright, N. T., and Michael F. Bird. *The New Testament in Its World: An Introduction to the History, Literature, and Theology of the First Christians*. Grand Rapids, MI: Zondervan Academic, 2019.

EIGHT

Did Jesus Christ Rise Miraculously from the Dead?

Saint Paul said, "If Christ has not been raised, then our preaching is in vain, your faith is in vain" (1 Corinthians 15:14, New American Standard Bible). The philosopher J. P. Moreland calls the claim that Jesus was crucified, died, and after three days miraculously rose from the dead "the foundation on which the Christian faith is built."[1] But is this foundation stone rationally credible? Are there good reasons to believe that it is true? The philosopher Richard Swinburne suggests one reason why this matters: one way God might put a stamp of approval on a specific religion would be to mark its historical birth with a verified and truly amazing miracle.[2]

To many educated people today, the Christian claim that Jesus Christ rose from the dead three days after his Crucifixion is absurd. Even if we accept the general historicity of the New Testament, they say, this part is too much. How, they ask, can there be any logical evidence for such a claim? For there are naturalistic ways to explain what happened after the Crucifixion — explanations that do not suppose that anything miraculous occurred.

Surprisingly, a number of respected philosophers and scholars associated with major research universities, all with impressive academic accomplishments, have examined the alternative naturalistic explanations in detail and found them wanting. The foundational miracle claim of Christianity, they argue, can be supported using the standard methods of historical research, ordinary common sense, and carefully applied inference to the best explanation. Although these scholars argue in their own distinctive ways, in this chapter, I summarize the main core of their reasoning.

PART 1: DOCUMENTED FACTS IN NEED OF EXPLANATION

The Christian Gospels make a number of specific historical claims that are accepted as historically reliable by nearly all scholars—conservative, liberal, and atheist—who study ancient documents and the books of the New Testament. Each claim is supported by solid historical data that has passed the gauntlet of standard historical research. Here is a partial list as assembled by the philosopher William Lane Craig.

1. Jesus Christ was a real person who lived in first-century Palestine.

2. Jesus was a popular religious teacher who led a group of dedicated followers.

3. Jesus was charged with blasphemy and sedition and crucified by the Romans.

4. Jesus died and was buried in a tomb owned by a well-known member of the Jewish community, Joseph of Arimathea.

5. After his death, his closest followers hid themselves away, despondent and frightened.

6. Women were among the group of people who first testified that they had found the tomb empty three days after the Crucifixion.

7. No alternative burial site was ever venerated as Jesus's final resting place.

8. Soon after the Crucifixion, many of Jesus's followers reported that they had actually seen and spoken in person with the risen Christ.

9. Within a matter of weeks, his closest followers emerged in a joyous mood and confidently stated to large crowds that Christ had risen from the dead. Some in these crowds had been eyewitnesses to the Crucifixion.

10. These individuals certainly at least *believed* that Jesus had appeared to them after the Crucifixion.

11. His closest followers, the apostles, traveled around the region at great personal cost and risk proclaiming that Jesus had miraculously risen from the dead.

12. The apostles refused to recant their belief, even when threatened with torture and death.

13. At least three went to their deaths rather than renounce or retract their claim that Jesus had risen miraculously from the dead. The apostle Peter, for example, was martyred in Rome.

Note that none of these facts includes the claim that something miraculous happened. It is theoretically possible that all of these claims are true, yet Jesus did not rise from the dead and nothing miraculous happened. The inference to the best explanation that I am about to make does not cover every established fact on the list; some are presented for further study, and some appear in more than one of the arguments to follow in this chapter.

Was the Tomb Found Empty on the Third Day?

Most scholars who study the New Testament documents would add the following claim to the list of facts that are based on reliable historical evidence: the specific tomb in which Jesus was buried was found empty three days after his death.

Again, note that this claim does not by itself include any miraculous element and does not by itself imply that Jesus rose from the dead. Like the previous thirteen points on the list, this claim is well supported by generally accepted historical evidence. Since this point is so crucial to the argument I am about to present, a short discussion is called for. Craig sums up the commonsense argument for the empty tomb, addressed to nonspecialists, in the form of an inference to the best explanation.[3] The empty tomb hypothesis, he argues, is the best overall explanation of the following generally accepted facts.

- The location of the tomb was widely known.
- The belief in the empty tomb flourished in Jerusalem, the city in which Jesus was buried.
- If the tomb had *not* been empty, opponents very probably would have pointed out the fact.
- The apostles very probably would *not* have preached the empty tomb to crowds if the body were lying inside a nearby and well-known tomb.
- Scholars regard Jesus's burial in Joseph of Arimathea's tomb as a well-attested historical fact.
- The historical evidence makes it highly unlikely that Joseph of Arimathea was an invention; the evidence indicates that he was a well-known figure in the Jewish community.
- Jesus's burial is reported in early independent sources appearing in the synoptic Gospels (Matthew, Mark, and Luke).
- Women were not regarded as credible witnesses at the time. Yet women are said to have first discovered the empty tomb.
- One recorded argument against the Christian story was that the Christians had stolen the body—an argument presupposing that the tomb was indeed found empty (Matthew 28:11–15, New American Standard Bible).
- No one on record denied that the tomb was empty. The empty tomb appears to have been assumed by all in the discussions that followed.

Craig argues in detail but with plain reasoning that it is not possible to explain the totality of these points on any reasonable hypothesis other than the supposition that the tomb was indeed empty three days after the Crucifixion.[4]

Now if the empty tomb is the best overall explanation of the historical data just cited, then it is reasonable to conclude that the tomb was indeed found empty. Of course, the mere fact that the tomb was empty does not, by itself, prove that Jesus miraculously rose from the dead. The empty tomb is just one more historical fact in need of explanation, one piece of the puzzle, one piece of the cumulative argument that is forming.

PART 2: EXPLAINING THE EMPTY TOMB

So what is the best explanation of the empty tomb? Is the gospel claim—that Jesus miraculously rose from the dead—the best explanation? Or can the empty tomb be explained naturalistically, that is, without reference to God or to anything supernatural? In the discussion that follows, the well-established historical facts cited above will come into play.

Among the naturalistic attempts to explain the empty tomb, the following eight hypotheses are perhaps the most popular competitors to the gospel claim that Christ miraculously rose from the dead.[5]

1. Jesus was a mere human being. He did not die on the cross; rather, he fainted (swooned) from exhaustion and from the injuries, loss of blood, and pain of the brutal scourging and Crucifixion. Thinking that he had died, the Roman guards took him down and allowed his followers to take his apparently dead body away.

This is the core idea that can be found among a group of hypotheses gathered under the title of the "swoon theory." But what happened next? From here there are many possibilities. An advocate of this theory might add that Jesus's followers mistakenly thought he was dead and buried him in a nearby tomb. Shortly after this, Jesus revived, regained his strength, rolled the covering away, and found his disciples. After convincing them that he had miraculously risen from the dead, he quit his ministry and disappeared into obscurity in a faraway land while his duped followers started a new religion.

If we let our imaginations run wild, many variations are possible. Perhaps after recovering in the tomb, Jesus returned to his followers (who could see that he had not died) and conspired with them to spread the lie that he had miraculously been raised by God from the dead as a "hook" to lure people into joining the new religion. After the fake news had spread, Jesus retired to a remote village to live the rest of his life in obscurity, working quietly as a humble carpenter while others built the new church. (Imagine that Elvis did not die on August 16, 1977, but instead secretly left Graceland, grew a beard, and lived out the rest of his life working unnoticed at a burger joint in Iowa.)

Or perhaps Jesus died from his wounds shortly after the conspiracy formed and was secretly buried and quickly forgotten.

However, many technical problems need to be overcome if you adopt a version of the swoon hypothesis. For instance, Roman guards placed at crucifixions were trained and disciplined killers. They were also merciless. They could tell when someone was dead and when someone had merely fainted or was faking it. They had strict procedures designed to ensure that no one was taken down alive from a cross.

One way a swoon theorist might handle this and related difficulties would be to hypothesize that the followers of Jesus bribed the Roman guards to let them take him down while he was still alive. Or perhaps the guards were secret followers of Jesus in the first place and winked as the followers carried him away alive. Perhaps the guards were drunk. Maybe the disciples ganged up on the guards, beat them up, and forced them to yield. Or perhaps a sympathetic superior officer ordered the guards to cooperate with the disciples.[6]

Assessment. Every version of the swoon theory faces the following formidable problem. It is virtually certain that Jesus physically died on the cross. The *Journal of the American Medical Association* is the most prestigious medical journal in the world. In 1986, it published a study by William D. Edwards, MD; Wesley J. Gabel, MDiv; and Floyd E. Hosmer, MS, AMI, titled, "On the Physical Death of Jesus Christ." These experts concluded:

> Jesus of Nazareth underwent Jewish and Roman trials, was flogged, and was sentenced to death by crucifixion. The scourging produced deep stripelike lacerations and appreciable blood loss, and it probably set the stage for hypovolemic shock, as evidenced by the fact that Jesus was too weakened to carry the crossbar (patibulum) to Golgotha. At the site of crucifixion, his wrists were nailed to the patibulum and, after the patibulum was lifted onto the upright post (stipes), his feet were nailed to the stipes. The major pathophysiologic effect of crucifixion was an interference with normal respirations. Accordingly, death resulted primarily from hypovolemic shock and exhaustion asphyxia. Jesus' death was ensured by the thrust of a soldier's spear into his side. Modern medical interpretation of the historical evidence indicates that Jesus was dead when taken down from the cross.[7]

This medical finding is nothing new. The authors of this study were merely confirming what scholars have known for centuries: from the perspective of medical science, the probability that Jesus survived his Crucifixion is extremely close to zero.

Furthermore, each variation of the swoon hypothesis leaves many things unexplained. Once we assume that Jesus was an ordinary human being, it becomes very hard to believe that after the Crucifixion the guards would not have noticed that he was still alive. It is equally hard to believe that the guards were bribed, drunk, or forced. It is harder still to believe that after a brutal Roman crucifixion a wounded and enfeebled Jesus barely able to walk could have recovered enough to convince his followers that he had risen miraculously from the dead. It is equally hard to explain the post-Resurrection appearances and to explain how his followers could have become so convinced by them that they set out to inform the world at great personal cost and risk of death while Jesus retired in obscurity.

And what would Jesus have done in his secret retirement? It makes no sense to suppose that "he would have gone to live in some remote non-Jewish village and taken no further interest in [the church his apostles were building]."[8] Swinburne asks, "Is it really plausible to suppose he would have taken no further interest in the mushrooming movement which his Passion and apparent Resurrection had inspired?"[9] Given what we know of him from the Gospels, "would he really have colluded for the rest of his life with a massive deception and a phony religion?"[10] Swinburne argues that on the basis of our background knowledge of human nature and the way the world works, it is extremely unlikely that any version of the swoon hypothesis is true.

Going still further, if we adopt a swoon hypothesis, then we cannot credibly explain the dramatic change in the behavior of the disciples after the Crucifixion, established facts 5 and 9 on the list, of which more below. And of course, the evidence that Jesus was taken from the cross and buried directly in a well-known tomb owned by Joseph of Arimathea—a tomb sealed by Roman guards—counts against all swoon hypotheses.

Of course, all kinds of improbable, unsupported, and imaginative clauses can be added to any swoon hypothesis to explain all the various data. For instance, to explain the vivid post-Resurrection experiences, we could suppose that Jesus recovered from his horrendous wounds in record time and looked positively glorified a few days later, that he was an excellent actor (and a good deceiver), and that the disciples had very poor vision. To explain the claim that after the Crucifixion Jesus hid himself away and took no further interest in the movement he had started, we could suppose that he escaped to a remote location such as India and took up birdwatching as a hobby to replace the intense activity of his ministry. To explain the behavior of the disciples immediately after the Crucifixion and their dramatic change a few days later, we could assume that the disciples were lying deceivers, or we could assume that they were the victims of a mass hallucination. I'll examine these proposals shortly.

However, the more clauses we add to any swoon hypothesis, the more complicated the theory becomes, which in turn makes the simpler Christian explanation more and more reasonable. I am employing Ockham's razor here — the principle that when two hypotheses explain the same data, the simpler hypothesis, the one with fewer assumptions, is the more reasonable of the two. With all of its necessary qualifications, the more complicated swoon hypothesis, on the basis of the total evidence, is far less likely than the Christian explanation. Swinburne adds that in view of what we know of Jesus's moral character from the New Testament, the various swoon theories become even less likely.[11] This point deserves a moment of further reflection.

Recall an idea raised in the previous chapter. The disciples were followers of a person universally acknowledged to be one of the greatest ethical teachers in history. Furthermore, the authors of the Gospels placed his stunning moral principles at the center of their message. It is very hard to believe that students and advocates of such a high morality were conniving liars engaged in a conspiracy to create a phony religion based on known falsehoods. The question raised by Josh and Sean McDowell is worth recalling in this context: "Are we to believe that some of the world's greatest ethical teachings came from unethical people? While possible, this hardly seems the most reasonable conclusion. Secondly, there's no reason to suggest that they had motives for material or societal gain."[12]

2. Jesus died and was buried. However, without realizing it, the disciples accidentally went to the wrong tomb, which was empty, and concluded that the burial tomb was empty.

This hypothesis leaves many things unexplained. Wouldn't the owner of the tomb, Joseph of Arimathea, have spotted the mistake and informed

> The swoon theory was first put forward in the late eighteenth century by a small group of German scholars that included Karl Friedrich Bahrdt (1741–92), Karl Venturini (1768–1849), and Heinrich Eberhard Gottlob Paulus (1761–1851). Variations appeared in the nineteenth century. However, by the end of the nineteenth century, the theory had been thoroughly rejected by serious historians. The swoon theory circulates now mainly in popular internet discussions, student papers, and pop culture books.[13] It is not considered a realistic option by serious academic scholars today.

the disciples? There is no recorded tradition with this theme. Wouldn't others have checked out the real tomb to see for themselves if it was empty? New Testament scholars agree that the burial site was no secret and was probably located not far from the place of the Crucifixion. The philosopher William Paley, in his eighteenth-century defense of Christianity, made interesting observations that bear on the point. Christianity could not have come into existence in Jerusalem, he argued, if the body lay in a nearby tomb whose location was known by many, including many who had witnessed the Crucifixion, for the opponents or Roman authorities would probably have produced the body to refute the Christian claims.[14]

In addition, given our knowledge of human nature, could the disciples really have believed strongly in Jesus's Resurrection, which they certainly did, if the body lay dead in a nearby tomb visible and known to many? This hypothesis not only leaves unexplained the dramatic change in the demeanor of the disciples, it also leaves the credible post-Resurrection appearances unexplained. These data points would then need separate explanations, making this naturalistic explanation much more complicated and disjointed than the simpler and more unified Christian account.[15]

3. Enemies of the Christians stole the body so that it could not be used to start a new religious cult.

If enemies had stolen the body, what would they probably have done after the Christian church began to grow? Being enemies, wouldn't they have revealed the truth in order to show everyone that the new religion was a fraud? Moreland argues:

If the enemies of Jesus had stolen his body, they could have produced it or alluded to the fact that they had taken it. No evidence exists that [opponents] ever used this strategy against the early church. Their only counterargument implies that they did not take Jesus's body (see Matt. 28:11–15). No motive could possibly suggest itself for such a silence if, in fact, they had taken it. [16]

Indeed, the author of the Gospel according to Matthew writes:

While the women were on their way, some of the guards went into the city and reported to the chief priests everything that had happened. When the chief priests had met with the elders and devised a plan, they gave the soldiers a large sum of money, telling them, "You are to say, 'His disciples came during the night and stole him away while we were asleep.' If this report gets to the governor, we will satisfy him and keep you out of trouble." So the soldiers took the money and did as they were instructed. And this story has been widely circulated . . . to this very day. (Matthew 28:11–15, New International Version)

This hypothesis has further problems. First, it leaves unexplained the dramatic post-Easter change in the disciples. Second, it cannot account for the post-Resurrection appearances of the risen Christ. And again, if separate naturalistic clauses are added to cover these facts, then we are left with a naturalistic account that is far more complicated and less unified than the simpler and more integrated Christian explanation. Ockham's razor again comes into play.

Some suggest that this hypothesis can be rescued by adding the following supplement. Perhaps enemies stole the body and then decided that exposing the lies of the Jesus movement was not worth the bother. After all, Christianity was a small religion when it began. The enemies might have decided to just ignore it and let it die out. The problem here, of course, is that this suggestion leaves unexplained the post-Resurrection appearances and the dramatic change in the conduct of the disciples, among other things.

Some critics focus on and reject the apologetical claim that *if* enemies had stolen Jesus's body, they would later have produced it to prove that the new religion was based on fraud and trickery. The critics' argument is that bodies decay rapidly, so the corpse would probably have been unrecognizable just a week or two after the Crucifixion.[17]

But wouldn't the demands to produce the body have started within days? And bodies certainly do not decay *that* fast. Groothuis's reply to the objection sounds sensible.

> But this is far from certain. Even if Jesus' face were decomposed at this point to some degree . . . his physique, hair color, and crucifixion wounds would still be visible and recognizable. Moreover, the burden of proof would have been placed on the disciples to show that this was not Jesus. But we have no indication that anything like this ever occurred.[18]

4. Grave robbers stole the body.

Although grave robbing was common, Swinburne writes that grave robbers "would have identified themselves to the Jewish leaders in the reasonable hope of being rewarded for this information." More importantly, "grave robbers were not interested in bodies, only in valuables put in graves."[19]

Craig argues, "We know of no third party with a motive to steal the body. Robbers had no reason to break into the tomb, since nothing of value was interred with the body, nor would they have carried away the dead man's body."[20]

In addition, like the previous hypothesis, this one does not explain the post-Easter appearances of the risen Christ, which would then need a separate explanation. Nor does it explain the dramatic change in the behavior of the disciples after the first Easter (mentioned in fact 9).[21]

5. The disciples stole the body from the tomb and then lied when they announced that Jesus had risen. In short, the whole Resurrection story was a deliberate hoax.

Many people are attracted to conspiracy theories these days. But this one is extremely implausible, given our background knowledge of conspiracies and human nature. First, conspiracies typically unravel over time as one conspirator after another breaks their silence and turns against their fellow conspirators. People break from conspiracies for many reasons, some because of feelings of shame, others out of a desire for notoriety or gain. Some might break away seeking revenge against those who ensared them in the first place. Feelings of guilt is another reason some might break from a conspiracy: they know they were wrong to participate and want to repent and warn others of the evil operation. But nothing like this happened in the case of the early church.

Moreland reflects:

> If the empty tomb and resurrection was a fabrication, why did not at least one of the disciples break away from the rest and start his own version of Christianity? Or why did not at least one of them reveal the fraudulent nature of the whole enterprise? If bad motivation was involved in the fabrication, one is hard pressed to explain the continued unity of the early leaders, in light of the human tendency to want to promote oneself. The assumption that they were all committed to the truth of their message is the only adequate explanation of their continued unity and the lack of any revelation of fraud.[22]

And isn't it part of our background information, Moreland adds, that "those who lie for personal gain do not stick together very long, especially when hardship decreases the benefits"?[23]

Michael Rota offers an additional consideration when he points out that the followers of Jesus had no incentive to lie and make up a new religion. Not only were there great costs; there was no profit to be made.

> People lie when they have an incentive or reason to lie. And here the incentives are all wrong. Proclaiming the resurrection of Jesus exposed the early Christians to ridicule, abuse and mortal danger. Jesus' teachings had led to his torture and crucifixion, and the earliest disciples would have known that more of the same would likely be in store for them if they continued to proclaim his teachings, challenging as they were to existing religions and the power of Rome. Moreover, Paul, Peter and the other apostles appear to have benefited little, in worldly terms, from their leadership positions in the new religion of Christianity. This stands in stark contrast to the experiences of the founders of many other religions.[24]

Consider the apostle Peter. Is it reasonable to believe that he gave up his career in commercial fishing, knowingly traveled around the Mediterranean for years lying about Jesus, and then accepted a horrible death by crucifixion in Rome rather than recant his story—all for a lie? Other close followers of Jesus spent the rest of their lives after the Crucifixion proclaiming the news that Jesus had risen from the dead, giving up everything in the process and in many cases facing terrible persecution. Again, isn't it part of our general knowledge of human nature that rational people don't usually sacrifice so much for something they know is a lie? The lying conspiracy theory is "extremely implausible in view of the readiness of the first Christian leaders to die for their faith."[25]

In the eighteenth century, Paley added interesting thoughts to the case against the liar hypothesis: "Would men in such circumstances pretend to have seen what they never saw; assert facts which they had no knowledge of, go about lying to teach virtue, and, though not only convinced of Christ's being an imposter, but having seen . . . his crucifixion, and so persist, as to bring upon themselves, for nothing, and with full knowledge of the consequence, enmity and hatred, danger and death?"[26]

Moreland cites another consideration: the followers of Jesus were Jewish theists. "It seems easy, for a modern agnostic, to think about making up a new religion for gain. But to a first century Jew, such an act was tantamount to lying against the God of Israel. . . . Lying against God and perverting his revelation would mean risking the damnation of one's soul to hell."[27] No first-century Jew in his right mind, argues Moreland, would risk damnation "for a few years of prestige as a leader of a new [and phony] religion."[28] In addition,

> the disciples had nothing to gain by lying and starting a new religion. They faced hardship, hostility, and martyrs' deaths. In light of this, they could have never sustained such unwavering motivation if they knew what they were preaching was a lie. The disciples were not fools and Paul was a cool-headed intellectual of the first rank. There would have been many opportunities over three or four decades of ministry to reconsider and renounce the lie.[29]

This "lying liars" hypothesis has yet more problems. The picture we get of Jesus in the Gospels "was not in keeping with [then] current conceptions of what the Messiah was expected to be like, which was a theocratic ruler who would deliver Israel from Gentile oppression." Craig notes that ordinary Jews "had no idea of a Messiah who dies and then rises from the dead but does not conquer the world."[30] Devout Jews, he argues, would not make up a story like this.

Yet another fact cited by Craig casts doubt on the lying conspiracy hypothesis: the Gospels were written and proclaimed in close proximity to the events they described.

> Anyone who cared to could have checked out the accuracy of what they reported. The fact that the disciples were able to proclaim the resurrection in Jerusalem in the face of their enemies a few weeks after the crucifixion shows that what they proclaimed was true, for they could never have proclaimed the resurrection under such circumstances had it not occurred.[31]

Now we go back to fact 6. According to the Gospels, women were among the first to find the empty tomb. Craig argues that this in itself is a good reason to doubt that the disciples made the story up, for women were not considered credible witnesses. If the disciples were making the whole thing up, surely they would not have made women the ones who discovered the key piece of evidence.

One last point deserves consideration. As many commentators have noted, the gospel account of the empty tomb is plain. A made-up story would likely have many embellishments. For instance, good storytellers could have presented Jesus appearing to the high priest, to the Roman emperor, or to crowds all around Jerusalem. Craig raises a number of good questions. If you were creating an elaborate hoax, would you make it as simple and unadorned as the gospel account? Or would you make men the ones to discover the empty tomb? Would you add some exciting twists and turns to the story, such as an appearance of the risen Christ to Pilate, who then becomes a closet believer? For many reasons, the lying conspiracy hypothesis is very improbable.

6. A Syrian brown bear frightened the guards, pushed the rock away, broke into the tomb, unwrapped the body, and dragged it away. The bear escaped undetected because a dust storm covered its tracks.

Students have suggested this hypothesis during class discussions.

7. Jesus's body was taken down from the cross, thrown into a common graveyard, and lost.

Neither this nor the previous hypothesis can explain most of the agreed-upon facts already cited, such as the known location of the tomb, the dramatic change in the behavior of the apostles, and the well-established post-Resurrection appearances.

8. Unbeknownst to history, Jesus had a twin brother who grew up in another family, isolated from Jesus. After many years, the non-Jesus twin finally went to Jerusalem to meet his long-lost brother. Unfortunately, he arrived at the moment of the Crucifixion. A few days later, realizing he had a golden opportunity, he decided to impersonate Jesus and pretend that *he* had risen from the dead. This is one version of the "evil twin" theory.

I leave it to the reader to assess the logical plausibility of this imaginative account.

These are the naturalistic hypotheses most often claimed by critics of Christianity to be more plausible than the Christian account. If each one leaves too many facts unexplained and if the verified facts as a whole are explained more reasonably and more simply by the Christian explanation—that Jesus miraculously rose from the dead three days after the Crucifixion—then that is a commonsense reason to accept the traditional Christian claim.[32]

John Dominic Crossan

John Dominic Crossan is an example of a noted biblical scholar who strongly favors naturalistic over supernaturalistic explanations. In *Jesus: A Revolutionary Biography*, he states matter-of-factly that the followers of Jesus "created" the burial and Resurrection accounts in order to make their story fit prophecy they found in the Hebrew scriptures.[33] After discussing certain dilemmas the disciples probably faced after the Crucifixion, Crossan continues, "The first problem was how to create a story in which Jesus was buried by his friends. If they had power, they were not his friends; if they were his friends, they had no power. Mark 15:42–46 solves that dilemma by creating one Joseph of Arimathea."[34]

On the next page we learn that "Matthew and Luke, each using Mark as a source, try to improve on that creation."[35] What actually happened, according to Crossan, is that after the Crucifixion, Jesus's body was either "left on the cross or [placed] in a shallow grave barely covered with dirt and stones" to eventually be eaten by wild dogs and other scavenging animals.[36] Nothing miraculous occurs on Crossan's naturalistic account of the death and burial of Jesus. In particular, no miraculous resurrection from the dead.

Crossan also prefers naturalistic explanations when it comes to explaining the gospel reports of Jesus miraculously healing the sick and disabled. In the same book, he draws a distinction between a disease and an illness. Disease is the biological "malfunctioning" of some part of the body. Illness is the "psychosocial" experience associated with a disease, including the personal and social responses to those with that disease. Thus, a medical cure for AIDs would heal the disease itself; a refusal to ostracize and condemn those with AIDs and acts of empathetic understanding and abiding respect and love toward those stricken with the disease would heal the *illness*. With this distinction in hand, Crossan explains in a strictly naturalistic way the accounts of Jesus healing the sick and disabled.

> The leper who met Jesus had both a disease (say, psoriasis) and an illness, the personal and social stigma of uncleanness, isolation, and rejection.... Was he curing the disease through an intervention in the physical world, or was he healing the illness through an intervention in the social world? I presume that Jesus, who did not and could not cure that disease or any other one, healed the poor man's illness by refusing to accept the disease's ritual uncleanness and social ostracization. Jesus thereby forced others either to reject him from their community or to accept the leper within it as well. Since, however, we are ever dealing with the politic body, that act quite deliberately impugns the rights and prerogatives of society's boundary keepers and controllers. By healing the illness without curing the disease, Jesus acted as an alternative boundary keeper in a way subversive to the established procedures of his society.[37]

All of which raises the question: What led Crossan to so strongly favor naturalistic explanations? In chapter 6, we examined the role that background beliefs play in the evaluation of evidence. That discussion suggests that philosophical presuppositions might have led Crossan to favor the naturalistic over the miraculous. Crossan's philosophical views are brought out in a famous debate he had with William Lane Craig that aired on WGN radio, Chicago, in March 1995.[38] During the exchange, Craig quotes public statements Crossan has made indicating his philosophical predilections—statements Crossan does not repudiate in the debate. For instance, "God does not act directly for me, physically, in the world in the sense in which the miracles taken literally would seem" and "I myself... do not believe that there are personal, supernatural spirits."[39]

Now, I am sure that Crossan, who is a theist and also a professing Christian, albeit of a very liberal kind, has reasons for his philosophical beliefs. The man is a serious scholar. The point, however, is that philosophical presumptions appear to motivate his strong inclination to favor naturalistic explanations at almost any cost.

PART 3: EXPLAINING THE DRAMATIC CHANGE IN THE DISCIPLES

Let's go back to verified facts 5 and 9. Reliable historical data indicates that after the Crucifixion, the disciples were terribly despondent and frightened. With their hopes crushed, they hid themselves away. Suddenly, shortly after the first Easter Sunday, they emerged into the public square giving bold and confident speeches proclaiming Christ's Resurrection. How are we to explain this dramatic change in the disciples, who "went from the depths of despair and doubt to a joyful certainty of such height that they preached the resurrection openly and boldly and suffered bravely for it."[40]

Many historians have observed that the Christian movement probably could not have gotten off the ground unless its founders had strong and deeply felt beliefs. But where did these beliefs come from, if not from the direct observation of real events?

The historian Pinchas Lapide puts the issue this way. One minute the disciples were a frightened group of men in hiding; the next minute they turned into a confident mission society convinced of salvation and able to work with much more success after Easter than before Easter. . . . No vision or hallucination is sufficient to explain such a revolutionary transformation. For a sect or school or order, perhaps a single vision would have been sufficient—but not for a world religion which was able to conquer the Occident thanks to the Easter faith.[41]

Again, what could plausibly explain the well-documented dramatic emotional change in the disciples other than the miraculous events they claimed to have actually witnessed?

PART 4: EXPLAINING THE POST-RESURRECTION APPEARANCES

The reports of Christ's appearances after the Crucifixion deserve a closer look. Given the extremely low probability that the apostles were all liars engaged in a massive conspiracy, how are we to explain the statements of those who sincerely testified that Jesus had appeared to them in person after the Resurrection? Some critics have offered naturalistic accounts. Gerd Ludemann writes, "One must understand the appearance to the more than five hundred brothers at one time as the report of a mass ecstasy that took place in the early period of the community."[42] Ludemann is one of many who explain the reported appearances of the risen Christ as mere hallucinations.

However, all hallucination theories face severe problems. Moreland notes that "some of the claimed appearances were to a single person; one was to a group of five hundred. . . . [T]hey are reported to have taken place during a very specific period of forty days. After this, however, they end abruptly, except for some appearances to the apostle Paul."[43] Furthermore, "the appearances don't just happen to believers. It is true that everyone who saw an appearance recorded in the New Testament became a believer, but they were not necessarily believers at the time of the appearance. Several of the Twelve were unbelieving even after one appearance."[44]

It is extremely improbable, Moreland argues, that the appearances were hallucinations, for many claimed to see Jesus at the same time, and "it is extremely unlikely that two or more people would have the same hallucination at the same time."[45] After examining documented cases of real psychological hallucinations, Moreland argues that accounts of the post-Resurrection appearances of Christ do not have the same characteristics.[46]

The philosopher Stephen Davis adds that hallucinations normally tend to affect a particular type of person, but a wide variety of people reported that they actually saw the risen Christ.[47] Such facts are hard to explain if we suppose that the appearances were all simply hallucinations.[48]

In addition, Rota argues that "hallucinations among healthy people do sometimes occur in situations of bereavement . . . [but they] don't lead to a firm belief that the deceased spouse has been resurrected." More importantly, "if the resurrection appearances were hallucinations, then the disciples experienced group hallucinations. For each of the three group appearances mentioned by Paul ('the twelve,' the 'more than five hundred,' and 'all the apostles'), those involved would have had to each experience a determinate, convincing hallucination with similar content at the same time. This is monumentally unlikely."[49]

Of course, if the appearances were veridical, that would explain all the facts cited above—facts left unexplained by the hallucination theory. The argument against the hallucination theory is an inference to the best explanation.

PART 5: THE HIGH COST OF DISCIPLESHIP

This is another point that deserves emphasis. Recall that the apostles refused to recant their belief in the risen Christ even when threatened with terrible consequences. Some actually went to their deaths rather than renounce their claim that Jesus had risen from the dead. Again, isn't it common sense that a large group of rational people is not normally going to give up their careers, suffer persecution, and even risk death for the sake of something they know is a lie? Is it reasonable to believe that the apostles were conspirators perpetrating a gigantic hoax at great personal cost and risk and for little or no material gain?

Against this possibility, history reveals that large conspiracies tend to unravel over time as members exit to tell the truth. The Mafia is a contemporary example. And a large conspiracy in which the members are suffering greatly for their lie, with no incentive to lie, and with no foreseeable profit, would seem to be the kind of conspiracy most likely to unravel. Yet when scholars, such as the historian and sociologist Rodney Stark, study the birth and early history of Christianity in depth, they find no evidence of a giant conspiracy unraveling.[50]

A GREMLIN OBJECTION TO THE OVERALL ARGUMENT OF THIS CHAPTER

Someone might object to the argument of this chapter as follows: Yes, the Christian account of the Resurrection is by far the most likely explanation, of all the explanations offered. However, the inference to the best explanation argument of this chapter assumes that someone cannot reject the Resurrection unless they already have an alternative explanation of what happened that is at least as good as the Christian explanation. But this is wrong, the objection continues. For in everyday life, when something highly unusual happens and we can't think of a good explanation, we may nevertheless reject suggested explanations on the basis of our background knowledge alone—even though we lack an explanation.

For instance, as you prepare to leave for work, you can't find your keys anywhere. Although you have no good explanation for why they are missing, you know they were not stolen by a squad of tiny gremlins. That hypothesis is ruled out by your background knowledge alone—even if you have no alternative explanation and are totally at a loss as to what happened. Unless someone produces a lot of evidence for the gremlin theory, the right thing to say is, "I'm not sure what happened to my keys; it's just weird."

Likewise, so the objection continues, a reasonable response to the gospel story is simply to say, "I can't think of a good explanation. I'm just not sure what happened. Despite the general reliability of the gospel texts, maybe the gospel writers got this part of the story wrong and we'll never know what really happened. I'm totally at a loss."[51]

This is a strong objection, but I believe it is based on a mistake. Consider again the lost keys. Yes, even without an alternative explanation, you can rule out the gremlin theory on the basis of your background knowledge alone. Before the keys went missing, you already knew that gremlins don't exist and therefore that gremlins don't sometimes steal keys. And you can reject the gremlin hypothesis even though you are at a loss and cannot think of an alternative explanation to account for the lost keys.

However, I submit that our logical relation to the gospel story of the Resurrection is radically different. As I argued in chapters 2, 3, and 4, our background information includes strong reasons to believe that God exists. It is also reasonable to suppose that God has good reason to intervene in history to help mankind, given the awful mess humans have made of things. And it is also logical to suppose that God would mark his intervention with a notable miracle, both to get our attention and to place a stamp of authority on the intervention. These background considerations alone raise the likelihood that the Christian account is a credible explanation and not a fantastical one.

Furthermore, as I argued in chapter 6, not only can miracles, at least in principle, be confirmed by sufficient circumstantial evidence; they are actually expected given that God exists and given the mess we humans have made of things. At a minimum, I contend, this justifies looking further into the details to see if the Christian account turns out to be the overall best explanation of the data, all things considered. Which is what we are doing in this book.

Now return to the case of the missing keys. Suppose that while you are looking everywhere for them, a trusted friend in full possession of their faculties and with no reason to lie calls and tells you something strange. "At the party last night," your friend says, "one of the guests confessed that he had an uncontrollable compulsion to steal people's keys, and he said he was especially attracted to key chains like yours." Three others who were present at the party confirm the testimony. Given your background knowledge (that keys do not disappear into thin air and that gremlins do not exist), this new information gives you an *obvious* solution to the puzzle: the compulsive key stealer took the keys. If the new explanation is supported by enough circumstantial evidence and if no other explanation explains the facts overall, the key stealer hypothesis is the obvious choice.

I contend that our logical situation with respect to the gospel story of the Resurrection is strongly analogous. Our review of Hume's argument shows, I believe, that highly improbable events can be confirmed by a combination of different lines of circumstantial evidence. Next, given our background knowledge (that God exists, that God has reason to intervene in history to help mankind, that God would mark his intervention with a miracle, that miracles are expected, etc.) and given the sum total of all the circumstantial evidence, the Christian account stands out above all the others as the obvious solution. And if it is, then the burden of proof shifts to those who reject it. Their burden is to produce an explanation that accounts for a broader array of facts. Certainly none of the naturalistic explanations we surveyed does the job.

To put it another way, I am claiming here that *if* you agree that God exists, that God has good reasons to intervene and would mark his intervention with a notable miracle, that miracles are expected and can at least in principle be confirmed on the basis of circumstantial evidence, and so forth, then the Christian account stands out above all the others as the obvious solution, upon a fair appraisal of all the historical and circumstantial evidence.

Going further, I submit that the following principle of explanation is reasonable: If we have important data in need of explanation and after serious and wide-ranging research one explanation stands out as the most obvious explanation of all the data, then it is our logical duty as rational beings to accept that explanation. I admit that this is a pretty convoluted principle. Here is the short form: After a serious and wide-ranging investigation of all the evidence and the most plausible alternative explanations, it would be irrational to reject the most obvious explanation consistent with our background information for no good reason. Science would not exist if no one followed this principle or one very much like it. Imagine Einstein saying, "My general theory of relativity is by far the best explanation of all the data, out of all the most plausible theories available, and my theory is the obvious solution, but I am going to shelve it and leave gravity an unexplained mystery." The principle of explanation that I am suggesting is also employed in every academic subject, not just in theoretical physics. We employ it constantly in everyday life too, whether we realize it or not. I see no good reason why it does not also apply in the case of the Christian claim that Jesus Christ rose miraculously from the dead three days after his Crucifixion.[52]

CONCLUDING REFLECTION

In this chapter, we've seen that many modern scholars are inclined to favor naturalistic over supernaturalistic explanations when interpreting the Gospels. In some cases, this inclination is so strong that it leads them to adopt a naturalistic explanation even when the Christian account explains many more facts and does so in a simpler and more obvious way. What motivates this modern tendency to favor the natural and resist the supernatural? I contend that this inclination, or bias, is ultimately due to the philosophical views some biblical scholars bring to the subject.

If you do not believe that God or anything supernatural exists, then you will consider only naturalistic explanations of phenomena. Supernatural explanations will be ruled out from the start. If you believe that miracles are impossible, then your attitude toward miracle claims will be the same. And you will have the same bias toward the natural and away from the supernatural if you agree with Hume that it is never reasonable to believe that a miracle has occurred.

On the other hand, suppose you hold that God exists, that divine intervention is expected given the mess we humans have made of things, and that God would likely put a stamp of authority on the intervention with a notable miracle that can in principle be confirmed by circumstantial evidence. You will then be open to the possibility that the gospel writers were simply telling the truth as best they could about the life, teachings, death, and bodily resurrection of Jesus Christ. The case for Christianity presented here, I contend, is common sense combined with a realistic view of human nature. Religious experience, as well as faith formation, may also play a role when an individual concludes, perhaps after quite a journey, that the Christian message is actually true.[53]

I am suggesting that the philosophical commitments a scholar brings to the study of scripture explain a good deal of the difference between those who take the Gospels in full—miracle claims and all—as serious historical evidence for the Christian faith and those who either reject them outright or accept them minus the miraculous claims. This is why the philosophical arguments we have examined in this book are part of the case for Christianity.

I further contend that if the theistic arguments we have examined in this book are sound, then two things follow. First, it is reasonable to accept a supernatural explanation when it is the most reasonable explanation of all the data. Second, the truth of the Christian claim, that Jesus rose miraculously from the dead three days after the Crucifixion, follows when commonsense reasoning is applied to the relevant historical evidence combined with a realistic view of human nature.

The overall argument of this book is therefore cumulative: the case grows from the first chapter to the last, with the arguments of this chapter resting ultimately on all the arguments preceding it, including the philosophical ones. In this book, philosophy and the Socratic method take their place at the core of the Christian apologetical enterprise.

So what is the best overall explanation of the accepted historical facts we've examined? Is it the foundational Christian claim that Jesus rose miraculously from the dead? Does this conclusion tie all the information together in the simplest way so as to make the best overall sense of the facts at hand? Or is one of the naturalistic hypotheses a more reasonable explanation?

It is a fact that Jesus founded a religion and made the apostle Peter the first head of that church. Was the Resurrection of Jesus God's stamp of approval on the new religion? Does the evidence as a whole support the claims to divinity that Jesus made, according to the authors of the books of the New Testament? Or is there a better explanation for all the relevant facts considered as a whole? The question combines philosophy, ancient history, textual exegesis, common sense, and inference to the best explanation.

When reflecting on this issue, it is good to keep in mind that the Gospels were written to offer to ordinary people commonsense evidence that Jesus was indeed miraculously raised from the dead, appeared in person to many after his bodily death, and founded a church.

Many say that the Resurrection can be accepted as a matter of faith but not as a matter of history or reason. However, if the overall argument suggested in this chapter is solid, then the Resurrection can be accepted in faith and at the same time with confirmation from history, reason, and common sense as well.

FOR FURTHER STUDY

Bauckham, Richard. *Jesus and the Eyewitnesses: The Gospels as Eyewitness Testimony*. 2nd ed. Grand Rapids, MI: Eerdmans, 2017.

Copan, Paul, ed. *Will the Real Jesus Please Stand Up? A Debate between William Lane Craig and John Dominic Crossan*. Grand Rapids, MI: Baker Books, 1998.

Copan, Paul, and Ronald K. Tacelli, eds. *Jesus' Resurrection: Fact or Figment? A Debate between William Lane Craig and Gerd Ludemann*. Downers Grove, IL: InterVarsity Press, 2000.

Davis, Stephen T. *Risen Indeed: Making Sense of the Resurrection*. Grand Rapids, MI: Eerdmans, 1993.

Habermas, Gary R. *On the Resurrection*. Vol. 1: *Evidences*. Brentwood, TN: B & H Academic, 2024.

———. *Risen Indeed: A Historical Investigation into the Resurrection of Jesus*. Bellingham, WA: Lexham Academic, 2022.

Habermas, Gary R., and Michael Licona. *The Case for the Resurrection of Jesus*. Grand Rapids, MI: Kregel, 2004.

Licona, Michael. *The Resurrection of Jesus: A New Historiographical Approach*. Downers Grove, IL: InterVarsity Press, 2010.

McDowell, Josh, and Sean McDowell. *Evidence for the Resurrection: What It Means for Your Relationship with God*. Grand Rapids, MI: Baker Books, 2008.

McDowell, Sean. *The Fate of the Apostles*. New York: Routledge, 2016.

Rota, Michael. *Taking Pascal's Wager: Faith, Evidence, and the Abundant Life*. Downers Grove, IL: InterVarsity Press. 2006.

Stewart, Robert B., ed. *The Resurrection of Jesus: John Dominic Crossan and N. T. Wright in Dialogue*. Minneapolis: Fortress Press, 2006.

Swinburne, Richard. *The Resurrection of God Incarnate*. New York: Oxford University Press, 2003.

———. *Was Jesus God?* New York: Oxford University Press, 2008.

Wright, N. T. *The Resurrection of the Son of God*. Vol. 3: *Christian Origins and the Question of God*. New York: Fortress Press, 2003.

For skeptical and alternative views on the Resurrection

Baigent, Michael. *The Jesus Papers: Exposing the Greatest Cover-Up in History*. New York: HarperSan Francisco, 2007.

Crossan, John Dominic. *Jesus: A Revolutionary Biography*. New York: HarperOne, 2009.

D'Costa, Gavin, ed. *Resurrection Reconsidered*. Oxford: Oneworld, 1994.

Ehrman, Bart. *How Jesus Became God: The Exaltation of a Jewish Preacher from Galilee*. New York: HarperOne, 2014.

Joyce, Donovan. *The Jesus Scroll*. Melbourne, Australia: Ferrell Books, 1972.

Martin, Michael. *The Case against Christianity*. Philadelphia: Temple University Press, 1991.

Schonfield, Hugh J. *The Passover Plot: A New Interpretation of the Life and Death of Jesus*. New York: Bantam, 1965.

Shapiro, Larry. *The Miracle Myth: Why Belief in the Resurrection and the Supernatural Is Unjustified*. New York: Columbia University Press, 2016.

NINE

Reason to the Best Explanation

The case for the Christian faith that I have been making in this book contains many separate lines of inference to the best explanation reasoning. Considered together, these arguments add up to a cumulative case argument for Christianity generally conceived. As I mentioned in chapter 1, we are all familiar with this kind of reasoning. Each time you consider a group of facts and decide what to conclude by thinking about what would best explain those facts, you make an inference to the best explanation. Most of what we believe about the world is based on inference to the best explanation reasoning. And almost every day we see separate arguments woven together into a cumulative overall case in courtroom trials and crime scene investigations covered on TV. An imaginative example will add a final bit of clarity to the idea.

DISCOVERING ANCIENT TEMPLES

The Oxford University philosopher Basil Mitchell (1917–2011) illustrates the concept of a cumulative case argument with the following thought experiment.[1] Imagine that two explorers hiking deep in a remote forest come upon a series of depressions in the ground. Looking at the uneven lay of the land, the first explorer thinks he sees a pattern. The depressions form what looks like a square. He proposes this hypothesis: the dips in the ground were left by the pillars of an ancient temple.

The first explorer is doing what all human beings do—trying to make sense of the world by forming hypotheses. The temple hypothesis, if true, would explain the depressions. The second explorer shakes his head. He thinks the depressions are merely random dips with no significance whatsoever. He sees no need to formulate a hypothesis. The dips are there, they are random, and that is all there is to it. No further explanation is needed.

However, the first explorer is not content to leave the dents as unexplained or "brute" facts.[2] Something about them beckons him to look further. After examining the area more closely, he begins to uncover additional things. First, he finds a rock that looks like it might have once been part of a pillar.

Of course, one piece of evidence usually never proves a hypothesis. Considered all by itself, this one unusually shaped rock does not prove anything. It might be only a coincidence that it is shaped like part of a temple's pillar. Its shape may be due to nothing but random forces of nature. However, the added evidence raises slightly the probability that the temple hypothesis is true.

Now the first explorer finds a chunk of marble that looks like it broke off an ancient statue. This too might be a pure coincidence. Certainly, this one piece of evidence—considered in isolation—doesn't prove that a temple once stood on the spot. But this additional piece of evidence raises the probability that the hypothesis is true. As he finds more pieces of marble, the explorer feels more confidence in his theory.

Mitchell observes that each item of evidence is an element in an interpretation, or explanation, of the depressions seen in the ground. Although any one item of evidence proves nothing, in the end, after much evidence has been collected, it may be that the best overall explanation of the depressions, and all the other discoveries, is that a temple once stood on the spot. The explorer's case grows with each new piece of evidence. At some point, if enough data are best explained by one hypothesis and if the data as a whole cannot be adequately explained any other way, the hypothesis qualifies as the *best explanation*. If a hypothesis is the best explanation of all the accumulated evidence, that is a good reason to believe it is true.

Keep in mind that best explanation arguments do not claim that the conclusion *must* be true with complete mathematical certainty. Rather, they claim that the conclusion is so probable that it is the most reasonable conclusion to draw based on the evidence.

In the opening chapter, I suggested that cumulative case arguments can be compared to lengths of rope. One thin strand of fiber may not support much weight, but when the fibers are interlaced or woven together, the rope that is produced may support a great deal of weight. Likewise, a single piece of evidence or a single argument considered in isolation from the rest of the case may not prove much, but when all the evidence and reasoning is interlaced and considered as a whole, the resulting argument may be logically compelling. Put another way, the weight of the evidence might eventually accumulate to show that the conclusion is true beyond reasonable doubt.

FINAL QUESTIONS

Time to sum up. What conclusion should a reasonable person draw if it is eminently reasonable to believe that God exists, if miracles are actually expected if God exists, if a life after bodily death is prefigured in the human soul, if the books of the New Testament are historically reliable when judged by the usual standards of historical research, and if the most logical explanation of the historical data is that Jesus Christ did indeed rise miraculously from the dead three days after his Crucifixion? Going further, if there are sensible responses to the major philosophical objections that have been raised against belief, is the Resurrection of Jesus evidence that God placed a seal of endorsement on the new religion that began with the preaching of Peter and Paul in Judea during the first century AD? What is the best overall explanation of the many lines of data we have examined in this book?

I realize that these are intellectual questions. Perhaps reason alone doesn't prove the Christian message true with sufficient certainty. Maybe it only points the way, leaving the next step not only to the intellect but also to the heart, the will, and perhaps support from friends, God's grace, or whatever it is in life that eventually leads the soul toward the end of the journey, which Christians believe is God as revealed through Jesus Christ.

FOR FURTHER STUDY

Bible. Many translations and editions are available. Examples follow.

Barker, Kenneth L., Mark L. Strauss, Jeannine K. Brown, Craig L. Blomberg, and Michael Williams. *New International Version Study Bible*. Fully rev. ed. Grand Rapids, MI: Zondervan, 2020.

Bellinger, W. H., Jr., and Todd D. Still, eds. *Baylor Annotated Study Bible*. Waco, TX: Baylor University Press, 2019.

Coogan, Michael, Marc Brettler, Carol Newsom, et al., eds. *New Oxford Annotated Bible with Apocrypha: New Revised Standard Version*. 5th ed. New York: Oxford University Press, 2018.

Senior, Donald, John Collins, and Mary Ann Getty, eds. *The Catholic Study Bible*. 3rd ed. New York: Oxford University Press, 2016.

For thoughts on the spiritual life

Boda, Murray, OFM. *Surrounded by Love: Seven Teachings from Saint Francis*. Cincinnati, OH: Franciscan Media Books, 2018.

Clark, Kelly James. *Philosophers Who Believe: The Spiritual Journeys of 11 Leading Thinkers*. Westmont, IL: InterVarsity Press, 1994.

De Waal, Esther. *Living with Contradiction: An Introduction to Benedictine Spirituality*. Harrisburg, PA: Morehouse Publishing, 1997.

John Paul II. *Crossing the Threshold of Hope*. New York: Alfred A. Knopf, 1994.

Peacock, Barbara L. *Spiritual Practices for Soul Care: 40 Ways to Deepen Your Faith*. Grand Rapids, MI: Baker Books, 2023.

Tomaine, Jane. *St. Benedict's Toolbox: The Nuts and Bolts of Everyday Benedictine Living*. 10th anniversary ed. Harrisburg, PA: Morehouse Publishing, 2015.

Willard, Dallas. *The Divine Conspiracy: Rediscovering Our Hidden Life in God*. New York: HarperOne, 2009.

For inspiration

Blight, David W. *Frederick Douglass: Prophet of Freedom*. New York: Simon & Schuster, 2018.

Bunson, Margaret R. *Father Damien: The Man and His Era*. Rev. ed. Huntington, IN: Our Sunday Visitor Publishing Division, 1997.

Chervin, Ronda. *Treasury of Women Saints: A Devotional Companion*. Cincinnati, OH: Franciscan Media Books, 2020.

De Volder, Jan. *The Spirit of Father Damien: The Leper Priest—A Saint for Our Times*. San Francisco: Ignatius Press, 2010.

Maynard, Theodore. *Too Small a World: The Life of Francesca Cabrini*. London: Papamoa Press, 2018.

Missionary Sisters of the Sacred Heart. *An American Saint of Our Day: Mother Frances Xavier Cabrini*. Whitefish, MT: Kessinger Publishing, 2010.

Oursler, Fulton, and Will Oursler. *Father Flanagan of Boys Town*. Garden City, NY: Doubleday, 1949.

Reilly, Hugh, and Kevin Warneke. *Father Flanagan of Boys Town: A Man of Vision*. Boys Town, NE: Boys Town Press, 2008.

NOTES

Introduction

1. Bertrand Russell, "A Free Man's Worship," in *The Meaning of Life*, ed. E. D. Klemke (New York: Oxford University Press, 1981), 56.

ONE. *What Is Apologetics?*

1. Many people believe that critical thinking is the solely negative practice of criticizing others—trashing them in debate, attacking their beliefs, and so forth. This is not accurate. In academic contexts, critical thinking carries its original Greek meaning: "criterial thinking" or "thinking based on criteria." A criterion (from the Greek word *kriterion*) is a standard of evaluation. As practiced by Socrates and by those who came after him in the Western philosophical tradition, not just any criteria will do. Critical thinking is thinking based on rational standards connected to reality. Socrates is often called the founder of critical thinking because he was the first person in recorded history to spend his life explicitly teaching the subject and the first to be executed for encouraging others to practice it in daily life. Thus, the highly respected Center for Critical Thinking (www.criticalthinking.org) begins its "Brief History of the Idea of Critical Thinking" with this statement: "The intellectual roots of critical thinking are as ancient as its etymology, traceable, ultimately, to the teaching practice and vision of Socrates 2,500 years ago." The rational criteria or standards employed in critical thinking are examined in detail in the academic subject also founded and named by the ancient Greeks, logic. For those interested in further study of critical thinking and logic, I recommend two textbooks that I wrote: *Think with Socrates: An Introduction to*

Critical Thinking (New York: Oxford University Press, 2015) and *Introduction to Logic* (New York: Oxford University Press, 2012).

2. Benjamin K. Forrest, Joshua D. Chatraw, and Alister E. McGrath, *The History of Apologetics: A Biographical and Methodological Introduction* (Grand Rapids, MI: Zondervan Academics, 2020), 34.

3. The church fathers were scholars who established the intellectual and doctrinal foundations of Christianity during the first several centuries of the church's existence. For further research into Christian Platonism, I recommend Alexander J. B. Hampton and John Peter Kenney, eds., *Christian Platonism: A History* (Cambridge: Cambridge University Press, 2021).

4. The fact that Lewis went on to incorporate Platonic themes into the *Narnia* books and his works of apologetics indicates that Plato's philosophy remained an influence for the rest of his career. It is no exaggeration to say that echoes of Plato can be found in just about every one of Lewis's written works. Indeed, Lewis's journey from atheism to theism to Christianity was Platonic. Plato had argued that the Highest Reality calls us in subtle ways, quietly attracting our souls like a magnet attracting iron. This is exactly the way Lewis described his own journey to Christianity in his spiritual autobiography, *Surprised by Joy: The Shape of My Early Life* (New York: Harcourt Brace Jovanovich, 1955).

5. William Lane Craig, *Reasonable Faith: Christian Truth and Apologetics*, 3rd ed. (Wheaton, IL: Crossway Books, 2008), 17.

6. Douglas Groothuis, *Christian Apologetics: A Comprehensive Case for Biblical Faith* (Westmont, IL: InterVarsity Press Academic, 2022).

INTERLUDE ONE. *The Socratic Method and the Christian Examination of Conscience*

1. A cognitive bias is an unconscious impulse or mental process that causes a person to jump to a conclusion or make a hasty decision based on an inadequate review of the relevant information. For an introduction to cognitive biases, I recommend Paul Herrick, *Think with Socrates: An Introduction to Critical Thinking* (New York: Oxford University Press, 2015), chap. 4.

2. As I submitted in chapter 1, philosophy in ancient Greece was more than mere intellectual speculation; it was considered a way of life — and a religious one at that. See Pierre Hadot, *Philosophy as a Way of Life: Spiritual Exercises from Socrates to Foucault*, ed. Arnold Davidson (New York: Wiley Blackwell, 1995).

3. Many books have been written offering guidance to those who want to make an effective examination of conscience; one example is Mindy Caliguire,

Soul Searching (Downers Grove, IN: InterVarsity Press Bible Studies, 2010). Since the sixteenth century many Catholics have examined their consciences with help from the spiritual prompts of Saint Ignatius of Loyola. See Sean M. Salai, S.J., ed., *The Spiritual Exercises of St. Ignatius of Loyola: With Points for Personal Prayer from Jesuit Spiritual Masters* (Charlotte, NC: Tan Books, 2020).

TWO. *Does God Exist? Part 1*

1. Keep in mind that by "argument," I mean one or more premises offered as evidence for or reasons to believe that a further statement, the conclusion, is true.

2. Kurt Godel, Alvin Plantinga, Saul Kripke, Peter van Inwagen, Peter Geach, Elizabeth Anscombe, Robert Audi, Eleanor Stump, Linda Zagzebski, Richard Swinburne, Robert Adams, Marilyn McCord Adams, William Alston, Alasdair MacIntyre, Bas van Fraassen, and Nicholas Rescher, to name only a few.

3. One example is Isaac Newton (1642–1726), founder of modern, mathematical physics, in his masterpiece, *Mathematical Principles of Natural Philosophy*. Published in 1687, the *Principia* (as it is called) is considered one of the greatest works of science ever published. On Newton's significance in the history of ideas, I recommend I. Bernard Cohen, *The Birth of a New Physics* (New York: Norton, 1985).

4. Frances Collins, *The Language of God: A Scientist Presents Evidence for Belief* (New York: Free Press, 2007).

5. Jerry Walls and Trent Dougherty, eds., *Two Dozen (or so) Arguments for God: The Plantinga Project* (New York: Oxford University Press, 2018).

6. Richard Swinburne, *The Existence of God* (New York: Oxford University Press, 1979; 2nd ed., 2004).

7. See Xenophon, *Conversations with Socrates*, with an introduction by Odysseus Makridis (New York: Barnes and Noble, 2005), chap. 4, "Socrates Proveth the Existence of a Deity."

8. Steven Weinberg, *Dreams of a Final Theory* (New York: Vintage Books, 1994), 6. Most leading physicists today believe that the universe displays one overall, comprehensive order. See James Trefil, *Reading the Mind of God: In Search of the Principle of Universality* (New York: Doubleday, 1989); Paul Davies, *The Mind of God: The Scientific Basis for a Rational World* (New York: Simon and Schuster, 1992); P. C. W. [Paul] Davies, *The Accidental Universe* (New York: Cambridge University Press, 1982), chap. 2; and J. H. Mulvey, *The Nature of Matter* (Oxford: Oxford University Press, 1981).

9. According to ancient historians, Pythagoras discovered that the tone intervals on the musical scale reflect whole number mathematical ratios between vibrating physical objects rather than the material properties of the physical objects themselves. For instance, an octave results when the ratio between the lengths of vibrating strings is 2:1, the fourth note is produced by a 3:2 ratio, and the fifth by a 4:3 ratio. The beauty that emerges within musical harmony is thus a function of abstract mathematical structure rather than of anything purely physical. During the seventeenth century, Pythagoras was honored by many of those who founded modern science for his early insights into the mathematical structure of the world, including his pioneering work that launched the science of acoustics by connecting math, physics, sound, and beauty.

10. The philosopher C. Stephen Layman gives a deeper defense of Ockham's razor (which he calls "the Principle of Simplicity" and its indispensability for science in *Letters to a Doubting Thomas: A Case for the Existence of God* (New York: Oxford University Press, 2007), chap.1, 26–37.

11. The ancient Greek philosopher Epicurus (341–270 BC) hypothesized that this happened an infinite number of times in the past, producing in time every possible combination of atoms. But even a chance process like this requires a background order that appears intelligently designed. Think for a moment about the precision that must be intelligently built into a properly functioning roulette wheel. On the surface, the wheel appears to be spinning randomly. But beneath the surface, operating in the background, lies a fine-tuned governing mechanism that ensures every possibility has an equal chance of occurring.

12. Michio Kaku, *The God Equation: The Quest for a Theory of Everything* (New York: Doubleday, 2021), 187–88.

13. J. E. Gordon, *Structures: Or Why Things Don't Fall Down* (London: Folio, 2013).

14. David Hume, *Dialogues concerning Natural Religion* (Indianapolis, IN: Hackett, 1980), 48.

15. Hume, 36.

16. Weinberg, *Dreams of a Final Theory*, 6. See also Trefil, *Reading the Mind of God*; Davies, *The Mind of God*; and Davies, *Accidental Universe*, chap. 2.

17. Craig J. Hogan, *The Little Book of the Big Bang: A Cosmic Primer* (New York: Springer Verlag, 1998).

18. I am using David Hume, *Enquiries concerning the Human Understanding and concerning the Principles of Morals*, 2nd ed., ed. L. A. Selby-Bigge, reprinted from the Posthumous Edition of 1777 (Oxford: Oxford University Press, 1902), 136.

19. References are provided at the end of the chapter.

20. Specifically, in the considerations that rule out the natural necessity hypothesis. Theists offer a further consideration on this issue. There is a definite

sense in which the God hypothesis is theoretically simpler than the hypothesis of an intrinsically ordered material universe. In philosophical theology, scholars ask questions about the nature of God and see how far reason and scripture can take them. There is a large consensus in this field that God, understood as the ultimate source of all, as the ultimate explanation, must be noncomposite—not composed of substantial or separable parts and thus not composed of separable parts arranged in an order. Our orderly universe, on the other hand, is composed of many billions of substantial parts arranged in an *improbable* order—an order that could have been otherwise. A being not composed of substantial parts would seem to be a simpler source of order. At the end of this chapter I suggest resources for further study of this fascinating branch of philosophy. See, in particular, Thomas P. Flint and Michael C. Rea, eds., *The Oxford Handbook of Philosophical Theology*, chap. 5, "Simplicity and Aseity," by Jeffrey E. Brower, 105–29. For a longer and more in-depth response to the question, Who designed the designer?, see William Lane Craig and Chad Meister, eds., *God Is Good, God Is Great* (Downers Grove, IL: InterVarsity Press, 2009), chap. 1, "Richard Dawkins on Arguments for God," loc. 361–91, Kindle ed.

21. David Hume, *Dialogues concerning Natural Religion*, 89.

22. "Hoyle on Evolution," *Nature* 294, no. 583 (1981), 105.

23. See John Polkinghorne, "Providence," in *Science and Providence* (Boston: New Science Library, 1989), chap. 3. Polkinghorne is a former professor of mathematical physics at Cambridge who became an Anglican priest. See also Richard Swinburne, *The Existence of God* (Oxford: Clarendon, 1979).

24. See Davies, *Accidental Universe*, chap. 2. See also John Barrow and Frank Tippler, *The Anthropic Cosmological Principle* (New York: Oxford University Press, 1986); and Joseph Silk, *The Big Bang*, rev. ed. (New York: W. H. Freeman, 1989).

25. See John Gribbin and Martin Rees, *Cosmic Coincidences: Dark Matter, Mankind, and Anthropic Cosmology* (New York: Bantam Books, 1989), 4.

26. See Davies, *Accidental Universe*; Barrow and Tippler, *Anthropic Cosmological Principle*; Gribbin and Rees, *Cosmic Coincidences*; George Greenstein, *The Symbiotic Universe* (New York: William Morrow, 1987); and Paul Davies, *God and the New Physics* (New York: Simon and Schuster, 1983).

27. Quoted by Alvin Plantinga, *Where the Conflict Really Lies: Science, Religion, and Naturalism* (New York: Oxford University Press, 2011), 195. From Brandon Carr and Martin Rees, "The Anthropic Principle and the Structure of the Physical World," *Nature* 278 (1979): 695.

28. Paul C. W. Davies, "The Unreasonable Effectiveness of Science," in *Evidence of Purpose*, ed. John Templeton (New York: Templeton Press, 1997), 49.

29. Barrow and Tippler, *Anthropic Cosmological Principle*, 360.

30. Heinz Pagels, "A Cozy Cosmology," reprinted in *Physical Cosmology and Philosophy*, ed. John Leslie (New York: Macmillan, 1990), 174.

31. Gribbin and Rees, *Cosmic Coincidences*, 269.

32. Gribbin and Rees, 10.

33. Barrow, *The Artful Universe*, 34–35.

34. Greenstein, *Symbiotic Universe*, 64–65.

35. Greenstein, 64.

36. Greenstein, 64.

37. Greenstein, chap. 3; Gribbin and Rees, *Cosmic Coincidences*, chap. 1.

38. Quoted in Paul Edwards, *Physical Cosmology and Philosophy* (New York: Macmillan, 1990), 16.

39. See Gribbin and Rees, *Cosmic Coincidences*, 18.

40. Gribbin and Rees, 18.

41. Gribbin and Rees, 26.

42. See Freeman Dyson, "The Argument from Design," reprinted in Dyson, *Disturbing the Universe* (New York: Basic Books, 1981), 250. Dyson argues that the improbable arrangement of the fundamental constants is evidence of design.

43. Dyson, "Argument from Design," 250.

44. Stephen Hawking, *A Brief History of Time*, 10th anniversary ed. (New York: Bantam, 1998), 129.

45. Kaku, *God Equation*, 188.

46. *Discontinuous* means that no signals or information or entities can pass from one mini-universe to another.

47. For more depth on the many worlds hypothesis, see Davies, *God and the New Physics*, 164–76; George Gale, "Cosmological Fecundity: Theories of Multiple Universes," in Leslie, *Physical Cosmology and Philosophy*; and Davies, *Accidental Universe*, chap. 5. See also the discussion in Peter van Inwagen, *Metaphysics* (Boulder, CO: Westview Press, 1993), chap. 8. For those with a physics background, I recommend Simon Saunders, Jonathan Barrett, Adrian Kent, and David Wallace, eds., *Many Worlds: Everett, Quantum Theory, and Reality* (New York: Oxford University Press, 2010).

48. Robert Spitzer, *New Proofs for the Existence of God: Contributions of Contemporary Physics and Philosophy* (Grand Rapids, MI: Eerdmans, 2010), 80.

49. Spitzer, 67–73. I review further problems theorists have raised for multiverse theory in Paul Herrick, *Philosophy, Reasoned Belief, and Faith: An Introduction* (Notre Dame, IN: University of Notre Dame Press, 2022), chap. 5.

50. Davies, *Accidental Universe*, 128.

51. Robert Martin, *Epistemology: A Beginner's Guide* (London: Oneworld, 2014), 65.

THREE. *Does God Exist? Part 2*

1. Bertram Wolfe, *A Life in Two Centuries* (New York: Stein and Day, 1981), 82. Wolfe was one of the first members of the American Communist Party. He worked for a time in the party's secret underground sector and attended meetings in Moscow chaired by Joseph Stalin himself. Wolfe later broke with the party and wrote a number of works critical of communism. His autobiography is colorful and provides many insights into the history of the twentieth century.

2. See John Leslie and Robert Lawrence Kuhn, eds., *The Mystery of Existence: Why Is There Anything at All?* (Malden, MA: John Wiley & Sons, 2013), 1; emphasis in original.

3. Leslie and Kuhn, *The Mystery of Existence*, 135.

4. See Steven Weinberg, "A Designer Universe?," in *Science and Religion: Are They Compatible?*, ed. Paul Kurtz (Amherst, NY: Prometheus Books, 2003), 33.

5. Michio Kaku, *The God Equation: The Quest for a Theory of Everything* (New York: Doubleday, 2021), 187–88.

6. In modal logic, a circumstance counts as "logically possible" as long as it is not self-contradictory and implies no self-contradictions. For example, it is logically possible that someone wins the New York State lottery ten times in a row. Although highly improbable, this statement counts as logically *possible* because the state of affairs (someone winning the lottery ten times in a row) is not self-contradictory and implies no self-contradiction. Put another way, the state of affairs counts as logically possible because it is consistently describable—describable without self-contradiction. On the other hand, it is not logically possible that two brothers exist each older than the other. It is also not logically possible that a square circle exists. Now, it can be proved mathematically, using what mathematicians call a "proof by contradiction," that 1 + 1 = 2 (assuming the standard meaning of the terms) is necessarily true. The proof shows that a self-contradiction logically follows if we suppose that 1 + 1 = 2 is false. This shows that 1 + 1 = 2 cannot be false in *any* consistently describable context, since (a) it is a law of logic that any proposition that implies a self-contradiction must itself be a self-contradiction, and (b) a self-contradiction is a paradigm case of the impossible. Of course, this proof, like all proofs by contradiction in mathematics and logic, assumes the law of noncontradiction. This is the principle stating that a self-contradiction is not, and cannot ever be, true in any context or circumstance. Mathematics and logic both presuppose the law of noncontradiction; mathematical and logical proofs are invalid without it. The law makes sense: A self-contradiction is a statement of the logical form "P and it is not the case that P." For instance, "The number is even and it is not the case that the number is even" (assuming the words retain

their same meaning throughout the statement). Notice that a self-contradiction asserts one specific thing in its first clause and then retracts that claim in the second clause, leaving nothing asserted in the end (and nothing to even possibly be true). As Aristotle pointed out, we can't reason from P to Q, we can't do mathematics, we can't even communicate, without presupposing the law of noncontradiction at some level. The principle is a presupposition of all rational thought. Whether they realize it or not, those who try to refute the law presuppose it each time they speak. Many examples of necessary truth exist: all the truths of pure mathematics are necessarily true.

7. For the reader interested in exploring modal logic, necessary existence, and the way philosophers have employed these concepts in search of an ultimate explanation of existence, I offer suggestions for research at the end of the chapter.

8. Richard Purtill presents this argument in his *Reason to Believe* (Grand Rapids, MI: Eerdmans, 1974), chap. 3. Some people claim that quantum events and virtual particles have no causes. They are mistaken. Quantum events and virtual particles occur only within, and because of, preexisting quantum fields. They do not come into existence out of nothing.

9. Michael Rota, *Taking Pascal's Wager: Faith, Evidence and the Abundant Life* (Downers Grove, IL: InterVarsity Press Academic, 2016), 114–15.

10. Peter van Inwagen, *Metaphysics* (San Francisco: Westview Press, 1993), 103.

11. Van Inwagen, *Metaphysics*, 98.

12. Kaku, *The God Equation*, 187–88.

13. If an argument is wanted, consider this. One hydrogen atom is clearly a contingent being. If the laws of physics had been sufficiently different, hydrogen would never have existed. If we take one hydrogen atom and add another to it, the two atoms together still exist contingently. If we add a third hydrogen atom, the three still exist contingently, and so on. The same can be said for any kind of atom, any subatomic particle, and any bit of energy. Nothing necessary emerges when we add one contingent being to another contingent being—no matter how many we add. A vast logical gulf exists between necessary and contingent existence; adding contingent beings to contingent beings does nothing to bridge that gulf.

14. Craig J. Hogan, *The Little Book of the Big Bang: A Cosmic Primer* (New York: Springer Verlag, 1998).

15. Bertrand Russell, *Why I Am Not a Christian: And Other Essays on Religion and Related Subjects* (New York: Touchstone, [1927] 1967), 6.

16. See Carl Sagan make the point at https://www.youtube.com/watch?v=Ag6fH8cU-MU.

17. See van Inwagen, *Metaphysics*, 98.

18. Van Inwagen, *Metaphysics*, 98.

19. William Lane Craig and Quentin Smith, *Theism, Atheism and Big Bang Cosmology* (Oxford: Oxford University Press, 1993), 63–64.

20. The refracting telescope was invented by Dutch lens makers in about 1608, but the Italian mathematician, physicist, and astronomer Galileo was the first to build a model and observe the heavens with it in 1609. The reflecting telescope was invented by the English mathematician, physicist, and astronomer Isaac Newton. A refracting telescope uses lenses to magnify images; the reflecting telescope uses a mirror and a lens.

21. An excellent account of the rise of modern science is I. Bernard Cohen, *The Birth of a New Physics*, rev. ed. (New York: Norton, 1985).

22. This law states that the entropy (disorder) of a closed system must increase over time.

23. John Farrell, *The Day without Yesterday: Lemaître, Einstein, and the Birth of Modern Cosmology* (New York: Thunder's Mouth Press, 2005), 80.

24. Farrell, *The Day without Yesterday*, 90.

25. I thank an anonymous reviewer for the University of Notre Dame Press for pointing out the name change to me. The International Astronomical Union officially changed the name of Hubble's law to "the Hubble-Lemaître law."

26. It is true that before Lemaître published his theory, some astronomers had raised the possibility that the nebulae might be receding from each other. However, the data had been inconclusive, and everyone had been reluctant to drop the assumption of a static universe.

27. Dominique Lambert, Académie Royale de Belgique, "Einstein and Lemaître: Two Friends, Two Cosmologies," *Interdisciplinary Encyclopedia of Religion & Science*, http://www.inters.org/einstein-lemaitre, accessed February 7, 2024.

28. The Hooker telescope at Mount Wilson remained the largest telescope in the world until 1949.

29. Some may wonder how Hubble was able to discover, just by analyzing light, that other galaxies are moving away from ours (and from each other) at great speeds. His discovery was based on something physicists called the Doppler effect. As a speeding train approaches, the pitch of its whistle increases, and as it speeds away, the pitch drops. The explanation for the change in pitch was discovered in 1842 by Christian Doppler (1803–53), an Austrian physicist. If a source emitting sound waves is moving toward an observer, the waves are bunched up, which increases their frequency and hence the pitch. If the source of waves is moving away from an observer, the waves are stretched out, which causes the frequency and pitch to decrease. Hubble reasoned that since light is a wave phenomenon, it must also display a Doppler effect. Thus, if a light source is moving toward us, its light waves should be crunched up and thus shifted toward the higher frequency (blue) end of the spectrum. If the source is moving away, its light should be

spread out and thus shifted to the lower frequency (red) end of the spectrum. After finding that the light from distant galaxies is shifted toward the red end of the spectrum and after measuring the degree of the "redshift," he concluded that other galaxies are moving away from ours and from each other at great speeds.

30. Farrell, *The Day without Yesterday*, 104.

31. Farrell, *The Day without Yesterday*, 106.

32. Farrell, *The Day without Yesterday*, 106.

33. Farrell, *The Day without Yesterday*, 100.

34. "In the beginning God created the heavens and the earth" (Genesis 1:1, New International Version).

35. Farrell, *The Day without Yesterday*, 115.

36. Farrell, *The Day without Yesterday*, 164.

37. I review these theories and the reasons they were abandoned in Paul Herrick, *Philosophy, Reasoned Belief, and Faith: An Introduction* (Notre Dame, IN: University of Notre Dame Press, 2022), Interlude 1.

38. Joseph Silk, *The Big Bang*, rev. and updated ed. (New York: W. H. Freeman, 1989), 108.

39. Farrell, *The Day without Yesterday*, dust jacket.

40. Steven Duncan, *Analytic Philosophy of Religion: Its History since 1955* (Penrith, CA: Humanities-Ebooks, 2010), 165.

41. For Craig's full presentation, see William Lane Craig and J. P. Moreland, eds., *The Blackwell Companion to Natural Theology* (Oxford: Wiley-Blackwell, 2012), chap. 3, "The Kalam Cosmological Argument," 101–201. A more compact version can be found here: William Lane Craig, "The Kalam Cosmological Argument," in *Two Dozen (or so) Arguments for God*, ed. Jerry Walls and Trent Dougherty (New York: Oxford University Press, 2018), 389–405.

INTERLUDE TWO. *Christianity's Contributions to World Culture*

1. Rodney Stark, *How the West Won: The Neglected Story of the Triumph of Modernity* (Wilmington, DE: ISI Books, 2014), 303–21.

2. Thomas Woods Jr., *How the Catholic Church Built Western Civilization* (Washington, DC: Regnery, 2005), 4–5. See also James Hannam, *The Genesis of Modern Science: How the Christian Middle Ages Launched the Scientific Revolution* (Washington, DC: Regnery, 2011).

3. Woods, *How the Catholic Church Built Western Civilization*, 5. Essentially the same thesis is also supported by the pathbreaking research of such respected contemporary specialists in medieval science as Lynn White Jr., Donald

Cardwell, and Edward Grant. See Donald Cardwell, *Wheels, Clocks, and Rockets: A History of Technology* (New York: Norton, 2001); Lynn White, *Medieval Religion and Technology: Collected Essays* (Berkeley: University of California Press, 1986); and Edward Grant, *The Foundations of Modern Science in the Middle Ages: Their Religious, Institutional and Intellectual Contexts*, Cambridge Studies in the History of Science (New York: Cambridge University Press, 1996). See also David Lindberg, *The Beginnings of Western Science*, 2nd ed. (Chicago: University of Chicago Press, 2007).

4. Charles Homer Hoskins, *The Rise of Universities* (New Brunswick, NJ: Transaction Publishers, [1922] 2002), 29.

5. Read the transcript in Alfred North Whitehead, *Science and the Modern World* (New York: Macmillan, 1946), 22 ff.

6. Ian G. Barbour, *Religion and Science: Historical and Contemporary Issues* (San Franscisco: HarperSan Francisco, 1997), Kindle ed., 46.

7. Ian Barbour, *Religion and Science*, 47. After noting the decline of Arabic premodern science, Barbour writes, "The West had greater confidence in human reason, and its universities allowed considerable freedom of inquiry as long as basic theological doctrines were not rejected. China, the other region of the world where science might have developed, made impressive advances in practical technology but not in theoretical science; higher education was controlled by state officials and was based on the authority of the [ancient] classics, which said little about science" (47).

8. For those who want to investigate, a good place to start is Rodney Stark, *The Victory of Reason* (New York: Random House, 2005), chap. 1. I also recommend Alfred North Whitehead, *Science and the Modern World* (New York: Free Press, [1925] 1997).

9. See Pierre Hadot, *Philosophy as a Way of Life: Spiritual Exercises from Socrates to Foucault*, ed. Arnold Davidson (New York: Wiley Blackwell, 1995).

10. Thomas Aquinas ranks with Socrates, Plato, and Aristotle as among the greatest philosophers of all time. In treatises that would fill more than fifty volumes in a modern college library, he raises some of the most difficult philosophical questions ever stated, critically examines answers from almost every school of thought in his day, and offers original arguments touching on almost every area of philosophy. At the height of his productivity, he was writing four manuscripts at a time, dictating to four different secretaries. Today some scholars spend their careers drawing new insights from his writings, and new research into his thought is published every year.

11. Steven Marrone, "Medieval Philosophy in Context," in *The Cambridge Companion to Medieval Philosophy*, ed. A. S. McGrade (Cambridge: Cambridge University Press, 2003), 23.

12. Marrone, "Medieval Philosophy in Context," 22.

13. Marrone, "Medieval Philosophy in Context," 28.

14. Of course, this theocentric conception of knowledge was not invented by medieval Christianity; it can be found in ancient Greece and Rome. The great mathematician Pythagoras believed that mathematics and philosophy, properly studied, elevate the mind, heart, and soul toward the highest being, God, the source of all truth. In the religious communities that he founded, mathematics and philosophy were practiced as spiritual disciplines that lead the soul toward God. Again, Socrates, Plato, Aristotle, and the Stoic philosophers of Greece and Rome all considered philosophy an ascent of the mind, heart, and soul toward God.

15. I consulted the following books on the history of mathematics: Carl B. Boyer, *A History of Mathematics*, 2nd ed. (New York: Wiley, 1991); Nicolas Bourbaki, *Elements of the History of Mathematics* (New York: Springer Verlag, 1993); Florian Cajori, *A History of Mathematics*, 5th ed. (New York: Chelsea, 1991); Victor Katz, *A History of Mathematics: An Introduction* (New York: HarperCollins, 1993); Morris Kline, *Mathematical Thought from Ancient to Modern Times*, 3 vols. (New York: Oxford University Press, 1972); David E. Smith, *History of Mathematics*, 2 vols. (New York: Dover, 1958); Dirk J. Struik, *A Concise History of Mathematics* (New York: Dover, 1967).

16. In the Old Testament, see Genesis 9:6 and 1:27. In the New Testament, consult the teachings of Jesus, especially the parable of the Good Samaritan and the Beatitudes. I note in passing that Jesus preferred to mix with the poor and sinners rather than with the high and mighty. During the Middle Ages, the monasteries of Europe pioneered the world's first hospitals as institutions serving the poor and sick regardless of social status. One can also see the doctrine of the *imago Dei* lived out in the lives of the saints, whether the incident is Saint Francis jumping down from his horse to hug the poor man with leprosy, Father Damien building a colony for the outcast lepers of Hawaii, or Father Maximilian Kolbe giving his life to the Nazis so that a fellow concentration camp prisoner with a family might live.

17. J. M. Roberts, *The Triumph of the West: The Origin, Rise, and Legacy of Western Civilization* (London: British Broadcasting Corporation, 1985), 72. Roberts's classic is now available in many editions.

18. The modern concepts of individual liberty; elected, constitutionally limited government; universal human rights possessed regardless of social status; and the rule of law were simply not being debated or even considered outside Europe during this formative period. Classical liberal ideas spread to the rest of the world during the nineteenth and twentieth centuries as individuals in other societies saw the results of their implementation, however imperfect it may have been.

19. Richard M. Weaver, *Ideas Have Consequences* (Chicago: University of Chicago Press, 1948).

20. For a philosophical account of Las Casas's work, I recommend Willam J. Talbott, *Which Rights Should Be Universal?* (New York: Oxford University Press, 2008), chap. 4, "An Epistemically Modest Universal Moral Standpoint," 47–87.

21. Faith M. Martin and Charles R. McBurney, *The White Chief of Cache Creek* (Pittsburgh, PA: Crown & Covenant, 2020), xi. The authors are citing Samuel Rutherford, *Lex, Rex: The Law of the Prince* (1664), 51.

22. From an editorial in *Reformed Presbyterian* 1, no. 8 (October 1837): 226, quoted in Martin and McBurney, *White Chief of Cache Creek*, xi. I thank Karen Olson for drawing Martin's fascinating research to my attention.

23. Martin and McBurney, *White Chief of Cache Creek*, xii.

24. See John Locke, *Two Treatises of Government* (New York: New American Library, 1965), 42.

25. A. C. Grayling, *Toward the Light of Liberty: The Struggles for Freedom and Rights That Made the Modern Western World* (New York: Walker Publishing, 2007). Grayling argues that philosophical ideals championed by classical liberals altered the course of history and changed the world. Modern history, Grayling argues, has been driven by philosophical ideas originating in Europe, including the biblical doctrine of the *imago Dei*.

FOUR. *Why Would God Permit Evil?*

1. Hitler's crimes against humanity are well known, in mind-numbing and horrifying detail. Under his orders, at least 6 million unarmed, innocent people were murdered. Crimes against humanity committed by moral monsters on the other side of the political spectrum are less well known. Historians, such as Robert Conquest and Simon Montefiore, have documented that Stalin was directly responsible for at least 20 million deaths. In Ukraine alone, Stalin intentionally starved to death approximately 6 million farmers for not following his orders. Incidentally, as shown by the archival research of the noted Harvard historian Richard Pipes, Stalin learned many of his lessons in mass murder from his predecessor, Vladimir Lenin, founder of the Soviet Union. And during his first three years in power, Mao Zedong had approximately 3 million political opponents executed without trial. The total number who died during just one of his social engineering experiments (the so-called Great Leap Forward) certainly exceeds 45 million—unnecessary deaths Mao knew were occurring. Three million were executed without trial in Communist China during this period (1958–62) just for not carrying out Mao's orders. During the twentieth century, Communist governments around the world

killed without trial between 80 and 100 million unarmed civilians and political opponents. Most people who hear this statistic find it hard to believe. For the reader who wants to research the topic, there is no better place to begin than Stéphane Courtois, Nicolas Werth, Jean-Louis Panné, Andrzej Paczowski, Karel Bartosĕk, and Jean-Louis Margolin, *The Black Book of Communism: Crimes, Terror, Repression*, ed. Mark Kramer, trans. Jonathan Murphy (Cambridge, MA: Harvard University Press, 1999). The authors, all scholars and former Communists, provide archival documentation and eyewitness testimony. On the crimes against humanity committed specifically by Stalin and Mao, in addition to the *Black Book*, I recommend the following: Anne Applebaum, *Red Famine: Stalin's War on Ukraine* (New York: Doubleday, 2017); Jasper Becker, *Hungry Ghosts: Mao's Secret Famine* (New York: Henry Holt, 1996); Robert Conquest, *Harvest of Sorrow: Soviet Collectivization and the Terror Famine* (New York: Oxford University Press, 1987); Frank Dikotter, *Mao's Great Famine* (New York: Bloomsbury, 2010); Richard Pipes, *Communism: A History* (New York: Modern Library, 2001); and for background, Richard Pipes, *The Unknown Lenin: From the Secret Archive* (New Haven, CT: Yale University Press, 1996). The amount of moral evil in this world is indeed mind-boggling. For many, the big question is: Why would God allow *so much*?

2. Philosophers distinguish *intrinsic* and *extrinsic* values, or goods. Something is extrinsically valuable if it is valuable only as a means to something else that is valuable. It is valuable only as a means to an end. Something is intrinsically valuable if it is valuable in itself, apart from anything it leads to or produces.

3. In human beings, the first hint or inkling of love might be *occasioned* by external factors, but in its fullness, love is an act of will.

4. It is part of our common notion of free will that if a person at a particular moment does something and the person could not possibly have done otherwise at the moment, given all the prior causes and conditions that led up to that moment, then the person is not acting of their own free will. An action might be *influenced* by external and preexisting factors, and it might be partly caused by outside factors, but it cannot be wholly caused by prior factors and remain an act of free will. Thus, if a person at a particular moment does something of their own free will, then that person *could* have done otherwise, given the very same antecedent causes and conditions leading up to the moment. So, if God fully determined each of your actions before you were born so that at any moment in your life you could not have done otherwise, then you are not acting of your own free will. This common account of free will goes back at least to the medieval philosopher Anselm (1033–1109) and is known today as the "theory of agent causation." If the theory is correct, then free will is the power within a person to cause something without being fully caused to do so by the sum total of all prior causes at

work in the universe at the moment. If so, then an act of free will introduces into the world a new line of cause and effect, one that was not preprogrammed into the universal script in the beginning. On this view of the freedom of the will, the causes and effects that result from an act of free will literally originated with the agent's choice. I defend agent causation theory in *Philosophy, Reasoned Belief, and Faith: An Introduction* (Notre Dame, IN University of Notre Dame Press, 2022), chap. 11. For an in-depth historical study, see Katherin Rogers, *Anselm on Freedom* (New York: Oxford University Press, 2008). For an advanced defense of agent causation theory, see Timothy O'Conner, *Persons and Causes: The Metaphysics of Free Will* (New York: Oxford University Press, 2002).

5. I find this theodicy in Augustine, but other philosophers disagree and interpret him differently. It is a matter of some debate whether Augustine endorsed a free will theodicy. For those who want to dig deeper, see Augustine, *City of God* (New York: Random House, 1950), bks. 11–12. For secondary treatments, see Michael Peterson, ed., *The Problem of Evil: Selected Readings* (Notre Dame, IN: University of Notre Dame Press, 1992), 191–97; Christopher Kirwan, *Augustine* (New York: Routledge, 1989); and John Hick, *Evil and the God of Love* (New York: Palgrave Macmillan, 2010), part 2.

6. C. Stephen Layman, *Letters to a Doubting Thomas: A Case for the Existence of God* (New York: Oxford University Press, 2007), 189. In his first work of Christian apologetics, *The Pilgrim's Regress*, and in his spiritual autobiography, *Surprised by Joy*, C. S. Lewis develops a profound argument for immortality that I examine in the next chapter.

7. J. R. Lucas, *Freedom and Grace* (Grand Rapids, MI: Eerdmans, 1976), 39.

8. Augustine, *City of God*, Loeb Classical Library (Cambridge, MA: Harvard University Press, 1957), 1:22. I was drawn to this passage when reading Anthony Meredith, SJ, *Christian Philosophy in the Early Church* (New York: T&T Clark, 2012).

9. The story of Joseph and his brothers, told in the first book of the Hebrew scriptures (Genesis 37–50), is a biblical illustration of sinful people committing an evil act, which God uses to further his plan of salvation. Joseph said to his guilty brothers, "But now, do not therefore be grieved or angry with yourselves because you sold me here, for God sent me before you to preserve life. . . . And God sent me before you to preserve a posterity for you in the earth, and to save your lives by a great deliverance. So now it was not you who sent me here, but God" (Genesis 45:5, 7–8a, New King James Version). Thanks to Karen Olson for bringing these verses to my attention.

10. Consider that on a traditional theistic interpretation of life, God gives each individual a unique set of hurdles and temptations, in keeping with the fact that each individual person is an utterly unique creation of God.

11. Hick, *Evil and the God of Love*, 324–25.

12. And thus consistent with God being all-good.

13. For the full argument, see William L. Rowe, "The Problem of Evil and Some Varieties of Atheism" and "The Evidential Argument from Evil: A Second Look," in *The Evidential Argument from Evil*, ed. Daniel Howard-Snyder (Indianapolis: Indiana University Press, 1996), 1–11 and 262, respectively. See also William L. Rowe, "Ruminations about Evil," in *Philosophical Perspectives*, vol. 5, *Philosophy of Religion*, ed. James E. Tomberlin (Atascadero, CA: Ridgeview, 1991), 69–88. My summary of the argument has been influenced by Chris Tweedt, "Defusing the Common Sense Problem of Evil," *Faith and Philosophy* 32, no. 4 (2015): 391–403.

14. Rowe, "Problem of Evil and Some Varieties of Atheism," 4.

15. Rowe, "Problem of Evil and Some Varieties of Atheism," 4.

16. For the full argument, see William Alston, "The Inductive Argument from Evil and the Human Cognitive Condition," in Howard-Snyder, *Evidential Argument from Evil*, 97–126.

17. Thus, skeptical theism does not justify skepticism with regard to *everything* we think we know.

18. For a number of excellent articles dealing with the issues raised by Rowe's argument, see Howard-Snyder, *Evidential Argument from Evil*.

19. In my view, skeptical theism supplements the other theodicies.

20. C. Stephen Evans and R. Zachary Manis, *Philosophy of Religion: Thinking about Faith*, 2nd ed. (Downers Grove, IL: InterVarsity Press, 2009).

21. Richard Swinburne, *The Existence of God*, 2nd ed. (New York: Oxford University Press, 2004). For an opposing view, see J. L. Mackie, *The Miracle of Theism* (New York: Oxford University Press, 1983).

FIVE. *Hasn't Science Proved That Life after Death Is Impossible?*

1. Quoted in Anthony Flew, ed., *Body, Mind, and Death* (New York: Macmillan, 1964), 5.

2. Research conducted in the evolutionary study of religion indicates that "humans are everywhere intuitive dualists and, unless inculcated otherwise, separate the intentional minds from the bodies of persons and some animals." Michael Bergmann and Patrick Kain, *Challenges to Moral and Religious Belief: Disagreement and Evolution* (Oxford: Oxford University Press, 2014), 259. As I explain in a moment, in this context dualism is the belief that human beings possess an immaterial mind or soul that is distinct from the material body.

3. Kathleen Weldon, "Paradise Polled: Americans and the Afterlife," June 15, 2015; updated December 6, 2017, https://www.huffingtonpost.com/kathleen-weldon/paradise-polled-americans_b_7587538.html.

4. This part of the view is common sense: it is obvious that a decision or act of will, which is a mental phenomenon, can cause the body to move; likewise, damage to the brain can cause changes in the mind. Mind and brain clearly affect each other.

5. Recently, philosophers referred to as Christian materialists have developed theories claiming to explain how life after death and heaven are still possible even if we assume that the human mind is composed of nothing but particles of matter. I discuss this view briefly below.

6. The work by Bergmann and Kain cited in note 2 also states that most people throughout history "when confronted with death . . . recognize the death of the body, but nevertheless continue to entertain the survival of the mind—or soul—of the deceased." See Bergmann and Kain, *Challenges to Moral and Religious Belief*, 259.

7. For Descartes's most noteworthy work, see *Meditations on First Philosophy* (Indianapolis: Hackett, [1641] 1979). For further study, see John Cottingham et al., *The Philosophical Writings of Descartes*, trans. A. Kenny (Cambridge: Cambridge University Press, 1985). A good study of Descartes's philosophy is Margaret Dauler Wilson, *Descartes* (London: Routledge & Kegan Paul, 1978). Also valuable is John Cottingham, ed., *The Cambridge Companion to Descartes* (Cambridge: Cambridge University Press, 1992).

8. René Descartes, *Meditations on First Philosophy*, trans. Laurence J. Lafleur (Indianapolis: Bobbs-Merrill Educational Publishing), 81. Descartes broke with the philosophical emphasis of the medieval period by making epistemological rather than metaphysical and religious issues basic. In doing so, he took Western philosophy in an epistemological direction and inaugurated what historians call the "modern" period in philosophy.

9. I am using x and y here as variables ranging over any things whatsoever.

10. Laurence BonJour, "Against Materialism," in *The Waning of Materialism*, ed. Robert C. Koons and George Bealer (New York: Oxford University Press, 2010), 6.

11. BonJour, "Against Materialism," 6.

12. For further exploration of the identity theory, see Cynthia Macdonald, *Mind-Body Identity Theories* (London: Routledge, 1989). See also Keith Campbell, *Body and Mind* (Garden City, NY: Doubleday, 1970); and Paul Churchland, *Matter and Consciousness* (Cambridge, MA: MIT Press, 2013), 26–36. An important early defense of the theory is David Armstrong, *A Materialist Theory of the Mind* (London: Routledge & Kegan Paul, 1968).

13. See J. J. C. Smart, "Sensations and Brain Processes," in *Materialism and the Mind-Body Problem*, ed. David Rosenthal (Indianapolis: Hackett, 1987), 54.

14. Thomas Nagel, *What Does It All Mean?* (New York: Oxford University Press, 1987), 33; emphasis in original.

15. Robert C. Koons and George Bealer, eds., *The Waning of Materialism* (New York: Oxford University Press, 2010), 18.

16. The neuroscientist John C. Eccles, who was awarded the Nobel Prize in physiology or medicine, defends a dualist account of the mind-brain relationship in Karl Popper and John C. Eccles, *The Self and Its Brain: An Argument for Interactionism* (New York: Routledge, 1984). Dualism is also defended in John Foster, *The Immaterial Self: A Defense of the Cartesian Dualist Conception of the Mind* (New York: Routledge, 1991). See also John C. Eccles, *How the Self Controls Its Brain* (New York: Springer Verlag, 1994). Eccles's account incorporates the latest scientific understanding of the brain's structure while offering an explanation of how a nonmaterial mind might act on the physical brain to bring about voluntary action.

17. For more depth on the Aristotelian account, see Patrick Lee and Robert P. George, *Body-Self Dualism in Contemporary Ethics and Politics* (Cambridge: Cambridge University Press, 2007), Kindle ed.

18. For those who would like to explore recent philosophical arguments for dualism, including those we just examined, I recommend Andrea Lavazza and Howard Robinson, eds., *Contemporary Dualism: A Defense* (New York: Routledge, 2016); Jonathan J. Loose, Angus J. L. Menuge, and J. P Moreland, eds., *The Blackwell Companion to Substance Dualism*, Blackwell Companions to Philosophy (Oxford: Wiley-Blackwell, 2018); John Foster, *The Immaterial Self: A Defense of the Cartesian Dualist Conception of the Mind* (New York: Routledge, 1991); and Howard Robinson, *From the Knowledge Argument to Mental Substance: Resurrecting the Mind* (Cambridge: Cambridge University Press, 2016). A famous philosophical essay arguing for mind-body dualism that created a big sensation in philosophy during the 1970s is Thomas Nagel, "What Is It Like to Be a Bat?," reprinted in Thomas Nagel, *Mortal Questions* (New York: Cambridge University Press, 2012).

19. C. S. Lewis, *Surprised by Joy: The Shape of My Early Life* (New York: Harcourt Brace Jovanovich, 1955); and C. S. Lewis, *The Pilgrim's Regress: An Allegorical Apology for Christianity* (Grand Rapids, MI: Eerdmans, 1958). The "Preface to Third Edition" of Lewis's *Pilgrim's Regress* contains an excellent discussion of Lewis's overall argument. See also Richard Purtill, *C. S. Lewis's Case for the Christian Faith* (San Francisco: Harper and Row, 1985). Of related interest is the view Lewis develops concerning the afterlife in *The Great Divorce* (New York: Macmillan, 1946).

20. Lewis also calls the feeling *sehnsucht* (German for "a prolonged unfulfilled desire or need"; vocabulary.com).

21. C. S. Lewis, *The Weight of Glory and Other Addresses* (Grand Rapids, MI: Eerdmans, 1975), 6.

22. C. S. Lewis, *Mere Christianity* (New York: HarperOne, 2023), Kindle ed., 136–37.

23. Harry Kemp, "God the Architect," in *Masterpieces of Religious Verse*, ed. James Dalton Morrison (New York: HarperCollins, 1948), 46–47.

24. Fulton Oursler and Will Oursler, *Father Flanagan of Boys Town* (Garden City, NY: Doubleday, 1949), 34.

25. For a survey of the field, see Bergmann and Kain, *Challenges to Moral and Religious Belief*.

26. In "Does the Scientific Study of Religion Cast Doubt on Theistic Beliefs?," Joshua C. Thurow argues that although research in the cognitive science of religion does not undermine belief in God, it casts grave doubt on Lewis's argument from joy, specifically, on his claim that joy is a natural desire analogous to our other natural desires such as hunger and thirst. Although I am tempted to enter this debate here, it is not appropriate for the present volume. For those interested in pursuing this issue, see Thurow's paper in Bergmann and Kain, *Challenges to Moral and Religious Belief: Disagreement and Evolution*, 277–92.

27. For further research on this argument, I recommend J. P. Moreland, *Consciousness and the Existence of God: A Theistic Argument* (New York: Routledge, 2010).

SIX. *Isn't It Illogical to Believe That a Miracle Occurred?*

1. David Hume, *Enquiry concerning Human Understanding* (1748), Kindle ed., loc. 1655.

2. In logic, a universal generalization is technically a statement of the logical form, "All A's are B's," for instance, "All cats are mammals." Scientific laws always contain suppressed *ceteris paribus* clauses of the form, "assuming standard conditions," "assuming no outside forces interfere," and so on.

3. Gerald O'Collins, SJ, *Revelation: Toward a Christian Interpretation of God's Self-Revelation in Jesus Christ* (Oxford: Oxford University Press, 2016), 98.

4. J. A Cover, "Miracles and Christian Theism," in *Reason for the Hope Within*, ed. Michael Murray (Grand Rapids, MI: Eerdmans, 1999), 345–74.

5. On the first class of background knowledge, see Richard Swinburne, *The Existence of God* (New York: Oxford University Press, 1979). On the second

class, see Richard Swinburne, *The Coherence of Theism* (repr. New York: Oxford University Press, 2016). On the third class, see Richard Swinburne, *Was Jesus God?* (Oxford: Oxford University Press, 2010) and *The Resurrection of God Incarnate* (Oxford: Clarendon, 2003).

6. Swinburne, *Resurrection of God Incarnate*, 25.
7. Richard Swinburne, ed., *Miracles* (New York: Macmillan, 1989), chap. 4.
8. Cover, "Miracles and Christian Theism," 356 ff.
9. Cover, "Miracles and Christian Theism," 357.
10. William Lane Craig, *Reasonable Faith: Christian Truth and Apologetics*, 3rd ed. (Wheaton, IL: Crossway, 2008), 257.

SEVEN. *Is the New Testament Historically Reliable?*

1. Here is a suggestion. This particular book passes all six tests. The best explanation is that it is truthful and generally accurate. Therefore, it is reasonable to conclude that the book is truthful and generally accurate.
2. Norman L. Geisler, *A Popular Survey of the New Testament* (Grand Rapids, MI: Baker Books, 2007), chap. 2, "The Gospel Record—History or Mythology?"
3. Geisler, *A Popular Survey of the New Testament*, 19.
4. Geisler, *A Popular Survey of the New Testament*, 19.
5. Geisler, *A Popular Survey of the New Testament*, 19.
6. Gary Habermas, *The Historical Jesus: Ancient Evidence for the Life of Christ* (Joplin, MO: College Press, 1996), 55.
7. Habermas, *The Historical Jesus*, 20.
8. Habermas, *The Historical Jesus*, 20.
9. Quoted in Geisler, *Popular Survey of the New Testament*, 21.
10. J. P. Moreland, *Scaling the Secular City* (Grand Rapids, MI: Baker Academic, 1987), 135.
11. Josh McDowell and Sean McDowell, *Evidence That Demands a Verdict: Life-Changing Truth for a Skeptical World* (Nashville, TN: Thomas Nelson, 2017), 56.
12. McDowell and McDowell, *Evidence That Demands a Verdict*, 56.
13. McDowell and McDowell, *Evidence That Demands a Verdict*, 56.
14. McDowell and McDowell, *Evidence That Demands a Verdict*, 56.
15. Geisler, *Popular Survey of the New Testament*, 19.
16. Geisler, *Popular Survey of the New Testament*, 20.
17. Josh McDowell and Sean McDowell, *Evidence for the Resurrection* (Grand Rapids, MI: Baker Books, 2009), 145.
18. Conservative biblical scholars date Matthew, Mark, and Luke to the 60s and John to the 90s. But conservative biblical scholars are in the minority in their

profession. Liberal scholars argue that Mark was composed around 70, with Luke and Matthew dating to approximately 80 and 90, respectively. These scholars date John's gospel to around 100. I thank an anonymous reviewer for the University of Notre Dame Press for information on this matter.

19. See McDowell and McDowell, *Evidence That Demands a Verdict*, 41–47. The authors provide a concise summary of the scholarship establishing the dates of composition for the texts of the New Testament.

20. McDowell and McDowell, *Evidence That Demands a Verdict*, 146. See also Sean McDowell, *The Fate of the Apostles* (New York: Routledge, 2016).

21. McDowell and McDowell, *Evidence That Demands a Verdict*, 148.

22. Quoted in Geisler, *Popular Survey of the New Testament*, 34.

23. David Turek, "What Everyone Should Learn from Gary Habermas," in *Raised on the Third Day: Defending the Historicity of the Resurrection of Jesus: Essays in Honor of Gary Habermas*, ed. W. David Beck and Michael Licona (Bellingham, WA: Lexham Press, 2020), 330–32.

24. McDowell and McDowell, *Evidence for the Resurrection*, 149.

25. The gnostic redeemers (from the Greek *gnosis*, "to know") were religious figures claiming to have special mystical knowledge of God, heaven, and esoteric matters.

26. Gary Habermas, *Risen Indeed: A Historical Investigation into the Resurrection of Jesus* (Bellingham, WA: Lexham Academic, 2022), 12.

27. McDowell and McDowell, *Evidence That Demands a Verdict*, 80.

28. Quoted by Geisler, *Popular Survey of the New Testament*, 29–30.

29. Craig Blomberg, *Can We Still Believe the Bible? An Evangelical Engagement with Contemporary Questions* (Grand Rapids, MI: Brazos Press, 2014), 2.

30. Gleason Archer, *The Encyclopedia of Bible Difficulties* (Grand Rapids, MI: Zondervan, 1982).

31. Bart Ehrman, *Misquoting Jesus: The Story Behind Who Changed the Bible and Why* (New York: HarperOne, 2005), Kindle ed., loc. 1452.

32. Blomberg, *Can We Still Believe the Bible?*, 15.

33. Blomberg, *Can We Still Believe the Bible?*, 16–17.

34. Blomberg, *Can We Still Believe the Bible?*, 26–28.

EIGHT. *Did Jesus Christ Rise Miraculously from the Dead?*

1. J. P. Moreland, *Scaling the Secular City: A Defense of Christianity* (Grand Rapids, MI: Baker Book House, 1987), 160.

2. Richard Swinburne, *The Resurrection of God Incarnate* (Oxford: Clarendon, 2003), Kindle ed. loc. 1713.

3. William Lane Craig, *Did Jesus Rise from the Dead?* (Pine Mountain, GA: Crossway, 2001).

4. For further thoughts, consult William Lane Craig, "The Empty Tomb of Jesus," in *In Defense of Miracles: A Comprehensive Case for God's Actions in History*, ed. R. Douglas Geivett and Gary Habermas (Downers Grove, IL: InterVarsity Press, 1997), chap. 15, 247–61.

5. My analysis draws on the arguments of Swinburne, Moreland, and Craig.

6. Bradley Bowen suggests these alternatives in the post, "Defending the Swoon Theory," Secular Outpost, June 1, 2019.

7. William Edwards, MD, Wesley J. Gabel, MDiv, and Floyd E. Hosmer, MS, "On the Physical Death of Jesus Christ," *Journal of the American Medical Association* 255 (11): 1455–63.

8. Richard Swinburne, *Was Jesus God?* (New York: Oxford University Press, 2010), 122.

9. Swinburne, *Resurrection of God Incarnate*, Kindle ed., loc. 2125.

10. Swinburne, *Resurrection of God Incarnate*, Kindle ed., loc. 2125.

11. Swinburne, *Resurrection of God Incarnate*, Kindle ed., loc. 175.

12. McDowell and McDowell, *Evidence That Demands a Verdict*, 80.

13. E.g., Bowen, "Defending the Swoon Theory." The theory is also considered in the *New York Times* best seller, Michael Baigent et al., *Holy Blood, Holy Grail: The Shocking History of Christ, the Shocking Legacy of the Grail* (New York: Delta Trade Paperback, 1983), 54 ff. An interesting variation on the theory appears in the popular 1960s book by Hugh J. Schonfield, *The Passover Plot: A New Interpretation of the Life and Death of Jesus* (New York: Bantam, 1965).

14. William Lane Craig, *Reasonable Faith: Christian Truth and Apologetics*, 3rd ed. (Wheaton, IL: Crossway, 2008), 338.

15. See McDowell and McDowell, *Evidence That Demands a Verdict*, 292–98, for a more detailed refutation of the wrong tomb theory.

16. Moreland, *Scaling the Secular City*, 171.

17. I thank an anonymous reviewer for the University of Notre Dame Press for suggesting this objection.

18. Douglas Groothuis, *Christian Apologetics: A Comprehensive Case for Biblical Faith* (Downers Grove. IL: InterVarsity Press, 2011), Kindle ed., 590.

19. Swinburne, *Was Jesus God?*, 122.

20. Craig, *Reasonable Faith*, 259.

21. See McDowell and McDowell, *Evidence That Demands a Verdict*, 279–87, for a more detailed refutation of the theft theory.

22. Moreland, *Scaling the Secular City*, 172.

23. Moreland, *Scaling the Secular City*, 172.

24. Michael Rota, *Taking Pascal's Wager: Faith, Evidence and the Abundant Life* (Downers Grove, IL: InterVarsity Press, 2006), 159.
25. Swinburne, *Was Jesus God?*, 123.
26. Quoted in Craig, *Reasonable Faith*, 340.
27. Moreland, *Scaling the Secular City*, 172.
28. Moreland, *Scaling the Secular City*, 172.
29. Moreland, *Scaling the Secular City*, 172.
30. Moreland, *Scaling the Secular City*, 172.
31. Craig, *Reasonable Faith*, 341.
32. See N. T. Wright, *The Resurrection of the Son of God* (New York: Fortress Press, 2003), for further criticism of naturalist attempts to explain away the Resurrection.
33. John Dominic Crossan, *Jesus: A Revolutionary Biography* (New York: HarperCollins, Kindle ed., 163.
34. Crossan, *Jesus*, 175.
35. Crossan, *Jesus*, 176.
36. Crossan, *Jesus*, 174.
37. Crossan, *Jesus*, 92–93.
38. For an edited transcript of the debate, see Paul Copan, ed., *Will the Real Jesus Please Stand Up? A Debate between William Lane Craig and John Dominic Crossan* (Grand Rapids, MI: Baker Books, 1998).
39. Copan, *Will the Real Jesus*, 30–31.
40. Craig, *Reasonable Faith*, 341.
41. Moreland, *Scaling the Secular City*, 178.
42. Gerd Ludemann. *The Resurrection of Christ: A Historical Inquiry* (Amherst, NY: Prometheus Books, 2004), Kindle ed., loc. 823–25.
43. Ludemann, *The Resurrection of Christ*, 173.
44. Ludemann, *The Resurrection of Christ*, 173.
45. Ludemann, *The Resurrection of Christ*, 177.
46. Ludemann. *The Resurrection of Christ*, 177–78.
47. Stephen T. Davis, *Risen Indeed: Making Sense of the Resurrection* (Grand Rapids, MI: Eerdmans, 1993), x. See also Gary R. Habermas, *Risen Indeed: A Historical Investigation into the Resurrection of Jesus* (Bellingham, WA: Lexham Academic, 2021).
48. See McDowell and McDowell, *Evidence That Demands a Verdict*, 287–92, for a more detailed refutation of the hallucination theory.
49. Rota, *Taking Pascal's Wager*, 160–61.
50. I recommend Rodney Stark, *The Rise of Christianity: How the Obscure, Marginal Jesus Movement Became the Dominant Religious Force in the Western World in a Few Centuries* (San Francisco: Harper, 1997).

51. I thank an anonymous reviewer for the University of Notre Dame Press for suggesting this objection to the overall argument of this chapter.

52. Another telling consideration is that the gremlin hypothesis is ad hoc while the Christian account is certainly not. A proposed explanation is ad hoc if it is put forward backed by no evidence at all, merely to explain something that would otherwise lack an explanation or to avoid an unwelcome explanation. The Christian account is not ad hoc, for it has a significant prior probability based on our background knowledge alone. It also rests on a good deal of historical evidence. In the subject of critical thinking, we tell students that it is never reasonable to accept an ad hoc hypothesis. See Paul Herrick, *Think with Socrates: An Introduction to Critical Thinking* (New York: Oxford University Press, 2015), chap. 11, 299.

53. Personally, I have come to believe that a program of faith formation plays an important role in the life of a Christian, especially in the life of young Christians. For faith formation, I contend, opens the mind as well as the heart to God's presence and calling.

NINE. *Reason to the Best Explanation*

1. Basil Mitchell, *The Justification of Religious Belief* (New York: Palgrave Macmillan, 2017).

2. In philosophy, a fact that has no explanation or that can be given no explanation is called a "brute fact." If an aardvark suddenly popped into existence in front of you out of absolutely nothing, and nothing caused it to be, its existence would be a brute fact.

INDEX

A
Acts of the Apostles, 6
agent causation, 224n4
Albert the Great, Saint, 92
Alcoholics Anonymous, 12
Alston, William, 112–13
analogical reasoning, 20–21
Anaximander, 16
Anaximenes, 16
ancient temples. *See* temple hypothesis
Anselm, 17, 224n4
antislavery crusade, world's first, 96
apologist
  Christian, 2
  defined, 2
Apology (Socrates), 1, 2
Aquinas, 17, 59, 67, 221n10
archaeological evidence for the reliability of the New Testament, 170–71
argument, defined, 3
arguments for existence of God
  cosmological
  —modal, 59–66
  —*kalam*, 73, 83–84
  from design
  —analogical version, 19–22
  —best explanation version, 22–26
  —fine-tuning version, 36, 43–45
  excess spiritual capacity, 143–44
  from joy (Lewis), 139–42
  from mind-body dualism to theism, 147–48
argument from evil. *See* evil: argument from, traditional
Aristotle, 4, 16, 30, 55, 59, 136
  version of mind-body dualism, 136–37
atomism, 26
Augustine, Saint, 4, 17, 106, 142, 225n5
Aurelius, Marcus, 5

B
background knowledge, 156–59, 185, 190, 195, 198–200
Barbour, Ian, 91, 221n7
Barrow, John, 39, 40
being, contingent, defined, 61
being, necessary, defined, 61
best explanation arguments. *See* inference to the best explanation

big bang theory, 80–83
   confirmation of, 82–83
Blomberg, Craig, 174, 175–76
Boethius, 17
Bonaventure, Saint, 4, 142
BonJour, Laurence, 127, 132
brute fact, 234n2

C

Caesar, Julius, 166, 168–70
Carr, Brandon, 39
Catholic Church, 89, 93
chance hypothesis, 26–28
charity, 97–98
Christian materialism, 137
Christian Platonism, 4, 212n3
church fathers, 4, 168, 212n3
cognitive bias, 12, 212n1
Collins, Francis, 18
conquistadors, critique of, 95
conspiracy theories of the
   Resurrection, 172, 184, 186,
   189–92, 197–98
contradictions, alleged in New
   Testament, 174
cosmic coincidences, 41–43
cosmic microwave radiation, 81–82
cosmological constant, 76, 81
Covenanters (Reformed
   Presbyterians), 96–97
Cover, Jan, 155, 160
   counter to Hume (on miracles),
   160
Craig, William Lane, 6, 73, 84, 180–
   82, 192
   reply to Hume (on miracles), 160–
   61
crimes against humanity, 110, 223n1
critical thinking, 1
   defined, 211n1

criteria, for evaluating historical
   accounts, 164–65, 173
Crossan, John Dominick, 193–95
cumulative case argument
   defined, 8
   of this book, 201, 205, 207

D

Darwin, Charles, 37, 40, 45
Davies, Paul, 39, 42
Davis, Steve, 197
demagogue, defined, 2
Descartes, 17, 93, 119–120,
   123–25, 136–37, 227n8
   divisibility argument of,
   120–23
Dialogues concerning Natural
   Religion (Hume), 31
dissociative identity disorder, 124
doppler effect, 219n29
dualism (mind-body)
   arguments for
   — Descartes's divisibility
     argument. (*see* Descartes:
     divisibility argument of)
   — from intentionality, 130–31
   — from privacy, 134–35
   — from qualia, 130
   — from subjectivity, 133–34
   challenges to, 123–129
   — argument from cognitive
     science, 123–25
   — argument from identity theory,
     128–29
   — argument from neuroscience,
     125–26
   — causal closure argument, 127
   defined, 118
   theory of Aristotle's, 136–37
   theory of Descartes's, 120–22

E
Eddington, Sir Arthur, 76, 80
Ehrman, Bart, 175
Einstein, Albert, 74–76, 80–81
empty tomb
   argument for, 181–83, 190, 192
   naturalistic theories of
   — body-theft, 187–92
   — evil twin, 193
   — swoon, 183–87
   — Syrian brown bear, 192
   — wrong tomb, 186–87
Enquiry concerning Human Understanding, An (Hume), 34
Epicurus, 214n11
evil
   argument from, traditional, 100–102
   — evidential, 110–12
   defined, 100
   gratuitous, 110
   natural and moral distinguished, 99
   problem of (introduced), 86, 99
evil twin theory of the Resurrection, 193
evolutionary science of religion, 144
examination of conscience, 13, 212n3
ex nihilo nihil fit, 63, 64

F
faith, 2–7, 49, 73, 179, 201–2
fideism, defined, 7
Flannagan, Father Edward, 143
Franklin, Benjamin, 117
free will, common notion of, 224n4

G
galaxy, defined, 79
Geisler, Norman, 167, 168–69

general relativity, theory of, 74–75
gnostic redeemer, stories of, 172
"God of the gaps" objection, 85
gospels, dating of, 167, 230n18
grave robbing theory of the Resurrection, 189–92
Grayling, A. C., 98
Greenleaf, Simon, 173
gremlin theory of the empty tomb, 198–200, 234n52
Gribbin, John, 38, 40, 42
Groothuis, Douglas, 7, 189

H
Habermas, Gary, 167, 171–72
Hadot, Pierre, 91
hallucination theories, of post-Crucifixion appearances, 196–97
Harrison, George, 143
Hawking, Stephen, 43, 56–57
Herodotus, 169
Hick, John, 106, 108
Hogan, Craig, 33, 68
Hoyle, Fred, 81
Hubble, Edwin, 77–79
Hubble-Lemaître law, 78
Hume, David
   argument against belief in miracles, 151–55
   critique of arguments from design, 30–36
   definition of miracle, 155
   surprising conclusion, 36

I
identity, numerical and qualitative distinguished, 122
identity theory, 128–29
imago Dei, 93–95, 98, 222n16

inference to the best explanation
  criteria for, 23–24
  defined, 7–8
  format for, 8, 23
infinite explanatory regression
  argument against, 35–36, 50–51
  defined, 35–36, 50–51
intentionality, 131–33
intentionality argument, 132–33
Irenaeus, Bishop, 106

J
Job, book of, 114

K
Kaku, Michio, 30, 46, 58, 67
kalam cosmological argument. *See*
  arguments for existence of God
Kant, 17, 158–59
Kemp, Harry, 142–43
Kenyon, Sir Frederick, 167–68
Krauss, Lawrence, 56–57

L
lambda. *See* cosmological constant
Lapide, Pinchas, 195–96
Las Casas, Bartolomé de, 95
law of noncontradiction, 217n6
Layman, C. Stephen, 104–5, 214n10
Leibniz, 17, 59, 84
Leibniz's law, 123
Lemaître, Georges, 18, 76–83
  first scientific paper, 77
  second scientific paper, 77–78
Leucippus of Miletus, 26
Lewis, C. S., 4, 5, 16, 139
  argument from joy (*see* arguments
    for existence of God)
  and Platonism, 212n4

liberalism (political), 94
  classical, 95
  modern, 95
Locke, John, 17
  and charity, 97
  and duties to the poor, 97
logical possibility, defined, 217n6
Lucas, J. R., 105
Ludemann, Gerd, 196

M
Machen, J. Gresham, 6
manuscript copies, 167–8
Marrone, Steven, 92
Martin, Faith, 96–97
Martyr, Justin, 2–5
  conversion, 3–4
Marx, Karl, 17
materialism (with respect to the
    mind), 118
  Christian, 137–38
McDowell, Josh, 169, 172, 186
McDowell, Sean, 169, 172, 186
Mere Christianity (Lewis), 16, 140
mere theism, 67
miracles
  Hume's argument against belief in,
    151–54
  Hume's definition of, 155
  problems with, 155
Mitchell, Basil, 205
modal cosmological argument. *See*
  arguments for existence of God
modality
  applied to being, 60–61
  and explanation, 61–62
modal logic, 59–60, 62, 70, 217n6
modern mathematics, birth of,
    89, 93

modern political philosophy, birth of, 93–94
modern science, birth of, 89–90
modes of truth, 59–60
monotheist, definition, 2
More, Henry, 4
Moreland, J. P., 168, 179, 187, 190–91, 196–97
multiverse hypothesis, 45–49
   mechanisms, 48

N
Nagel, Thomas, 13
naturalistic evolution, as an explanation of joy and our spiritual capacity, 144–45
natural necessity, as an alternative to design, 25–27, 44–45, 215n20
natural selection, 37, 40, 144
nebulae, 74, 78–79
neuroscience, argument from, 125–26
Newton, Isaac, 75, 79, 213n3
Nietzsche, Friedrich, 17

O
Ockham, William of, 24
Ockham's razor, 24, 33, 66, 68, 72, 84, 186, 188, 214n10
   and identity theory, 128–29
"One and the Many," problem of, 29
One over the Many, 49

P
Pagels, Heinz, 39
Paul, Saint, 2, 6, 152, 179
Penzias, Arnold, 81
Peter, Saint, 2
Philoponus, John, 84
philosophy, defined, 2–3

Pilgrim's Regress, The (Lewis), 16
pizza-making machine, 43
Plato, 1, 4, 16, 30, 59, 91, 118
privacy, 134
privacy argument, 135
Purtill, Richard, 64, 159, 214n9, 218n8, 222n14
Pythagoras, 23, 214n9, 222n14
Pythagoreans, 17

Q
qualia argument. *See* dualism (mind-body): arguments for

R
redshift, 82, 219n29
Rees, Martin, 38, 39
Reformed Presbyterians. *See* Covenanters
rights
   to life, liberty, and property, 94
   of workers, women, and children, 98
Roberts, J. M., 94
Rota, Michael, 65, 190, 197
Rowe, William L., 110
Russell, Bertrand, xi, 68–69

S
Sagan, Carl, 69
scientism
   critique of, 18–19
   defined, 17
Scotus, John Duns, 17
Shapely, Harlow, 77
skeptical theism, 112–14
Smart, J. J. C., 128–29
Socrates, 1, 2, 4, 11–13, 16, 19, 21–22, 24, 211n1 (chap. 1)
   trial of, 1–2

Socratic method
  and Christian life, 13
  defined, 11–12
Somme, Battle of the, 164
Spitzer, Father Robert, 48
split-brain syndrome, 124–25
Stark, Rodney, 89–90
Stoics, 17
subjectivity, 133
subjectivity argument, 134
Swinburne, Richard, 19, 114, 156, 179, 185–86, 189
  reply to Hume (on miracles), 156–60

T
Tacitus, 168–69
temple hypothesis, 205–6
Thales, 16, 29, 33
theodicy
  defined, 102
  free will, 103–5
  moral qualities, 106–8
  rug maker, 105–6
theology, philosophical, 35, 67, 157, 215n20

Thurow, Joshua, 229n26
Tippler, Frank, 39
truth
  contingent, 60
  defined, 3, 12
  necessary, 59–60
  possible, 60
Turek, David, 171

V
van Inwagen, Peter, 65–66, 69–70, 137
variations among New Testament manuscripts, 175–76

W
"Weight of Glory, The" (Lewis), 140
Weinberg, Steven, 21–22, 33, 57
Whitehead, Alfred North, 90
Wilson, Robert, 81
Wolfe, Bertram, 55
Woods, Thomas, 90

X
Xenophon, 19

PAUL HERRICK

is professor of philosophy at Shoreline Community College.
He is the author of multiple textbooks in formal logic,
critical thinking, and philosophy, including *The Many Worlds of Logic*,
Think with Socrates, and *Philosophy, Reasoned Belief, and Faith*
(University of Notre Dame Press, 2022).